GETTING TO SORRY

GETTING TO SORRY

THE ART OF APOLOGY AT WORK AND AT HOME

Previously published as *Sorry, Sorry, Sorry:*
The Case for Good Apologies

Marjorie Ingall and Susan McCarthy

Gallery Books

New York   London   Toronto   Sydney   New Delhi

Gallery Books
An Imprint of Simon & Schuster, Inc.
1230 Avenue of the Americas
New York, NY 10020

First Gallery Books trade paperback edition January 2024

Previously published as *Sorry, Sorry, Sorry: The Case for Good Apologies* in 2023

GALLERY BOOKS and colophon are registered trademarks of Simon & Schuster, Inc.

Simon & Schuster: Celebrating 100 Years of Publishing in 2024

For information about special discounts for bulk purchases, please contact Simon & Schuster Special Sales at 1-866-506-1949 or business@simonandschuster.com.

The Simon & Schuster Speakers Bureau can bring authors to your live event. For more information or to book an event, contact the Simon & Schuster Speakers Bureau at 1-866-248-3049 or visit our website at www.simonspeakers.com.

Interior design by Davina Mock-Maniscalco

Manufactured in the United States of America

10 9 8 7 6 5 4 3 2 1

The Library of Congress has cataloged the hardcover edition as follows:

Names: Ingall, Marjorie, author.
Title: Getting to sorry: the art of apology at work and at home / Marjorie Ingall and Susan McCarthy.
Description: First Gallery Books hardcover edition. | New York, NY : Gallery Books, [2023]
Identifiers: LCCN 2022020890 (print) | LCCN 2022020891 (ebook) | ISBN 9781982163495 (hardcover) | ISBN 9781982163518 (ebook)
Subjects: LCSH: Apologizing.
Classification: LCC BF575.A75 I46 2023 (print) | LCC BF575.A75 (ebook) | DDC 158.2—dc23/eng/20220624
LC record available at https://lccn.loc.gov/2022020890
LC ebook record available at https://lccn.loc.gov/2022020891

ISBN 978-1-9821-6349-5
ISBN 978-1-9821-6350-1 (pbk)
ISBN 978-1-9821-6351-8 (ebook)

For Jonathan, Josie, and Max
—MI

For Daniel, Joseph, Kitty and Nic Jay, and Asa Bea
—SMcC

Not everything that is faced can be changed,
but nothing can be changed until it is faced.
—James Baldwin

CONTENTS

GETTING TO SORRY

INTRODUCTION

Apologies are evidence of a society that cares about itself, a society that honors other people's experiences, thoughts, and feelings as precious. In tiny ways and larger ones, apologies move us toward justice.

Sounds lofty, we know. But, truly, apologies civilize us. In our day-to-day dealings and in the wider social sphere, they make things better. It's human nature to sometimes disappoint or betray others, but saying you're sorry—and doing it well—has the near-miraculous, super-heroic power to heal.

These are trying times. That's a cliché for a reason—all times try our souls, a necessary condition of living. But can we acknowledge that *these* times—what with their bitter partisan divides, climate-based disasters, widening economic gulf between haves and have-nots, collective attempts to wrestle or refuse to wrestle with historic injustice—are particularly difficult? We need all the strategies we can get to make our way through and make things better. Good apologies are one of the tools we could all be deploying more. We'll show you how. And when you start apologizing well—and learn to elicit and accept good apologies—you'll become a better friend, a better family member, a better coworker, and a better world citizen. Widespread adoption of good apologies can make the world a better place to live in.

No lie: apologies are wonderful, vital things.

Unless they're done very badly, in which case they're hideously ugly, catastrophic, messy things.

Kind of Like Duct Tape

We were about to compare apology to a "double-edged sword," but forget that metaphor: How many of us ever get around to swordplay these days? (So busy.) Let's instead think of saying you're sorry as superglue. It's amazing stuff, but if you use it wrong, you can wreak all kinds of destruction. Have you ever received a bad apology, one that made you say, "Okay, I was mad before, but now I'm *really* mad!"? Maybe it was a "Sorry if you took my suggestion the wrong way" apology, or a "Sorry, I didn't realize you were so sensitive" apology, or a "Sorry, but you always . . ." apology. The person apologizing to you has just glued their finger to their nose. Metaphorically.

Why Listen to Us?

The two of us, Marjorie Ingall and Susan McCarthy, have been studying and analyzing apologies in the news, pop culture, literature, and politics since 2012 on our website, SorryWatch.com. In pursuit of education, enlightenment, and entertainment, we have waded through so many of the worst apologies that we had to make up Bad Apology Bingo cards in an attempt to keep ourselves calm. Happily, we've also written about quite a few lovely apologies, the ones that make things better. By studying all those apologies and figuring out what went wrong or right, we came up with the golden rules for apology. Technically speaking, apologies are easy! We can teach you how to apologize beautifully in six simple steps. And we will! You do not need to download an app. You do not need a special screwdriver. A child can apologize well, if they choose to.

Yet apologizing well is agonizingly difficult for many (most?) grown-ups. We'll talk about why that is and how to succeed nevertheless.

How Did We Get So Obsessed with Apologies?

Both of us are longtime journalists and authors. Susan writes a lot about wildlife and animal behavior; Marjorie writes a lot about books and Jewish stuff. Marjorie didn't really start paying attention to apologies until her first child went to nursery school. Little Josie, a fierce toddler, spent the better part of that year in the Consequences Chair. Marjorie felt like she was constantly apologizing for her kid's biting, hitting, yelling, non-sharing. This prompted a lot of thought about how one teaches kids to apologize. (See chapter 5, " 'I'm Sorry I Chased You with a Booger': Teaching Children to Apologize.") Especially because, after her time as an editor at *Sassy*, Marjorie was way too familiar with the phenomenon of teenage girls who apologize for everything—for existing! For having opinions! Later, as a columnist at the *Forward* and then at *Tablet*, she learned that the subjects of apologies and of forgiveness (see chapter 8, "How to Accept an Apology and How to Forgive . . . and When to Do Neither") needed to be written about every single year at the High Holy Days. That's when, among other things, Jews apologize and/or ask for forgiveness from those they have wronged in the previous year. (We're always delighted when people tell us that rabbis quote SorryWatch in their sermons.) She wound up writing about apology *a lot*.

Marjorie's friend Susan came at the subject more out of long-standing resentments about bad apologies she'd gotten in relationships. (Let's not call them grudges, because . . . well, okay, yeah—grudges.) Things like "I'm sorry if anything I did or said hurt you. . . . Why are you still upset? I apologized! What else am I supposed to do?" She also found herself surprisingly, deeply pleased when she got a belated apology from friends who'd ghosted her in high school. It wasn't a perfect apology, yet it brought an astonishing sense of relief.

Then Susan wrote a humor piece for *Salon* making fun of "Sorry if..." apologies. It was tied to current news stories, so it became dated immediately, yet it had a significant afterlife. The thing had legs. People told her, "I made my mom read it" (because their moms tried to pass things off with a "Sorry you feel that way" apology). They emailed to say, "I printed it out and forced my boyfriend to read it" (because he couldn't see why his "Sorry but . . ." apology wasn't bringing smiles and rainbows), and "I sent it to my manager" (because surely the manager wants to know that the "Sorry if . . ." apology for the policy change is just making people madder . . . right?).

Susan likes to think people don't have to be forced to read her stuff. But she realized this was something a lot of readers felt strongly about. Knowing Marjorie also cared deeply about goodness and badness in apology, and that she wrote about it often and hilariously, Susan suggested they team up to do SorryWatch.

We started devouring books, studies, and articles about apology. (We both have a weakness for research.) Mostly we looked at hundreds, and by now even thousands, of apologies—all too many of them terrible—and analyzed what was wrong with the bad ones.

The Hideous Allure of Terrible Apologies—and the Dynamic Power of Great Apologies

As SorryWatch took off, people started sending us apologies and asking—*demanding*—that we parse them. We were led into controversies in subcultures we knew little or nothing about. Large-animal vets, doomsday preppers, comedy-tour organizers, drunken poets, Burning Man sound camp organizers . . . It's been edifying.

We marveled at the simplicity and effectiveness of the good apologies we saw—and were tempted to rant mouth-foamingly and often about the bad ones. Our furious tirades were frequently cathartic for us and tended to get more traffic than our levelheaded, admiring posts. But we began feeling increasingly strongly about the need to praise those less-frequent good ones. Starting in around 2016, when certain folks began insisting ever more loudly, both implicitly and explicitly, that apologies were a sign of weakness, we started seeing the need to promote good apologies as signs of strength and character.

Sadly, there are tons of people who see the refusal to apologize as muscular and tough. In fact, it's the opposite. Apologizing means letting your best self crash through the wall of your own defensiveness like the Kool-Aid Man. It takes real guts to apologize publicly *and* privately, and it takes valor to apologize to those with less status and power than you, especially when no one's making you do it. Apologizing well shows wisdom and honor. The aftermath of a good apology can improve the lives and spirits of everyone it touches. Everyone feels healed. This makes our planet a better place for everyone.

We also began to see that an unsolicited heartfelt apology is a potent thing. When you deliver a good apology, it can make you feel better about yourself and your own perceived past failings, it can make you feel a sense of release and redemption, and it can fill you with a sense of mission and purpose. When you receive a good apology, it can make you feel connected to the person who took the step of reaching out to you and risking rejection. It can make you feel seen. It can give you a small experience of justice.

There's a plethora of research on how potent good apologies can be—for the apologizer, for the recipient, and for the planet at large. Study after study—in the fields of psychology, medicine, law, and management—show that apologizing directly to those who are harmed has a huge, positive impact. We'll look at some of them in more depth in this book.

All the Deliciousness We Have for You Herein

We'll talk about apologies from kings and criminals, alcoholics and small children, corporations and parents, celebrities and your neighbors. We'll talk about apologies you might be given and apologies you might be called upon to make. We'll look at immediate apologies; apologies made after some thought; apologies made after earlier apologies bombed; and apologies made generations after the fact.

We'll offer guidance on how to deliver a perfect apology; look at the science behind whether apologies are accepted or rejected; explain which kinds of apologies work best; and examine great and lousy apologies in history and pop culture. We'll give you the tools to make your own determinations about how you want apologies and forgiveness to work in your life. We'll explicate the difference between apology and regret; discuss whether you can solicit an apology if you're owed one; and consider the psychology behind the anger we often feel even after getting an apology. We'll look at the role of apology in various religions. We'll ponder whether you should apologize even if you feel you've done nothing wrong or if you feel the other person was more to blame than you. We'll look at best practices for teaching children to apologize well. We'll look at how governments apologize for past wrongs, and why they so often refuse to. And we'll look at social media's role, for good and for ill, in fostering a culture that frequently seems to demand apologies and then dismiss them out of hand. Also, bingo cards.

A good apology uplifts not just the recipient but everyone the recipient tells. When you read about a beautiful apology on Facebook or hear about one in the media, it's almost as if you received the apology yourself. Good apologies have ripple effects. They make the world feel more humane.

Apologizing to Your Dog

Susan would like you to know that you apologize to a dog the same way dogs apologize to you. Susan's dog might nip too hard during a play fight. Susan yelps in pain/protest. The dog flattens his ears to show humility, belly crawls over, and frantically licks whatever he can reach. He abases himself, shows concern, and does his best to make things right by licking. That's his apology. So if Susan steps on the dog's toes (because he's *lurking underfoot*), and he yelps, she crouches to show humility, speaks tenderly, and strokes his lower face where a puppy might lick him. The dog forgives. Ideally, he'll also be more careful about *lurking underfoot*.

CHAPTER 1

THE IMPORTANCE OF APOLOGIES, GOOD AND BAD

When we started our site SorryWatch in 2012, people told us we were clever because apologies were "having a moment."

Thanks! But what does that really mean? Apologies were suddenly fashionable? Were 2012 humans somehow more acutely aware that apologies were important in life? Were there more bad apologies out in the world? Were people miraculously more attuned to rotten apologies? And what does it mean that, every year since, we've heard that apologies are having a moment?

In any case, it's true that people seem to be talking a lot more about public apologies than we did a few decades ago. There's no way to know if there are more—or better—apologies in private life. But, for sure, we started hearing a lot more "having a moment" comments when Donald Trump was elected. As a candidate, he was asked by Jimmy Fallon, "Have you ever apologized, ever, in your life?" He answered, "I fully think apologizing is a great thing, but you have to be wrong. . . . I will absolutely apologize, sometime in the hopefully distant future, if I'm ever wrong."

He then proceeded to not apologize for four years. Some people think this is great. Some do not.

Apologies Go Way Back

The forty-fifth president may have gotten more people talking about apologies, but we don't actually believe the topic is particularly trendy or timely. Plato wrote of his fellow philosopher Socrates's apology (really more of an *explanation* than an apology, but we'll come back to that), and the twelfth-century philosopher Maimonides wrote extensively about how to apologize, how to accept an apology, and how to forgive.

There's a Talmudic term for repairing the world: *tikkun olam*. Good apologies can help repair a broken world. In the Jewish tradition, God contracted the divine self to make room for creation, and God's light was placed in vessels, some of which shattered. Part of humans' purpose on earth is to gather those broken shards and sparks of wonder and beauty by doing acts of repair and healing. Good apologies are a huge part of that process.

Bad apologies? Well, not so much. A bad apology misses the point, sometimes deliberately. (The Hebrew word for "sin," *khet*, actually is an archery term meaning "missing the mark.") It's an act of self-defense, of doubling down, of half-heartedness; it's a deflection, a semi-disguised plea to move on rather than an attempt to mend hurt. And we all know people who refuse to apologize, even badly.

In fourteenth-century England, writer Geoffrey Chaucer apologized for his past depictions of sinful characters. (That money-grubbing Friar! That skanky Wife of Bath!) At SorryWatch, we've looked at an apology by a guilt-ridden Salem witch trial jury, by beetle-loving naturalist Charles Darwin, by President Abraham Lincoln, by hotheaded Russian novelist Leo Tolstoy, and by melancholy American poet Emily Dickinson (who could not stop for death but could stop to apologize).

Apologize or I Shoot

So yeah, apologizing has long been a subject of interest to human beings. Susan's fascinated by how apologizing fits into the rule of dueling. Formalized dueling goes back to the Roman Empire, but the best write-ups we've seen are from the eighteenth and nineteenth centuries. Here's the thing: the basic concept of the duel is that one person has insulted another, and the insulted person fights to uphold his (usually) honor or (sometimes) pride. But seconds, whom you *must* have in a proper duel, to say nothing of the doctor, are supposed to try their hardest to talk the duelists out of it and get them to apologize. In many cases, combatants would try to shoot in a nonlethal manner and *then* apologize.

In 1778, Generals Robert Howe and Christopher Gadsden were angry with each other over which of them should be commanding South Carolina troops. Gadsden called Howe names in a public letter and wouldn't take it back. Howe challenged him to a duel. Pistols at eight paces! On the day, Gadsden said Howe should shoot first. Howe shot and "grazed" Gadsden's ear. Gadsden then fired into the air. Howe declined to fire again. Gadsden then apologized to Howe, and if they didn't go off arm in arm, they parted on friendly terms. "Gadsden had the quixotic notion that, as a gentleman, he could not apologize until he had received his adversary's fire," writes William Oliver Stevens in *Pistols at Ten Paces: The Story of the Code of Honor in America*. Which is so bizarre. It's almost as if this was just showing off.

Social Media and Apology: Just, Wow

Talking about showing off definitely brings us to social media. Social media means that venomous acts can go viral in an instant. Apologies that once might have been private are now often world viewable. Demands to apologize—and *not* to apologize—come fast and furious. When the apology for said venomous act does appear, it's sometimes so lousy that it starts a brand-new round of hashtaggy opprobrium. A bad apology can pitch you right out of the frying pan of your own making into the fire of international hatred. If a video of your bad behavior is widely seen, and people are widely WTF, your apology had better not try to tell people that they did not see what they clearly saw. Social media can be excellent for accountability, which is bad for people who do not want to be accountable.

Social media can also be good for the art of apology—and it *is* an art. Discussing other people's apologies, teasing apart what makes them good or bad, can help us all in our own efforts to apologize well.

"Modern progress has brought unprecedented advances that make it easier for us technically to connect," writes Vivek H. Murthy in *Together: The Healing Power of Human Connection in a Sometimes Lonely World*, "but often these advances create unforeseen challenges that make us feel more alone and disconnected."

Being online makes it easier to be nasty and snarky when you don't see your target's face, when you're not likely to run into their family in your neighborhood. We perform for friends and allies. On some platforms, we don't really have conversations: we just blast our thoughts and images and videos through an emotional fire hose. Fury is rewarded— one 2017 Pew Research Center study found that Facebook posts expressing "indignant disagreement" received nearly twice as many likes and shares as posts containing no disagreement. Facebook knows this and catapults high-engagement bait into the top of your feed. So folks have become quick to attack other people's real-life behavior, work, social media activity, and apologies; it's exciting when everyone who shares your values is validating you and reacting to you. It's akin to getting high. (Literally: a 2019 study showed that excessive use of social media causes the same changes in the brain as drug addiction . . . and similarly leads to impaired judgment.)

Sometimes when a person gets attacked on social media and then apologizes for whatever their offense was, fellow social media users refuse to accept the apology, even if that apology is good. Some folks get addicted to the validation they get for flame throwing. And there's way less virtual applause for accepting an apology. Because the latter is boring. And if the apology *isn't* good, that leads to escalating attention. Sometimes folks are legitimately horrified by someone's conduct. Sometimes they see an opportunity to score humor points or feel holier-than-thou. There can be an element of magical thinking involved: If I call that person out, I will not only look virtuous, I will also be protecting myself from ever being attacked for my own conduct or content. (Ha.) It puts the caller-outer on record as being on the right side. Fury becomes an amulet.

SorryWatch began because Marjorie and Susan were impatient with reading about terrible apologies from politicians, celebrities, and all kinds of people who really ought to know better. How can people still be saying, "Sorry but . . ."? How can PR companies still be telling their clients to say, "Sorry if . . ."? But not all apologies that go viral on social media are from public figures. And some apologies go viral for being good instead of rancid.

A Bully's Apology out of the Blue

In 2015, ChadMichael Morrisette was minding his business—brand consultancy and visual design in West Hollywood—when he got a surprising Facebook message. (See "social media.") It was from someone who'd once been part of making his life a living hell. (We've kept the original spelling and punctuation of the messages.)

"Hey Chad, I was recently talking with my 10 year old daughter about bullies. She asked me if I ever bullied anyone and sadly I had to say 'yes'. What came to mind was how shitty and mean I was to you when we were in Jr. High. I want to apologize. If we lived in the same state I would apologize to your face. I don't even know if you remember, but I do and I am sorry."

Morrisette was shocked. He both did and didn't know what the writer, Louie Amundsen, was talking about. Morrisette had grown up in a small Alaskan town where he was constantly bullied in junior high school. "The entire football team bullied me. It wasn't one guy, it was six or seven guys who would follow me in the hallways, harassing me, insulting me, threatening my life," he said. "There were times I'd walk down the hallway and groups of guys would follow me, threaten me, humiliate me, push me." He said, "I was bullied for being gay. I was bullied for being little." It got so bad, he noted, "I couldn't even walk to classes without an adult escort or friends with me."

So he knew what Amundsen was talking about, but couldn't remember which tormentor he was or *which* shitty mean things he had said. Morrisette had left that town at fifteen and never looked back. For some reason. The Facebook message shook him up. He didn't answer for a few days. Then he replied.

"I'm quite moved by this. Thank you and accept your apology. In 20 years you are the only person to apologize for being a bully to me when we were younger. I hope you can proudly tell your daughter that you have also apologized for it, and that we are good. It's amazing what 20 years and children can do to us, no? Thank you again, and I hope you stand up to bullying anytime you see it. Have a great day!"

The answer: "Thank you. Your forgiveness means more than you know and I hope I am [not] the last to ask forgiveness from you. Cheers!"

This exchange caught people's attention, and various outlets interviewed both guys. Amundsen said his daughter was working on a student council skit about bullying. Asking him various questions on the topic, she finally asked if he'd ever bullied anyone. "I had to think about it for a minute and that's the first time I had thought about it in twenty-plus years, so I answered honestly and said yes," he said. Afterward he concluded it was his duty to try to apologize. "You can't change your past, but you do still own it. I can't take back the names I called him, and the threats I made toward him, but I can apologize. It doesn't excuse my behavior as a child in any way, but as an adult it's the best I can do to try to make it up to him. . . . I really didn't expect him to respond at all, and figured if he did it would be telling me where to stick the apology, kind of like 'too little too late.'"

But Morrisette said it's never too late. "A simple 'I'm sorry' can change everything," he said.

And Amundsen's apology was excellent. He said he was sorry and what he was sorry for (without repeating the ancient insults). He didn't make excuses. He didn't say, for instance, "I was just a kid myself." The apology and its acceptance empowered them both.

The story was gripping to many people. Most people haven't been tormented that badly in school, but many were bullied or ostracized or treated unfairly and never got an apology from anyone.

Thinking About Apologies Means Thinking About Power

Kids who bully are experimenting with power. (As are adults who bully, but they should have grown out of that.) Some parties feel that they are powerful because they *deserve* to be. Others feel that they lack power because those who do have power are hoarding it. People who are in charge rarely feel that they shouldn't be. Societally speaking, the way power shifts is often through a revolution, a war, a conquest, an uprising. Power shifts are rarely polite.

Questions of who has power are perpetually relevant, but every generation seems to think it's wrestling with conflicting ideas about power for the first time. Apologies are about power, too: to apologize well is to give some of your power away. (As hotheaded Russian novelist

Tolstoy might have put it, people who don't want to apologize are all alike; people who feel they're owed apologies are each pissed off in their own way.)

When someone powerful apologizes, oftentimes they're not actually apologizing to those they've hurt. They're apologizing for damaging the image of the institution they represent. Pro athletes who are caught on camera beating their wives don't usually apologize to their wives first in their public apologies. They usually start by apologizing to their team owners, to management, to the brands they endorse, and to the fans before they get around to saying their wives' names. Sometimes they say that the apology is from both the athlete and the wife, as if she's equally culpable for being beaten. This is because the wife has no power. The owners, management, brands, and fans are the ones who have the potential to destroy the athlete's career.

Acknowledging that you owe something (even if it's just two words: "I'm sorry") to someone else because you were cruel or ignorant, then apologizing well for it—that's hard. It puts you in a subordinate position. And it's why so many people resist apologizing. It's scary to look under your own hood and see that you've done wrong—and scarier still to talk openly about that wrong to the person or community you've harmed.

It does feel that we're at a moment in which power structures are being challenged in a meaningful way, more fundamentally than ever. #MeToo, #BlackLivesMatter, #OwnVoices, #TransWomenAreWomen—all these hashtag campaigns are indications that not only are greater numbers of disenfranchised and harmed people demanding to be listened to but also that we're in transition as a culture. Some folks who want to be perceived as allies are raising up voices that haven't been historically heard from, and some folks are digging in harder than ever to hold on to their place of supremacy. Lousy apologies are often insincere attempts to placate people demanding justice; good apologies acknowledge that other folks deserve justice. From you. You, the person apologizing.

No wonder good apologies are scary! But when facing cultural change, it's normal to be scared. And we need to be scared—at least a little—for power to shift in healthy ways that help us all grow.

If We Treated Indigenous People Badly, It Wasn't Because They Were Indigenous, Just Bad

In December 2019, Maxwell Johnson took his granddaughter to a branch of the Bank of Montreal (BMO) in Vancouver, British Columbia, to open her first bank account. He planned to transfer money to her electronically when she was traveling with her basketball team. He didn't foresee problems: he'd had an account there for five years. He had also just deposited $30,000 from an Aboriginal rights settlement package, due to his status as a member of the Heiltsuk Nation. He brought his tribal status card and his birth certificate. His granddaughter was too young to have her own tribal status card, but she was covered by her mother's card, so he brought that and also his granddaughter's medical card.

But there *was* a problem. There was a branch manager, Ms. S., who found the whole thing very suspicious. It seemed to her that Johnson's ID didn't exactly match the bank's records, and she didn't like the granddaughter's, either. Where did all that money in Johnson's account come from? She wasn't sure, but she wasn't going to let him take any of it out. She told the pair that she had to "verify" their cards, then went away and called the police and reported "fraud in progress."

Police arrived, took the two outside, and handcuffed them on the busy sidewalk. Grandfather and granddaughter were separated and patted down. They remained calm, although the child started to cry. The grandfather kept asking what the problem was. How could his ID not match when it had always matched before? They were arrested.

They were held on the sidewalk while one of the constables placed some calls from a police car. When he confirmed that the granddaughter was in official records as being twelve years old, as the grandfather and child had said, and not seventeen, as Ms. S. had speculated, she was uncuffed.

Things were checking out, so the constable went in to talk to Ms. S., who was still "adamant" that a scam was happening. He made more calls and reached the justice coordinator of the Heiltsuk Nation, who confirmed that Johnson and granddaughter were tribal members, that Johnson had recently received that totally legit money, that the girl was *supposed* to use her mother's card because SHE WAS ONLY TWELVE, and that everything was on the up-and-up. You know, if the police could make these calls, the branch manager could have.

So, after forty-five minutes, the police uncuffed Johnson and told him he was free to go. He and his granddaughter went to the local branch of the Vancouver Police Department (VPD), where the constable explained why they had been arrested in the first place. The VPD says the constable apologized.

But you know what? Johnson still wasn't happy. Not long after the incident hit the news, the VPD said it was "regrettable." The bank put out a statement saying they apologized "unequivocally" and that "recently, an incident occurred that does not reflect us at our best. We deeply regret this."

When a grandparent tries to open an account for a grandchild, there are often annoying demands for paperwork. But seldom are longtime customers arrested. Seldom are they and their grandchildren handcuffed and searched in public. Many people voiced the opinion that Johnson and his granddaughter were treated this way because they were Indigenous. The BMO denied it. The VPD denied it. They said Ms. S. told them Johnson and his granddaughter were "South Asian," which is odd when SHE WAS HOLDING THEIR TRIBAL STATUS CARDS. (No one actually argued that it was racism against South Asian people, not racism against Indigenous people, because that really would not have helped.) There were demonstrations outside the bank.

Some days after the arrests happened, the bank called Johnson to apologize, but he wasn't impressed. "The damage is already done. My granddaughter is going to be scarred for life." He was thinking of a lawsuit through Canada's Human Rights Tribunal.

Almost a month later the bank let it be known that they had formed an Indigenous advisory council. Bank executive Erminia Johannson said they had made a mistake in calling the police, and they were "heartfelt [sic], sad, disappointed, embarrassed and apologetic on this situation" but that their review had determined that the incident "cannot be characterized" as racist. In an impassioned press conference, Johannson referred to "the situation," the "unintended circumstances," "what happened," and "a series of events that we all know about." She never said "arrest" or "handcuffs." She never said "twelve years old."

That didn't help matters, and a lawsuit was indeed filed against the BMO and the VPD. The VPD said that they'd been told Johnson and his granddaughter were South Asian; that teenagers are "sometimes a flight risk," so handcuffing made sense; and that the VPD officers took Johnson and his granddaughter out of the bank and onto the street "to protect the privacy of those being arrested." Video of the scene shows many people walking past the handcuffed pair. It does not show any privacy.

The apologies Maxwell Johnson and his granddaughter received have so far been bad, delayed, evasive, and unconvincing. They haven't made the BMO or the VPD look any better.

Who has the power in this story? The big national bank and the police department. Once upon a time, such humiliating mistreatment of First Nations people would have gone unremarked upon. But with cultural change challenging power structures, powerful entities are fearful, defensive . . . and in full denial.

The World Spins Faster

The issue of timing is important here, and it may look like we're going to contradict ourselves. The Bank of Montreal dragged their feet in responding to the outcry against their treatment of Johnson and his granddaughter—whose name we know, because it was blurred out in only *some* of the VPD documents made public, but we're certainly not going to use it, even if it means we have to keep saying the unwieldy "Johnson and his granddaughter"—and that seems to have made Johnson feel disregarded and more insulted than ever.

They should have acted immediately. But acting immediately doesn't mean you have to act completely. What you *do*, if you're a decent person who learns that your business has handcuffed a twelve-year-old trying to open a bank account with her grandpa and treated them like criminals in broad daylight in a public place, is *instantly* go to them and say, "We're so sorry! We should *not* have called the cops about your confusing paperwork! You should *not* have been cuffed! You should *not* have been arrested! We're going to investigate and review and find out exactly how this happened and make sure it never happens again! What would you like us to do for you?" *Then* you do the review.

But in other cases of a different nature, it may be better to think deeply before embarking on an apology. Nowadays, for most of us, it's very hard to *sit* with anything. We don't take the time to breathe before reacting publicly to an insult . . . or to an apology. When a politician or celebrity does something wrong, they're urged to do one of two things: ignore the outcry or issue a statement instantaneously. It's a facet of a world in which we're expected to respond to bosses' questions 24-7, check our email every few minutes, never ignore a text, perpetually be up on the latest news.

But sometimes it's better to wait before saying you're sorry. Cynthia M. Frantz, a psychology professor at Oberlin College, studies the timing of apologies. In 2004 she published a study in the *Journal of Experimental Social Psychology* called "Better Late Than Early: The Influence of Timing on Apology Effectiveness." She had eighty-three students imagine that a friend had forgotten to meet them as promised. She then asked the students to imagine that the friend apologized as soon as they saw the student, or after the student had had a chance to vent to the friend about being blown off by them, or not at all. Study participants had the most positive feelings about the apology they received after having a chance to express their annoyance and irritation to the friend. It was important to them that they felt heard.

A friend of Susan's, a Black woman of considerable accomplishment, once asked Susan not to mention those accomplishments when introducing her. She preferred to get acquainted without that information being in the forefront. She also said she had the feeling that Susan didn't do the same thing when introducing white friends. Susan is white.

Susan got defensive. She agreed that of course she would introduce her friend in whatever manner was preferred—but! But! No! She tried to introduce everybody with a little information to start the ball rolling! She treated everyone the same way! Susan's friend accepted the promise to change the introduction style but did not seem to feel understood.

Susan kept thinking about it. And realized that her friend was right. It truly was often the case that she liked stressing her friend's accomplishments because they conflicted with possible stereotypes. She hadn't meant to be obnoxious, but she'd succeeded anyway. It was a racist microaggression.

She called her friend and apologized. The exact words are lost to memory, but she said something like, "I thought about what you said, and you were right. I'm sorry. I won't do it anymore—and now I understand why. Thank you for explaining." Her apology was accepted. This was a case where sitting and thinking was important and made things better.

Apologies tend to be terrible when they're knee-jerk. So many public apologies are bad because they come immediately, the public figure frantically reacting to angry Instagram and TikTok and YouTube comments, clearly without actually taking the time to ponder what precisely it was that they did wrong. Sometimes they deny what's clearly true, because lying is the first, visceral, panicked choice when one feels cornered. The next apology from the public figure comes a few hours or a day or two later, often as a longer screenshot shared across platforms, buffed to a shiny sameness, clearly crafted by a PR or crisis communication team, sounding very little like the person's own voice. The first apology is narcissistic; the second is self-serving.

The twenty-four-hour news cycle is not helpful to good apologies. We'd like to think there could be more private apologies if people take inspiration from the public apologies, even if it's the scornful negative inspiration of "I can do better than *that!*"

The Pleasures of Apologizing

One of our favorite things about apologies is that after you make a good one, you feel a sense of release. There's relief. A clean feeling. It's over. You don't have to avoid the subject. You don't find yourself secretly obsessing or agonizing or wishing it away anymore. Because you handled it. And you don't have to obsess about whether people in the limelight apologized well for their peccadilloes or not. Because you dealt with your own *mishegas* head-on.

There's currently a movement away from "call-out culture," which exists to point fingers and yell at people, toward "call-in culture," a term popularized by Smith College professor Loretta J. Ross. Call-in culture enlists a person who needs help in embracing difference and diversity and gives them a role in their own education and self-betterment. This kind of gentle guidance can create new allies from antagonists or sideline sitters. Folks from different backgrounds, age groups, races, and religions can work to support one another and build a more just world.

Social media may frequently be toxic, but it's also democratizing. Sure, some people will always be fiercer than others, more impatient for change. And some people will perpetually refuse to negotiate in good faith. But we all benefit when we refrain from tearing down the kind of people who apologize poorly because they don't really understand what they've done wrong, as opposed to the kind of people who apologize poorly because they're assholes who are sure they're right.

Again, public apologies are the ones we all hear about, and their analysis can be a useful public exercise. But private apologies are equally (probably more!) important and deserve the greatest respect. Good apologies mend the social fabric. We use the term "social fabric" for a reason. The very phrase means that none of us is on our own; we're all woven together in this world. What we do affects others and what they do affects us. We all need to behave well toward each other so that the world is an okay place to be. When the social fabric is torn (loose threads! people seeing skin you didn't want them to see!) emotions get raw, and the world feels cold and bad.

But if the person who wrongs us apologizes? Sincerely and with forethought? Then we feel like it's not a world where such indignities and assaults happen with no one caring. A well-knit apology warms us. It shows that we're not adrift, by our lonesome, in a freezing world. It acknowledges that we *should* be able to go through life un-kicked, seen. We all want to feel that we matter. Our dignity, our time, our feelings. They all matter. We're all tied together, with lovely knots in a beautiful afghan made from friendly sheep. This metaphor may have gotten away from us.

Apologies are small actions that are more powerful than most people guess. Sometimes it feels that changing the world is too daunting, too vast. There are too many moving parts. But tiny acts can have big repercussions, like a butterfly flapping its wings in the Amazon some-thing something typhoon something. We may see the positive impact of an apology in a sudden surprised smile, the smoothing of a furrowed brow, the dropping of shoulders squared for battle.

About That Moment We're Having

It seems to us that people say apology is having a moment because they're seeing so many more public apologies, and in a way that's a good thing. Work with animals has shown that one of the best ways to learn things is to see *others* schooled. Seeing other people attacked for saying leash laws are reminiscent of the Third Reich, seeing their snarkiness demolished, noticing how idiotic their defensiveness makes them look, makes many onlookers aware of the folly of such comparisons.

Sometimes people use the phrase "having a moment" with a little moue of distaste. Some seem slightly worried the moment is coming for them, maybe for dumb things they could easily have said in high school. Or on Usenet. Or in that private Prank'd Facebook group they used to be in. Although apology is timeless—as we've pointed out, dogs can do it! and wait till we tell you about the monkeys!—it *is* newly being spotlighted in action. We hope the outcome will be good. More and more people are hip to the horrors of "Sorry if . . ." (Come-dian Harry Shearer calls these "ifpologies," and so do we. We think he was first. But we think we beat you to "bropology," Harry Shearer! And "fauxpology"!)

Rather than say that apology is having a moment, perhaps it's better to say that apology's time of recognition has come.

ACTION ITEMS

❑ **Do you owe someone an apology?** Don't be knee-jerk about it and risk making things worse. Take a beat. Think about what you'll say. Read the rest of this book.

❑ **Did you screw up publicly?** You don't have to look at your social media mentions, you know. Log off, talk to friends you trust, ponder your next steps.

❑ **Breathe.** It sucks when people yell at you. But most of the time they move on. You can't consider the best course of action when your heart's pounding and you feel besieged.

❑ **If someone is mad at you, let them yell.** They need to feel listened to. Try to listen. If you can't listen, just shut up and do your best to record their words in your brain for later, when you can play them back and consider them. At least they're talking to you. When someone yells, they're giving you an opening to fix what you did wrong. When they ghost you, it's a lot harder to make amends.

❑ **Consider observing a social media Sabbath.** One full day a week, don't go on the internet and don't watch any news on TV. Focus on being present, on sitting with yourself and other human persons. You can do it.

Four Reasons Not to Apologize

1. *You don't mean it.* You'll just apologize badly and risk making things worse. Seriously, don't apologize. (You may want to check in with someone you trust about whether you *should* want to apologize, though.) If you don't feel bad for refusing to eat your friend's carob-beet cupcakes, don't apologize for refusing to eat your friend's carob-beet cupcakes. Apologize instead for hurting your friend's feelings, or for not asking them to bring their famous zucchini-flax loaf, which you love—assuming that you can tolerate the zucchini-flax loaf—or for yelling in front of the whole party, "If I wanted to eat something that tastes like dirt, I'd just go to the yard and yank up some sod!" like a sensitivity-free dickhead.

2. *It would hurt the other person.* Are you consciously or unconsciously using apology as a weapon to feel superior or to make the other person feel small?

3. *The other person doesn't want to hear from you.* Because then, if you apologize anyway, your apology isn't really about their feelings; it's about your own need for expiation.

4. *The other person is demanding too many apologies.* If the other person refuses to forgive but keeps insisting you grovel, you are allowed (nay, encouraged) to stop.

CHAPTER 2

SIX SIMPLE STEPS
TO GETTING IT RIGHT

A good apology corrects an imbalance, respects a person's value, and takes away an insult. A bad apology makes things worse. If my dog snaps at you, and I say, "I'm sorry, but you shouldn't have looked at her that way. Most dog people know not to do that," I decidedly made things a lot worse. I implied that it was your fault—so maybe *you* should apologize to *me*—and that you're ignorant, and not a dog person, or maybe just a lousy dog person.

(Incidentally, sometimes we write as if you are the person apologizing. In which case, no offense intended. Sometimes we write as if you are the person getting the apology. Which you richly deserve! Sometimes we write as if we are witnessing someone else's apology to others. An apology that may be good or bad! Confusing, and yet we are sure you can keep up. We believe in you.)

It Was Never My Intention Not to Be Flawless

Being in the wrong or being one-down (meaning at a disadvantage in a situation or having conceded a lead to someone else—it's British) is no fun. And for some people it's fucking agony. It's also uncomfortable to have to reexamine your assumptions. "My concept for the graphic novel wasn't racist, because I'm not a racist." "I couldn't have sounded conde-scending, because it's a thing with me to respect every human soul, even dipsticks like Jordan." "I'm shocked that anyone found me intimidating, since I'm a fluffy duckling at heart." "My political party—the Democrats/ Republicans/Conservatives/Liberals/Labour/Whigs/Tories/Federalists/ Anti-Federalists/Greens/Libertarians/The Rent Is Too Damn High Party—couldn't have done anything harmful, or at least nowhere near as bad as the other fellows, because we are the good guys on this issue." The work of acknowledging that your worldview is flawed can take some pondering.

Simple Steps to Great Apologies

We believe the good apology has six parts. Maybe six and a half. Here they are:

1. **Say you're sorry.**

2. **For what you did.**

3. **Show you understand why it was bad.**

4. **Only explain if you need to; don't make excuses.**

5. **Say why it won't happen again.**

6. **Offer to make up for it.**

Six and a half. **Listen.**

Let's unpack, shall we?

FIRST, say "I apologize" or "I'm sorry." Say it. Say those words. So basic, yet so often overlooked. Because those words take the blame, peo-ple will often avoid saying them without thinking about it. They say, "I regret the explosions!" without acknowledging that we *all* regret the explosions. People *blocks away* regret the explosions, and some of us are still picking shrapnel out of our socks. So the person who actually caused the explosions needs to say more than "regret." Psychologist Harriet Lerner, author of *Why Won't You Apologize?: Healing Big Betrayals and Everyday Hurts*, calls "I'm sorry" the "two most powerful words in the English language."

In *Never Hit a Jellyfish with a Spade*, British humorist Guy Browning writes, "If you can't stomach an apology, you can just say you regret something. This is shorthand for 'I regret being in a situation where an apology is called for.' " The fact that people use "regret" as a dodge is all too real. After the events of Kent State, where the Ohio National Guard fired on a student peace rally and killed four people and injured nine more, there were statements of regret from the Guard. Asked whether that was an apology, the adjutant-general of the Guard, Sylvester Del Corso, told a reporter, "There is no apology. We expressed sorrow and regret just as you would express condolences to the family of someone who died."

Regret takes no ownership. The point of saying you're sorry or that you apologize about a situation in which you were a prime actor is to acknowledge that *you caused or partly caused the thing that happened*. So if you actually intend to apologize, you must take responsibility and not merely hand-wave about your sorrow. Also, regret is about *your* feelings, not about the feelings of the person you're apologizing to. And the latter are what's important here. Later, *if and when you're forgiven*, you can flash your vocabulary words: you felt "rue" and "remorse" and "anguish" alongside your regret! But again, you do not get to say this NOW.

The apology should be *to the people harmed*. If you're a celebrity who got caught on camera licking the donuts in a display case, or a politician who spent public money to redecorate your deep-sea fishing boat, *The Lucky Loophole*, or a sports immortal who injected buttloads of steroids and called everyone else cheaters and sued anyone who suggested that you injected buttloads of steroids—your apology should *first* be directed to the donut workers and purchasers, the taxpayers, and your teammates, not to the fans/supporters you've disappointed. Not to the studio, not to the state party organization, not to the owner of the team. And not to your Instagram followers. You can apologize to them, too, but if you're going on and on about how you let your Fan Nation down and glide right over what you actually did to let them down, that shows a deep lack of understanding of the offense. Almost as if your real concern is your career.

SECOND, say what the something was. Specify! This is important. This is something that gets bungled a lot. People are embarrassed; they want to get it over with and they can't bring themselves to say what they did. "That was quite a situation, alas." Nope. Name it.

Say it simply. Expressing that you're sorry for what you did (and naming that thing) is not the same thing as saying it is regrettable if anyone got the wrong idea about the thing. You know, the thing. That happened.

A person who is apologizing might not name the offense because they don't want to think about the offense. But it's also true that in some cases, they're being wily. They apologize in vague terms because they're secretly only apologizing for part of what they did. "I'm sorry I messed up your dinner party," they say. And they are sorry they threw the chutney, but they're not sorry they called your sister a ferret-faced jizztrumpet—they're kind of proud of that, actually, and they'd enjoy doing it again.

Maybe you didn't care about the chutney, but you feel bad for your sister, who had been shy about meeting your cool artist friends, and now she never wants to again. Or maybe you didn't care about the chutney, and you actually think it was time somebody told your lousy sister what's what, but you're upset that they stormed out of the dining room and drove off in your car and ran it out of gas. In either case, you didn't actually get an apology for the thing that upset you, because the person apologizing was so vague.

Remember, apologize *for what you did*. Not for how the other person felt about it. You are apologizing for your actions, not how the other person responded to them. It's an important distinction. You're sorry for calling them a hypocrite, not for "upsetting" them. People mess this one up a lot. It's evasive, and it's lazy. As comedian Franchesca Ramsey writes, " 'I'm sorry you feel that way' will always be easier to say than 'I'm sorry I made you feel that way. I'll do better.' "

Here is another example of not naming the offense: If you are, say, an international fashion brand repeatedly accused of employing racist imagery, insulting LGBTQ families, and calling celebrities "ugly" and "cheap," and you release a series of racist videos showing a Chinese woman trying and failing to eat Italian food with chopsticks (including one where someone off-screen sneers and leers at her attempts with a cannoli and asks in Mandarin, "Is it too huge for you?"), your apology should consist of more than vague sentiments delivered somberly in Italian to a camera. Vague sentiments like "We have deeply reflected on how our words and deeds have affected the Chinese people and China," and "We feel sad." (Again: irrelevant, your feelings.) Adding, "I hope you can forgive us for the misunderstanding in our cultural understanding" and "We attach great importance to this statement of apology" is meaningless given your brand's repeated behavior. Plus, "cultural understanding"? It doesn't take much cultural understanding to refrain from calling China "the country of shit" in a leaked Instagram message—accompanied by five poop emojis!—or telling an Asian model distressed by your ad campaign that she is "China Ignorant Dirty Smelling Mafia" who eats dogs.

You had to drag in zombies

When you say what you did or said, say you did it; don't say "it was done." In other words, use the active voice, not the passive voice. Don't say "I'm sorry a toaster was dropped on your foot." Say "I'm sorry I dropped the toaster on your foot." If you say "Mistakes were quite possibly made by the administrations in which I served," you're going to sound like Henry Kissinger. You really want that?

One test for passive voice is the "by zombies" test. Does the sentence still work with the undead in it? Rebecca Johnson, a professor of culture and ethics at the United States Marine Corps University, explained that "if you can insert 'by zombies' after the verb, you have passive voice." So "I'm sorry a toaster was dropped on your foot by zombies" is a decent sentence with passive voice (but a bad apology). "I'm sorry I dropped the toaster on your foot by zombies" doesn't make sense at all, because it's not the passive voice. See?

There are even more ways to phrase things to avoid saying anyone did anything. "Old tweets came to light." "Shit happened." "An unscheduled chemical release occurred."

We commit to making a sad face

Naming what you did is part of taking responsibility. We've noticed that people, especially public figures and corporate representatives, have a tendency to say, "I take responsibility" (because they know that's a thing they are supposed to say), but they may not actually take responsibility at all. "I feel awful that our product made long-lasting fuzzy green splotches appear on people's skin, and I take full responsibility. The product formula was changed by others while I was out of town and the first I heard of it was when the polka-dotted plaintiffs got a lawyer. I feel terrible for the people who didn't read the label before rubbing the product all over their bodies." That person is not actually taking responsibility. Will they be paying medical bills? *Before* they get sued?

Just the same way, don't carefully detail how your Instagram post was the fault of your social media team, and then say you are taking responsibility, without saying how and in what way you are changing to take responsibility.

Similarly, if you are a grown-up sports announcer at a high school girls basketball game who calls the team that knelt during the national anthem "fucking [n-words]," you do not get to apologize for "this most unfortunate incident." Oh, what incident was this, the one where the concession stand ran out of popcorn? And you should not say in the second sentence of your apology that you thought your microphone was off. Even if you then say "that is no excuse," you have literally just excused yourself because you used the second sentence of your apology to tell us you had no idea the microphone was on, which sure seems to be giving away some prime apology real estate to something irrelevant. And you need to own that you said the n-word—you can do that without repeating the slur, simply by calling it "a racial slur"—and that you said it about teenage girls expressing their First Amendment rights whom you said should "get their ass kicked." But instead of saying that in your apology, you chose to say "I am a family man. I am married, have two children and at one time was a youth pastor. I continue to be a member of a Baptist church." That's all super-duper fascinating, but these attributes do not unsay the words you said. And then, the cherry on top of the shitty apology cake was your telling us you have type 1 diabetes and your blood sugar was spiking. Millions of diabetics have experienced blood sugar spikes and have inexplicably managed not to say the n-word. As for the sentences "While the comments I made would certainly seem to indicate that I am racist, I am not. I have never considered myself to be racist, and in short cannot explain why I made those comments," well, sir, let us help you. You made those comments because you are racist. Stating that "it is my sincere desire that I can obtain forgiveness" doesn't earn you forgiveness. You have to do the work, work you clearly are not doing if you "cannot explain" why you made those comments.

But now, a palate cleanser: Here's an example of what taking ownership of your misdeeds actually looks like. When a woman attending a wedding held in an Ohio historical museum was harassed by two staff members who insisted she couldn't breastfeed her baby where people (families!) could see, the museum follow-up showed what responsibility and commitment look like. They apologized to the woman, they posted about the incident publicly, they disciplined the two staff members (who had violated state law), they contacted a breastfeeding organization to provide training for all staff, and they posted images of historic clothing items designed and worn by earlier Ohio women to make breastfeeding simpler. That was a splendid apology, and it was accepted. No legal action is pending.

Notice that a good apology *focuses*. It doesn't just flop around and wallow in random dismay.

THIRD is showing you understand why what you did was bad. You understand the impact. You acknowledge the effects. If you took their pogo stick without permission, you should apologize for that. But if by taking their pogo stick, you left them stranded shoeless in the desert (hmm, this might be a Burning Man apology), you need to apologize for that too.

If you turned your phone off to take a quick nap and slept so long you missed the engagement party at Jordan's parents' place, you should apologize for that, and also, also, for how awkward it was for Jordan to have to say that the person they planned to marry hadn't shown up yet, and how Jordan was actually afraid you were DEAD, and called all the hospitals, and—you know what?—just ask Jordan what else you should apologize for. But don't pretend the only issue is that you were tired.

Shawna Potter's *Making Spaces Safer* (which includes a discussion of apology) gives an example of filling the dishwasher in shared housing. If last night I said I would clear the dishes and put them in the dishwasher, and today you come home and I didn't, I should apologize. Potter says I should not say "I'm sorry! I was in a meeting! Jeez!"

Potter suggests it's better to say, "I'm so sorry I forgot to load the dishwasher. I know how frustrating that is for you because you expected to come home late after a long day of work and be able to prepare your dinner without a big mess in your way." If I'm blaming the fact that I got home so late ("This meeting with the West Coast chapter went long, and I just couldn't get away"), then I might keep that in mind for the future, so next time I won't promise to do cleanup on meeting days. Finally, I can make an offer of repair: I could clear the dishes now, if they're still sitting there, or fix them dinner, or order a pizza.

Consider all the ways you may have caused offense. If you grab someone's Japanese naval officer's sabre to open a stubborn jar of pickles and snap the tip off, well. You broke their expensive sabre. You also showed contempt for their collection. Maybe they care that you demonstrated disrespect for the Japanese Navy, maybe they don't. But you need to take these matters into account when apologizing. Simply offering to share the pickles may not be enough.

Suppose Jordan has a few drinks at the lounge and gets drunker than expected and opts to be Really Careful driving home and yet somehow gets pulled over and blows .14 percent in the breath analyzer. "Where's the problem?" Jordan says. "Look, I messed up, but nobody got hurt, except me—I spent the night in a cell, the fine is huge, and my insurance rate is gonna go sky-high. If I apologize to anyone, it should be me!" Wrong. Jordan endangered everyone on the road that night.

THIS HURTS ME MORE THAN I HURT YOU

"I feel terrible!"

"I'll be doing some soul-searching."

"I am deeply ashamed of my uncharacteristic behavior."

"I wish that whole night hadn't happened."

"These events have left me so rueful."

"We are saddened."

"I'm heartbroken."

Remember, the apology is not about you and your feelings. When we say you should show you understand the impact, we mean the impact on the other person, not you. You must say what you did, not how you feel about it now. Do not leave out the spray paint, the turkey carcass, or the flamethrower. An apology is not about your saddened heartbrokenness. It's about the other person, and what you did to make *them* feel saddened and heartbroken. Or angry.

Actually, it's a long, kind of ironic story of why I took your piebald camel

The **FOURTH** part of a good apology is to explain why whatever it was happened—if necessary, and only if necessary. If I snarl at someone because I'm stressed by a bad day, I should apologize. I can mention that I've been having a bad day as explanation ("I'm sorry, that wasn't about anything you did"), as long as I don't then make them part of the bad day ("I had a nightmare day, and coming home some jerk cut me off on Banana Street, and then you asked if I've seen your shoes when I have said a million times I AM NOT YOUR GODDAMN SHOE CONCIERGE"), and as long as I don't divert the conversation to the details of my bad day and my endless, endless suffering ("It's like the dry cleaner never saw a belly-dance costume before!").

Sometimes explanations are very helpful. "My son has the exact same tricycle, and I thought my kids had left it out there on the sidewalk. I really wasn't trying to steal your kid's trike. I apologize! I don't blame you for being upset—I would be upset too. I should have noticed the fancy streamers on the handlebars."

It's also sometimes the case that people want and need explanations to make sense of things. "I ghosted you because I knew what you said about Jordan using me was true. I felt like I'd been a complete idiot. I wasn't mad at you, I just couldn't face you because you knew what I'd done."

But focus hard on not letting explanations drift into excuses. Keep in mind that "I didn't mean to!" is an excuse. It is not a get-out-of-jail-free card. Intent and impact are two different things, and the latter matters a lot more than the former. I didn't mean to let your rabbit out when I opened the door for fresh air, but the rabbit is just as gone.

Excuses are things like "Our algorithm didn't prioritize frontline staff to get the Covid vaccine, which is why we vaccinated some of the senior doctors who don't even come into the hospital instead of any of the hospital-based medical residents we also just asked to work extra shifts in the ER" and "Our organization was in transition and some things fell through the cracks" and "My comedy is edgy, and I should have known that some people simply don't understand incisive cultural commentary."

There's a continuum in apologies from explanations (sometimes good) to excuses (bad) to attacks (very bad). If I was late to your baby shower because the bus I was taking caught fire, that's an explanation. If I was late to your baby shower because I was hung over, that's an excuse. If I was late to your baby shower because baby showers are a saddening instance of brainwashed consumerism—come *on*, sheeple!—and it took me a while to force myself to get out the door, that's an attack.

If I say I was late to your baby shower because on the way someone hurled an angry skunk into my car while I was idling at a stoplight and I had to go back home and bathe in tomato juice before I came, that's implausible. Something about that doesn't smell right.

The **FIFTH** step is to say why whatever you did won't happen again. "I'll be sure to look at the trike handlebars next time." "We had everyone on the staff go through training with the Breastfeeding Alliance, and all new hires will learn about our policy." "Now that I know how you feel about that nickname, I'll never use it again." "We fired the manager." "I'm keeping the gun safe locked from now on." "I went to a 12-step meeting last night and I'm going again tomorrow night."

In some situations you might want to line up assistance from someone else. "Once you've committed to changing your behavior or repairing the harm that was caused, find one person who can hold you accountable," the Software Freedom Conservancy suggests. "This could be a business coach or mediator, or a counselor or therapist. You need to find someone who is not involved with your organization and not a friend. This is the only way to get an unbiased perspective."

Sometimes this step isn't needed. Sometimes it's obvious it can't happen again. What are the chances that you're going to rent another piano and I'm going to be able to get my hands on more gelignite in this nowhere town?

The **SIXTH** step is offering to make up for what you did—making reparations. Remember that guest who threw the chutney? They should be scrubbing everything you own to get the chutney out. If it's relevant, an apology might discuss how to make reparations in a broader way. A drunk driver can't bring back a loved one, but they might make a donation for the local emergency service to get a new ambulance with more modern equipment. (Remember, in the fifth step of our six-and-a-half steps, they joined that substance-abuse recovery program.) A hotel might arrange training in recognizing implicit bias for their staff—which means all their staff, not just the minimum-wage folks. Bad policies can be rewritten.

Clearly, not every step is needed in every apology. But never ever skip one and two—always say you're sorry and what you're sorry for.

In many lists of apology steps, the last step is asking for forgiveness. We emphatically don't agree. We don't think asking for forgiveness should be part of an apology at all. Asking for forgiveness is like asking for a gift; Miss Manners would tell you it's rude to ask for a gift. A gift should be freely given. You are the person in the one-down position, which means you do not get to ask the person you've harmed to make you feel better. Apologies are not negotiations. Just as excuses don't belong there, parleys for absolution don't belong there either.

SIXTH AND A HALF: Now, depending on the situation, there might be one more thing to do. Make sure the person you've apologized to can have their say. Listen. Do not interrupt; do not protest. Just listen.

Different delivery mechanisms send different messages: Which is right for you?

Handwritten letter. This is the most potent way to apologize. We rarely write letters these days, which means there's something about a hand-addressed missive on serious stationery that says, "This is important." You found a stamp and everything. If you have done something truly awful, a letter is how you apologize. If what you have done is only moderately awful, you can send a postcard featuring a poop emoji holding a sign that says "Sorry I was a giant turd" on it. Or you know, some other postcard.

Email. If you have a lot of background info to impart or explaining to do (though again, be wary of too much explanation, which can often read as making excuses for yourself), email is a good medium. Email gives you space to unroll and explore without all the weighty import of a handwritten note. Be sure to conclude with "You don't have to respond to this." As ever, *you're* the one who needs to sit with discomfort when you've screwed up; you do not get to ask for a response.

Text. This is often your best apology choice in our digital age. It's informal but thoughtful, and it doesn't have a ton of baggage. The person has the option to respond to you or not, on the spot or not. It's best for smaller offenses. A texted apology says: "I know I screwed up, but I also don't want to make you uncomfortable by turning this into a *thing*."

Face-to-face. The single most essential caveat about a face-to-face apology: the other person needs to be able to walk away from you. For instance, do not apologize in a car when you're going to be sitting next to that person for the next twenty minutes; you could make them uncomfortable and they're stuck. If someone walks away as you're trying to apologize, you have chosen the wrong way to apologize! Let them go! Do not follow! Talk to an apology-savvy friend about the specifics of your situation and consider giving the other person some time before you try again—in a text, an email, or a handwritten card, NOT face-to-face. The very last thing you want is for the other person to feel cornered. And if the person doesn't want to talk to you, period, respect that.

Regardless of how you apologize, DO NOT seek absolution from the other party or provide a lot of context in your missive. Again, you're supposed to be groveling here, not explaining or asking for a gift—a gift the person might not think you deserve.

Go forth!

Doing all six (and maybe a half) steps means doing something most people can't seem to manage. When you do, you'll be making an effort toward balance and fairness and making things right. Good on you.

ACTION ITEMS

Memorize this. Print it out and put it next to your computer. Make a note on your phone. Hire Lin-Manuel Miranda to put it to music and sing it on YouTube.

- ❑ 1. **Say you're sorry.**

- ❑ 2. **For what you did.**

- ❑ 3. **Demonstrate that you understand the impact and know why what you did was hurtful.**

- ❑ 4. **Offer explanation (if relevant) but no excuses.**

- ❑ 5. **Make clear why what you did won't happen again.**

- ❑ 6. **Make reparations.**

- ❑ Six and a half. **LISTEN.**

The exception to "An apology should say exactly what you did wrong"

What if, in saying what you did wrong, you do it again? If what you did involved ugly words, racist terms, or just *hilarious* insults, you'd do better to allude to them rather than repeat them in the apology. "What I said was insulting, and not true, and I apologize for saying it. You didn't deserve that." "I'm sorry I subjected you to a racist cliché." "I was trying so hard to be funny, and instead I was just stupid. I'm really sorry." If you had an affair with their spouse, and you're sorry and want to make it right, do not go into details about the fun you and their spouse had together.

The best "when to avoid specificity" advice is this timeless disclaimer from Monty Python: "We would like to apologise for the way in which politicians are represented in this programme. It was never our intention to imply that politicians are weak-kneed political time-servers who are concerned more with their personal vendettas and private power struggles than the problems of government, nor to suggest at any point that they sacrifice their credibility by denying free debate on vital matters in the mistaken impression that party unity comes before the well-being of the people they supposedly represent, nor to imply at any stage that they are squabbling little toadies without an ounce of concern for the vital social problems of today. Nor indeed do we intend that viewers should consider them as crabby ulcerous little self-seeking vermin with furry legs and an excessive addiction to alcohol and certain explicit sexual practices which some people might find offensive. We are sorry if this impression has come across."

CHAPTER 3

SORRY IF, SORRY BUT, SORRY YOU: THINGS NOT TO SAY

If good apologies have six (and a half) parts, how many parts do bad apologies have? Tons. So many. Too many to count without becoming intolerably cynical about humans and the things they do with words. This is why we try not to count.

SorryWatch has examined thousands of apologies, and people are still surprising us with new ways to mess them up. Pairing the words "I'm sorry" with "I only called you a hamster-brained cocknugget because you upset me first," or "When I said the gentleman was a witless fart lozenge, that was taken out of context," or "I only forgot the house key because *someone in this house* had to make sure the kids had their jackets," or "Just because she was new to the office, I was only being *friendly* to make her feel welcome," or "We had no intention of shooting down that passenger plane, but it was in our air space and it could have been a UFO," means the apology is inherently bad. It refuses ownership. The "why" is obvious: we're trying to make it look like our imperfections aren't imperfections at all and rather the fault of someone else.

I Would *Remember* Turning to the Dark Side

One factor that produces bad apologies is a deep belief in our own innocence. Most of us are prone to this. We've all been children and, wow, were we innocent! We had no bad thoughts about anyone. Our hearts were ridiculously pure. We were weak; we were as fluffy little bunnies.

Now, not so. But we may not have considered that today we are large, dangerous adults with horrifying vocabularies and that we may have absorbed all kinds of nasty assumptions during our long journey from bunnydom. So it's not hard to tap into a sense of clueless, blameless irresponsibility and move from there to a sense of grievance: *Why are you picking on me?* Sometimes we channel Miss Piggy: "*Moi*? Fragile *moi*? You want *moi* to apologize?" (Go ahead, do the voice. We know you want to.)

There can be an arrogance of innocence. "I know my heart is pure, so anything I say is okay." "I don't have a racist/sexist/homophobic/transphobic bone in my body." "I'm shocked that anyone could possibly think I meant it that way." This kind of hubris can be especially treacherous for certain people: "I don't think you understand. I'm professionally in the right. That's what I *do*. I'm the diversity *czar*." Or the youth minister. Or the dean of student life. Or the politician who has hired so, so many women.

Politicians, businesspeople, and celebrities all were innocent babies, too, so when they are called out for acting or speaking in a sexist, homophobic, ableist, ethnocentric, bullying, or otherwise invidious way, they are quite likely to be astonished. If it's pointed out that they said a racist thing, they're stunned, because babies aren't racist, and they don't personally recall ever having decided to become a racist. They were just kidding around! If they're accused of cultural appropriation, they can't believe it, because like, kids and Halloween costumes! Why do you hate Halloween? It was for fun! Yes, it was a noose, but it was a FUN noose!

This gives rise to the amazingly common claim "That's not who I am!" People say this so frequently that it prompted the making of the very first Bad Apology Bingo card. "That's not who I am" comes in other flavors: "That's not what we stand for." "Some of my best friends are [fill in the blank]." "This is not a reflection of my values." "Those who know me know that I'm not racist/sexist/antisemitic/anti-Muslim/someone who has sex with sheep; I only *like* sheep a lot."

"I'm Sorry" Can Be a "Perf Utto"

The unadorned words "I'm sorry" and "I apologize" can be terrifying to say because they're performative utterances. A performative utterance (we call them "perf uttos," because we're jaunty like that) is when the thing you say actually *does the action you're saying*. It's a concept that's easier to explain with examples: "I do," when said at the altar, means that you are married. The words are the action. When you say, "Fifty bucks says the Bears lose," the act of uttering that sentence is the act of placing the bet and also the act of promising to pay up if the Bears lose (which they probably will, because Marjorie is a Packers fan). "Ready, set, GO!" is not only three words, but also the actual start of the race. When your boss says, "You're fired," and you say, "I quit!," you've both just issued performative utterances. Saying "I apologize" is a performative utterance, and people can sense it even if they can't articulate why: to some folks, it *feels* like an admission of wrongdoing, and they don't want to admit they're wrong. Perhaps that's why Oakland's former mayor said she was "apologetic" about being caught (twice!) driving while holding her phone in her hand and using it to talk or text. "I'm apologetic" is not a performative utterance. It merely describes a feeling.

I'm the Victim Here

Also, sometimes people feel they're inherently innocent because they're a member of a marginalized group. No. When musician Questlove toured

Japan in 2014, he put up Instagram posts making fun of the way Japanese people speak English, with lots of switches of the letters *l* and *r*. Har har. Some folks had criticism to share, and Questlove made the choice to think about what they said. He took down the posts and made an excellent apology. He said he'd thought he was being "funny-cute" and that he was wrong. "Given that Black culture consistently finds itself at the butt end of so many offensive 'outsider' jokes, I should be way, way more sensitive (after all, who's zooming who)," he wrote. "I for one should never allow my cultural bias to take precedence over my 'examined life.'" Well done. There are different kinds of privilege, and different ways people can show bias. Being a victim does not mean you cannot also sometimes be a perpetrator.

Now back to you. If it's hard to believe that you, lovely you, messed up, it may also be hard to admit that your lovely nation did. We'll talk about this more in chapter 7, but here we'll just say that if you're ever proud of your country, you must also be willing to be ashamed of your country. And then willing to do the work to fix it.

They Never Let Me Forget It

Some bad apologies come out of the wish not to give others ammunition to use against you. Those others might be your political opponents, or they might be your beloved family. The fear of looking weak goes deep in us social animals. Looking weak can be dangerous. In the wild, animals that look weak are the ones predators target. When social animals appear weak, their beloved pack fellows may take the opportunity to stage a coup or steal a mate. We human animals seem to have an instinct to protect our image.

Being vague about what's being apologized for is a way of avoiding handing out ammo to our enemies. Instead of saying precisely what they're apologizing for, people may say they're sorry for how it all went down, for what happened, for the way things turned out. Because if I actually specify that I'm sorry for taking your car and going off with your girlfriend, or for telling the other kids not to play with you because you have cooties, or for instructing the manager not to rent to people like you, what if you then turn around and remind me of it constantly? What if you shout, "So you admit it!" Or, in the last case, what if you sue me?

It may *feel* safer just to apologize for "any misunderstanding"—except that bad apologies often leave people feeling vengeful. They're not appeased by "Sorry for how that worked out"; they're infuriated. Vagueness feels safer, but it's not. Instead of restoring mutual respect, you may have created a new cause for anger. As psychologist Harriet Lerner writes, "Sometimes, the failure of the other person to apologize when they should hits us harder than the deed they should apologize for."

One problem with vague apologies is the potential for misunderstanding what the apology is for. When Jordan said she was sorry for those things she said, she was thinking about how she called her friend a jackass. But since she didn't specify what she's sorry for, she doesn't find out that her friend wasn't bothered at all about being called a jackass. She's welcome to call him a jackass anytime! In reality, his feelings were hurt when she called him a bully. A *bully*! That's what was so wounding. Since her vague apology kept her from finding out what really upset him, she's liable to do it again.

Coming for You, Character Played by John Wayne!

Some people have gotten the idea that it's a character flaw to apologize. A weakness. Police chiefs shouldn't apologize, because it means they're not standing behind their officers. Teachers shouldn't apologize or they'll lose control of the class.

We disagree—strongly. We think a lot of the time such views are merely excuses not to do the hard thing and apologize. Cowardly excuses, even.

In *Sorry About That: The Language of Public Apology*, Edwin L. Battistella analyzes a John Wayne movie, *She Wore a Yellow Ribbon*, which seems to promote the idea that apologizing is lily-livered and unmanly. Wayne's character, Captain Nathan Cutting Brittles, keeps telling people, "Never apologize; it's a sign of weakness." This philosophy, Battistella notes, has "become associated with a certain type of masculinity that denies regret, empathy, and responsibility rather than the stoic who quietly bears them." But Battistella says that "Excuses are a sign of weakness" would be a better description of Brittles's outlook; the film's take on apology and masculinity is actually more nuanced than toxic. Self-professed John Wayne fans never seem to note that Captain Brittles says of himself, "Old men should stop wars," or that he takes responsibility for an underling's failures: "Only the man who commands can be blamed; it rests on me." Wouldn't it be great if more leaders listened to *those* lines in the movie?

Alas, we've learned a lot of bad apologies from the movies. "Love means never having to say you're sorry"? You know nothing, *Love Story*! Love means being willing to say you're sorry *constantly*!

Or what about HAL 9000's apology in *2001: A Space Odyssey*? Astronaut Dave Bowman tells the scary supercomputer, "Open the pod-bay door, HAL," so Dave can come back inside the spaceship. HAL responds in that unnerving, flat voice, "I'm sorry, Dave. I'm afraid I can't do that." HAL knows that Dave and his colleague Frank were planning to disconnect him. The lack of emotion in the "sorry" is possibly more terrifying than the knowledge that HAL is planning on letting Dave die slowly without oxygen. The moral: Never forget your helmet. No, wait. Don't plot to turn off your sentient AI when it has cameras everywhere and can read lips. Also, if you really want to infuriate someone with whom you're arguing, affect HAL's endlessly calm, patient, emotionless voice, which invariably makes the other person feel both condescended to and crazy.

One film did offer the lesson that an apology given under duress rather than given freely and thoughtfully tends to not be a good apology. In *A Fish Called Wanda*, John Cleese's character refuses to apologize for calling Kevin Kline's character stupid. Kline's character responds, "You pompous, stuck-up, snot-nosed, English"—here he looks Cleese up and down—"*giant* twerp scumbag fuckface dickhead asshole!" Cleese responds, "How very interesting. You're a true vulgarian, aren't you?" Kline snaps, "You're the vulgarian, you fuck!" But in the very next scene, we see Cleese apologizing beautifully!

> *I apologize. I'm really, really sorry. I apologize unreservedly. I offer a complete and utter retraction. The imputation was totally without basis in fact and was in no way fair comment and was motivated purely by malice, and I deeply regret any distress that my comments may have caused you or your family, and I hereby undertake not to repeat any such slander at any time in the future.*

The camera spins around during Cleese's speech, and we see that he's being held upside down by his ankles as Kline dangles him out of a window. We, the viewer, understand that while this apology ticks many of the boxes of an excellent apology, it is not. It uses the words "I'm sorry" and "I apologize," and the speaker commits not to err again, but it is an apology made solely to prevent imminent death. This is not an apology to be trusted. However, Kline responds, "Okay," and seems quite satisfied with this apology. The film has established that he is stupid.

Sorry If, Sorry But, Sorry You

When people want to pin a problem on a third party, bad apologies burst into blossom. "It wasn't my fault." "It was the fault of the gossip sites." "It was the fault of the kind of people who troll through old social media posts looking for stupid things I said, wore, or recorded myself eating when I was just a teenager." "It's cancel culture." "It's playing the gotcha game." "It's people who think they're so woke: *they're* the problem!" All ways to say: Don't get mad at me; get mad at *them*!

In the (ideally) less public sphere of the family, it was *obviously* the other kid's fault. "He started it!" "She cheese-touched me!" "He ate the fun-sized Milky Way I was saving!" "She drew a mustache on Barbie!" "They read my diary!" All these justifications for pinching a sibling, kicking them in the shins, giving them a swirlie, or gifting them with a purple nurple are bad justifications. Heaven forfend anyone just apologize. For what they themselves did.

Sometimes, when an offender does apologize, they can't seem to stop adding clauses to the word "sorry." Instead of letting the apology be a complete (and maybe even perfect) thing, they go on to make criticisms, to level charges of having provoked the bad thing that happened, or to suggest psychotherapy (the worst). "Sorry, but you made me so mad." "Sorry, but you have to expect that kind of thing when my candidate loses and yours wins. *Supposedly*." "Sorry, but I can't help myself when someone disrespects my religion."

"Sorry, but . . ." is a frequent problem in long-term relationships. (Ask us how we know.) "Yes, sorry I snorted rudely, but that's because you said my parakeet activism was trivial!" "I said your parakeet activism was trivial because you ignored my question about the car warranty, and that's urgent!" "I didn't ignore your question about the car warranty. I was trying to remember if we stuffed it in the drawer of detritus or filed it in the giant folder of takeout menus no one has looked at since 2002!"

It's wearisome to try to remember the chain of aggravations. So really it's good news that in a proper apology *you should not do that*. An apology for snorting rudely should leave out the excuse for snorting rudely. Just say, "I'm sorry I snorted. That was rude and uncalled-for." Do not use an apology as an excuse or justification for criticizing the other person.

This can be a huge challenge, we admit. Susan once pep talked Marjorie out of her desire to include in an apology her rationale for saying the mean thing she had to apologize for. Marjorie had *reasons* for saying that mean thing! But her reasons for saying the mean thing were not relevant to the content of the apology. They never are, no matter how much you—or Marjorie—want them to be. Sorry not sorry.

Once your snort-apology is out of the way, y'all can deal with the car warranty and the parakeet activism. There might be more apologies to come—parakeets are living creatures, for God's sake!—but these apologies should be separate from any apology-centered chain of events.

In *The Five Languages of Apology: How to Experience Healing in All Your Relationships*, Gary Chapman and Jennifer M. Thomas give the example of sisters Iris and Marie, who argued a lot. Iris often lost her temper with Marie, but when she apologized for flying off the handle, she'd end by complaining, "I just wish you would stop putting me down. I know I am not as educated as you, but that doesn't mean that you can treat me like dirt." Marie didn't feel apologized to; she felt attacked. "What kind of apology is that? She puts all the blame on me." We agree with Marie. Even if it's true that Marie sneers at Iris, and even if that is an issue that deserves discussion, that needs to be a *separate discussion* from the one about Iris flying off the handle.

When I Hurt You, I Hurt Myself—Only Worse

One family of bad apologies comes when the apologizer pays too much attention to themselves and their anguish over what they did. It's unfortunate, because this often comes from someone taking seriously whatever they did, which is good, but taking it too far, which is bad.

If Jordan did something mean to you, and you point it out, and Jordan comes back to you later with an apology that includes "I realize I was awful to you. I took your complaints so much to heart that I haven't slept for nights. I had to get medical treatment for exhaustion," the focus is now on Jordan, who apparently suffered a lot worse than you did. Maybe you should apologize to Jordan? This kind of apology comes from someone who's feeling justified or excused or at least distracted by their own anguish. This kind of apology can also be the hallmark of a narcissist.

Sadly, "all about me" apologies are frequently deployed when a white person has been informed that their words or conduct have hurt a person of color. The white person sobs about how they had no idea, they feel so terrible, they're sorry but the fact that their offense has been pointed out to them when they didn't mean anything RACIAL by it has caused them the Special Agony of being thought of as racist. . . . The white person is essentially asking for a blessing, reassurance, or immediate forgiveness from the person they've harmed. Similarly, when someone misgenders a trans person and then whirls into a shame spiral of apology and mortification and self-abnegation, they put the trans person into the position of having to soothe the person who just misgendered them. This isn't fair. Apologize briefly and nondramatically. Center the other person's needs, not yours.

Let's Put That Behind Us and Move On with Amnesia!

Some bad apologies come into being when the person apologizing is afraid of having "that conversation." They really don't want to examine the chain of events. They certainly don't want to dwell on what they said. They want an apology to sweep things under the carpet. Forever. (Which just leads to lumpy carpets. Lumpy carpets of the mind.)

Apologies like these avoid specificity like the plague. They apologize for "the events," "some of my posts," or "things that might have been said," and then hurry on. Often these apologies try to get everyone to agree to let bygones be bygones. "Glad we took care of that. Let's never speak of this again! Let's look ahead! Let's let us, together, in beautiful harmony, come together in healing, no matter what it was I did that was so long ago I can't even remember exactly what it was, even if it only happened last Tuesday! What's next on the agenda?"

For the Advanced Student

Come on, aren't there exceptions? Well, yeah. If another hockey parent overheard you saying their kid is an ugly little psychopath, you should apologize even if you genuinely think the kid *is* an ugly little psychopath. You're going to have to dig deep down into your insincerity and say that sometimes, when you're upset, the nastiest things fly out of your mouth and you're going to work on that; that their darling Jordan is actually a talented little skater who puts in the hours and never gives up; and you're really, really, really sorry. (You may be glad someday when the kid turns into a fine human being, which happens surprisingly often.) You don't have to lie. You have to tell a selective truth for the benefit of the team, for your own kid's future experience on the ice (because you don't want the little psychopath taking revenge on your spawn for what *you* said), and for the sake of modeling good apologies to others (to your kid, for the psychopath kid, for the psychopath kid's possibly psychopathic parent).

Or—in an obviously comparable situation—if you are a soldier and a wartime enemy has you in captivity and has been torturing you for days, you might be well-advised to say you are sorry for your actions even if you aren't sorry. You might hope that reading the apology just as your captors wrote it, including phrases like "I am a black criminal and I have performed the deeds of an air pirate," will tip some people off that the apology wasn't composed by you.

However, years later, if you're running for president and being urged to apologize for using racist slurs when referring to Asian people, and you initially dig in your heels and double down and refuse to apologize because "they" tortured you, you might wish to think hard about that refusal. Did all Asian people torture you? Did your torturers torture you *because* they were Asian?

Eventually, this candidate *did* elect to apologize, saying, "Out of respect to a great number of people whom I hold in very high regard, I will no longer use the term that has caused such discomfort. I deeply regret any pain I have caused. I apologize and renounce all language that is bigoted and offensive." Sometimes politicians apologize as a political strategy. (Sometimes they do *not* apologize as a political strategy; a certain other presidential candidate from a different party opted not to apologize for her record as a state prosecutor, when she opposed legislation to investigate police shootings.) Granted, the politician's apology for his use of racist language was only adequate. We're not crazy about his use of "any pain," since it allows for the possibility that there was no pain. When you *know* something has caused hurt, don't say you regret "any" hurt that was caused.

First Day with My New Lips

Some apologies are bad because the person apologizing simply has no practice. As we're going to argue a couple of chapters from now, many of us aren't taught how to apologize as kids and may not have seen good apologies happening around us. When psychiatrist Aaron Lazare was working on his book about apology, he said, "I freely discussed this subject with friends . . . and colleagues. These were discussions about why I thought the subject of apology to be so interesting and engaging, not advice or problem-solving sessions—so I thought. Months or years later, several of these people told me about apologies they offered that had profound impacts on their lives. Some of these people had not understood the apology process and literally did not know how to apologize."

There are also people who hope they won't have to say the Scary

Apology Words if they show remorse by their actions. Actions are good . . . but they should accompany actual words.

When we're suddenly on the spot, we're inept. We don't know when it's important to specify what we're apologizing for (most of the time) and when it's important not to (when describing our mistake is doing it again, as with that aforementioned politician's use of anti-Asian slurs: we don't need to hear the words one more time). And maybe we don't want to do the work to figure out how to apologize well on our own, because that is not fun. Or easy.

This is when the natural wily genius thing comes up, because if we're not careful, we'll find ourselves saying, "I'm sorry if you thought I did something inappropriate, but that was never my intention." "Long ago, when I was a very young man . . ." "Even though steroid use is widespread in this sport . . ." It just slips from our self-protective lips.

Did You See Me Man Up?

Think about, perhaps, Mark Wahlberg's 1993 press conference in which he apologized for the two crimes he was charged with as a teenager. "I just want to set the record straight," he said. (Heroic!) "In 1986, I harassed a group of school kids on a field trip. Many of the students were African Americans." This is a very vague apology for an incident in which Wahlberg threw rocks and chanted, "Kill the [n-words]." And if Wahlberg had been engaging in full disclosure, he could have added that he threw rocks and racial slurs at Black children on *two separate occasions*. (An overachiever!) He continued, "In 1988 I assaulted two Vietnamese men over a case of beer. Racist slurs and language were used during these encounters, and people were seriously hurt."

This is a super-fun use of the passive voice. Racist slurs were used by whom? People were seriously hurt by whom? (Zombies?) The non-minimizing apology would have specified that he, Marky Mark, used the racist slurs, and that he, Marky Mark, beat one of the Vietnamese men unconscious with a big stick and was initially charged with attempted murder. (He pled it down to felony assault.) "I am truly sorry for what I did," Wahlberg went on. "I was a teenager and intoxicated when I did those things, but that's no excuse." True, yet we notice that you mentioned it! However, you did not mention that in the latter incident, you were also reportedly high on PCP!

Wahlberg continued, "Nor is it okay to beat up people because your friends are doing it. I know there are kids out there doing the same stuff now, and I just want to tell them, don't do it." Again, what a hero! Such courage! When Wahlberg attempted to have the felony conviction struck from his criminal record, the outcry was such that he withdrew the request. Still, he persisted in casting himself as a hero for owning his past, saying that his choosing to leave the gang of Boston thugs he'd been hanging around with at the time "made it 10 times more difficult to walk from my home to the train station, to go to school, to go to work." Our hearts bleed for him.

When it comes to bad apologies, it's always smart to look for vagueness. Does the apologizer say what they're sorry for? Sorry about "all that"? "The incident"? Could mean anything. Look for minimizing. Maybe they say, "Sorry for the confusion," when it would be more appropriate to say, "Sorry I tried to get you thrown out of the conference because you criticized my last paper."

Damn It, Fritz, I'm a Campaign Manager, Not a Translator

Take, for example, the apology of Senator Fritz Hollings of South Carolina in 1983, after calling the Iowa supporters of his opponent Alan Cranston "wetbacks from California." Hollings responded to the public outcry with "I in no way intended those remarks to be a comment on Hispanics or Mexican Americans. I apologize for my choice of words, if they offended anyone." Pro tip: You have definitely offended people if you have to apologize. Hollings's Iowa campaign manager, Ken Purcell, did not help matters when he explained that Hollings "did not mean it in a racial sense. It was meant in the sense of people crossing the state border to do something in another state. I hope people will not take it as a racial insult. It was not meant as such." Stop talking, Ken.

Many bad apologies that we've seen recently are apologies for the feelings of others, not for the words or deeds of the person apologizing. A lot of apologies arising from the #MeToo movement fall into this category. "I'm sorry you were uncomfortable when I locked the office door and took off my clothes." "I would never want to intimidate anyone, and I'm sorry if anyone felt upset in any way when I answered your knock in my gaping bathrobe." "I apologize if anyone felt like their career was on the line when I asked about their sex life." (This is also known as the "believe women, but not the women who accuse *me* of anything" defense.) The problem is portrayed as coming from the uncomfortable, intimidated, frightened people who simply don't understand the situation or who overreact in our oversensitive times and therefore do not comprehend the beautiful, pure intentions of the apologizer.

Apologizing for the feelings of others is not merely the province of the rich and powerful. It happens in otherwise delightful family homes all the time. "I'm sorry you got upset when I didn't call." "I'm sorry Jordan thought I was making fun of their singing." "I'm sorry you didn't realize I was kidding when I said you were adopted from the circus." In some families, certain parties are fond of the rhetorical strategy of getting *other people* to apologize all the time. Take, for instance, the joke about the son who calls his mother to ask, "Ma, how are you?" "Not too good," the mother says sadly. "I'm very weak." The son asks, "Why are you weak?" The mother says, "Because I haven't eaten in thirty-eight days!" The son says, "Why haven't you eaten in thirty-eight days?" The mother answers, "Because I didn't want my mouth to be full of food if you should call!"

(This is a cue for the son to apologize. Same for the son who gets two neckties from his mother for his birthday, and he wears one the next time he goes to her house for dinner, and she greets him with "The other one you didn't like?")

I Apologized—What's the Problem?

Contemplating loving homes full of intelligent, creative people brings us to the subject of poisoned apologies. Poisoned apologies are even worse than plain bad apologies.

Poisoned apologies aren't just inadequate. They are bitter cruelty enrobed in sweet chocolate. Stuffed inside each one, instead of creamy nougat filling, is an insult: "I apologize for yelling at the dog, but you're overreacting again." "Sorry I snapped at you, but you're so whiny sometimes." "I'm sorry that discussion was so hard on you. If you're so easily triggered, you might want to consider getting counseling." "I apologize for hurting your FEEWINGS."

If you accept the apology—which is unlikely—you'd be accepting the insult too. The essence of a poisoned apology is that the feelings the hurt person has are bad feelings, and the hurt person is bad for having those feelings.

Poisoned apologies often suggest that it's wrong for people to be upset: "Apparently I crossed some invisible line." "I forgot that we are living in an age of political correctness." "Did they not know they were at a *comedy show*?" And there may be the suggestion that someone has demanded the impossible of them: "I never said I was perfect!" (Or "Like you're so perfect!"—which tends to lead to completely random attacks.) Nobody's perfect. Nobody thinks they're perfect—but they still may always think they're right in *this particular case*. Which particular case? Any particular case!

Forget Perfect—Try for Good

Perfect is the enemy of good, Voltaire (supposedly) said. Perfection is impossible, so it's not a reasonable goal. Failure is built in. And when you accept that everyone is flawed, you can accept that we all have the choice to apologize well or poorly or not at all. What's invariably true is that the cover-up is worse than the crime. Covering up is the hiding of imperfection and famously leads to trouble. Apology is the opposite of covering up.

Here's a suggestion: If you know you're likely to apologize badly, try practicing your apology to your mirror, your cat, a clump of dandelions. "I'm sorry, reflection." "I apologize, Fluffypants." "Dandelions, you were right. I was wrong. I should have listened to you." Once you've gotten a positive response from your reflection, Fluffypants, and dandelions—or at least not a negative one—practice on a sympathetic (to *you*) friend. Ask them to think how they'd respond if they received an apology like the one you're presenting to them. If they say they'd be irked, chances are the recipient you're practicing for will be irked too. Now it's on you to decide whether you're capable of apologizing well or whether you should opt not to apologize at all.

We would love to tell you that knowing how to apologize would make you perfect but, regrettably, we'd be contradicting ourselves. And setting a bad example.

"I'm Sorry" Can Be a Phatic Expression

A semi-aside: Some folks are critical of what they perceive to be insincere apologies that actually aren't. In linguistics, a phatic expression is speech that doesn't mean anything except that the speaker is being polite. Let's say your friend says, "I broke my toe!" or "The game I had tickets to was called on account of rain!" or "I thought I'd recorded the Oscars but I accidentally recorded the entirety of *Sex Lives of the Potato Men*!"

and you reply, "I'm sorry!" That doesn't mean *you* broke the person's toe, or made it rain, or tuned the telly to the 2004 comedy that the *Times* of London called "a masterclass in film-making ineptitude" and the *Sunday Telegraph* called "less a film than an appetite suppressant." Saying "Sorry" as phatic speech is a low-impact attempt to bond with another person. It serves a socio-pragmatic purpose. It shows you're listening. It is a form of small talk. It is a pleasantry, an attempt to create connection. For British people, saying "Sorry" before asking a question is usually phatic. For Canadians, the word "sorry"—pronounced with that delightful *o* sound, so sweetly mockable to us Americans—is often phatic. Try to be tolerant of phatic apologies even if they rub you the wrong way. "Don't be sorry: *you* didn't break my toe" is an impolite response to phatic speech.

Taking Responsibility Can Change Lives

Let's end this chapter on a powerful example of how healing a good apology can be. After the explosion of the space shuttle *Columbia*, NASA launch integration manager Wayne Hale publicly took the blame. Although he'd repeatedly raised safety questions privately—and was rebuffed by other NASA officials—he stepped up and apologized. He said:

> I am at fault. . . . I stand condemned in the court of my own conscience to be guilty of not preventing the Columbia disaster. We could discuss the particulars: inattention, incompetence, distraction, lack of conviction, lack of understanding, a lack of backbone, laziness. The bottom line is that I failed to understand what I was being told; I failed to stand up and be counted. Therefore, look no further; I am guilty of allowing Columbia to crash.

With these words, Hale took responsibility, acknowledged the impact, didn't try to pass the buck. Imagine the guts this took.

And almost three years later he apologized *again*. In the initial investigation of what caused the explosion, NASA investigators decided that improper installation of the foam insulation on the shuttle's fuel tanks was responsible. The media dutifully reported this. But then scientists discovered that improper installation wasn't the cause after all; the insulation had failed because of the completely normal expansion and contraction of a full tank of fuel. NASA had neglected to test the insulation on full tanks, only on partly full ones. Which meant that the guys who'd installed the foam were innocent. Hale flew to the foam installation plant in Louisiana to apologize personally, in an all-hands meeting, to all the assembly workers, for NASA's wrongful placement of blame. It wasn't their fault. He was so sorry. "Thin comfort for me to apologize: so late, so little," he reflected on his blog later.

Is it, though?

ACTION ITEMS

Before you apologize, check:

❏   Am I shifting the blame?

❏   Am I minimizing my offense?

❏   Am I sounding defensive?

❏   Do I really want to apologize here?

❏   Can I apologize without reminding the other person that they've sinned too?

I'm Sorry vs. I Apologize

In *Sorry About That*, linguist Edwin Battistella argues that the words "I'm sorry" "[do] not literally perform an apology" and that they only report on how the speaker feels. (Like "regret.") In contrast, "I apologize" is *the action* of apologizing. It's a performative utterance, in other words.

We think that, in colloquial usage, "I'm sorry" can have the same weight as "I apologize"—as long as it's not followed by cunning caveats like "if I upset you" or "if people mistakenly inferred that I was acting out of prejudice" or "that the media took my actions out of context."

Indeed, sometimes people getting an apology feel that "I apologize" is suspiciously formal. They think it sounds distancing, ritualistic, forced. "I'm sorry" works better, they feel, because it seems more heartfelt.

BAD APOLOGY BINGO CARD #1

never claimed	disheartened	not what I meant	not what I'm about	misrepresenting
move forward	intent	saddened	obviously	out of character for me
forgiveness	it distresses me that	**FREE SPACE**	if it sounded like	actually
humans make mistakes	how I expressed myself	sorry if	what I believe	despite
compassion	my own trauma	imperfect	inebriated	I feel guilty

CHAPTER 4

BLAME IT ON THE BRAIN: THE SCIENCE OF WHY WE SAY SUCH DUMB STUFF

One overarching reason we resist apologizing—and then apologize poorly when we do apologize—is that we have a compelling psychological need to see ourselves as the hero of our own story. To acknowledge wrongdoing, and to do so without offering up mitigating factors and rationalizations, means we have to cast ourselves as the villain in the narrative. And no one wants that. We will do pretty much anything to hold on to our heroic status in the book of our lives. Let's explore this notion! As a tribute to the fact that certain refrains persistently run through bad apologies, every subhead in this chapter is a song lyric.

There Goes My Hero

It's human nature to be self-protective. We don't want to get hurt . . . and that includes being psychologically hurt. And when the psychological hurt is self-inflicted? The worst.

Self-justification is a powerful drug. We didn't do anything wrong, we tell ourselves. But if we did do something wrong, there are extenuating circumstances! We had to do it!

So we are good, but we did a bad thing. How the heck do we reconcile these two contradictory notions? Cognitive dissonance, baby! Holding these two impossible-to-both-be-true facts in our head at the same time makes us feel ill at ease, uncomfortable, uneasy, regretful, ashamed. The worse the bad thing is, the more dissonance we feel. If our actions conflict with our sense of self, we'll bend over backward to create sense and logic out of the contradictions. It's how we cope, how we make it through the day. If we didn't see ourselves as good—or at least *trying* to be good—we'd be unable to function. We'd be flattened by depression, anxiety, guilt. (Those of us who *do* struggle with depression, anxiety, and guilt—Marjorie raises her hand to you, reader, in a cheery, antidepressant-fueled wave!—have to do quite a bit of work to figure out what elements of our self-image can be ameliorated by apology, forgiveness, and self-forgiveness. But more on that struggle in chapter 8.)

To a certain degree, *not* attempting to wrestle with cognitive dissonance is a smart choice. Delving into every single not-so-good or not-so-positively-motivated thing we've ever done would be utterly paralyzing. We'd never sleep again. We'd do nothing but cry and hate ourselves. But if we *never* addressed our sometimes disappointing behavior, we'd be sociopaths. We'd damage our relationships (again, consider how furious we are when people refuse to apologize to us when they really should, or when they apologize to us badly) and we'd miss the opportunity to become better, kinder, more thoughtful people. The journey to self-betterment can be very satisfying, which is why we enjoy stories in which a selfish person—say, Ebenezer Scrooge, Eleanor Shellstrop in *The Good Place*, Bill Murray's character in *Groundhog Day*, Amir in *The Kite Runner*, Faith in *Buffy the Vampire Slayer*—does the work of becoming more compassionate, learning to understand others, and earning forgiveness.

It's maddening when someone who *should* apologize has the opportunity to do so but refuses to. Take prosecutor Ken Starr, who was instrumental in destroying Monica Lewinsky's life during Bill Clinton's impeachment trial in 1998. A decade later, Lewinsky ran into Starr in a restaurant and wrote about the experience for *Vanity Fair*:

> *Starr asked me several times if I was "doing O.K." A stranger might have surmised from his tone that he had actually worried about me over the years. His demeanor, almost pastoral, was somewhere between avuncular and creepy. He kept touching my arm and elbow, which made me uncomfortable.*
>
> *Understandably, I was a bit thrown. (It was also confusing for me to see "Ken Starr" as a human being. He was there, after all, with what appeared to be his family.) I finally gathered my wits about me—after an internal command of Get It Together. "Though I wish I had made different choices back then," I stammered, "I wish that you and your office had made different choices, too." In hindsight, I later realized, I was paving the way for him to apologize. But he didn't. He merely said, with the same inscrutable smile, "I know. It was unfortunate."*

"It was unfortunate"? What a jerk. He wasn't being recorded. There was no journalist taking notes. Starr could have acted like a human being and given even a B-minus apology, like, "I know those hearings were agonizing for you, and I'm so sorry we put you through that." Even if he thought that she was necessary collateral damage in the pursuit of justice, or that she was stupid for having an affair with the president in the first place—even though the president was married and she wasn't, and he was twice her age and held all the power in the relationship, and at the time people acted like he was a manly horndog but she was a dumb bimbo, and the country went *off* on making Jewish and fat jokes about her while Democrats merely muttered that Clinton's prosecution was politically motivated and Republicans tut-tutted that he was a liar and she was a slut in a stained blue dress (hey, apparently we're still mad about this)—Starr could have apologized. He could've even avoided taking personal responsibility by saying "we" or "my office" in a way that might not get an A-plus grade from SorryWatch but would at least have potentially gone a long way toward making Lewinsky feel seen as a human being. But nope.

Presumably Starr, like most of us, saw himself as the hero in his own story rather than a villain in Lewinsky's. If he ever felt bad about what he had done to a young woman who was betrayed by a friend and became the focus of every late-night comedy monologue for months, he tamped down those feelings or rewrote the story in his head to conform to his self-image as someone just doing a job, or someone single-minded in his pursuit of justice, or a man righting a wrong that affected the entire country.

And if he'd felt even a tiny stab of guilt, he'd probably done what most of us do and spent years filing down the troubling memory, smoothing its rough edges, turning it into a story that conformed precisely to what he wanted it to be and who he wanted to be. "The more a person recalls a memory, the more they change it," wrote novelist Lidia Yuknavitch in *The Chronology of Water*: "Once you open your mouth, you are moving away from the truth of things. According to neuroscience. The safest memories are locked in the brains of people who can't remember. Their memories remain the closest replica of actual events. Underwater. Forever."

Weird Science

Yuknavitch is right about the neuroscience. Psychologists tell us that if there's an inconsistency in our behavior or attitudes that conflicts with who we tell ourselves we are, we are compelled to take action to eliminate the inconsistency or to create harmony in all these inharmonious aspects of our lives/brains/experiences/storytelling. We crave cognitive consistency. If something pops up—a feeling, a bit of evidence, an action we've taken—that contradicts our pretty picture of ourselves and the world, we do everything possible to discredit this new piece of evidence. Confirmation bias is the belief that, oh, yep, this new thing shows me exactly what I already thought to be true. Even if that's patently ridiculous.

There's a meme that explains confirmation bias in one panel. An old crone in Puritan garb is sitting on a witness stand. She says, "It makes no difference what I say. You've already decided I'm guilty." A man in buckled shoes and a Pilgrim hat gasps, "THE WITCH CAN READ MINDS!"

Voilà. Confirmation bias.

Feeling justified in our beliefs and doings can lead to some piss-poor apologies. *Ugh, fine*, we think. *I'll say I'm sorry to keep the peace. But I'm only doing this out of pity for you, because you are the idiot in this exchange.* Or: *Sure, whatever, I'll say some nebulously regretful-sounding words out of expediency, because I want to get past this already.* (Our term for something that vaguely resembles an apology but is not one is Apology-Shaped Object.)

Our ability to feel sure we're in the right is compounded, because overwhelmingly we tend to talk on social media to people who agree with us. And we choose to get our political and election news from sources that support our views. According to a 2019 Pew Research Center survey, 93 percent of people whose main news source is Fox News identify as Republican, and 95 percent of people who watch MSNBC identify as Democrats. (*New York Times* readers and NPR listeners, at 91 percent and 87 percent, also tended to be left leaning. Shocking, we are sure.)

If you agree with me and the way I view the world, clearly you are smart and trustworthy. If you disagree with me and the way I view the world, I pity you in your idiocy and venality. It's like living in Garrison Keiller's Lake Wobegon, "where all the women are strong, all the men are good looking, and all the children are above average." Statistically, this is not possible. Yet almost all of us believe ourselves to be more attractive than average, smarter than average, kinder than average. (This is known as "illusory superiority," or the Lake Wobegon effect.)

Everybody Plays the Fool

Our sometimes unconscious insistence on protecting our worldview is backed up by MRI studies. In one such study, conducted shortly before the 2004 presidential election, clinical psychologist Drew Westen at Emory University gave MRIs to thirty men who strongly identified as Republicans and thirty men who strongly identified as Democrats. The men were presented with statements by then candidates George W. Bush and John Kerry, in which both men clearly contradicted themselves. (Politicians? Contradicting themselves? Unheard-of!) The Republican subjects found ways to discount Bush's inconsistencies and highlight Kerry's, and the Democrats did the opposite. Feelings, not logic, held sway.

"We did not see any increased activation of the parts of the brain normally engaged during reasoning," Westen said in an Emory press release about the study. "What we saw instead was a network of emotion circuits lighting up, including circuits hypothesized to be involved in regulating emotion, and circuits known to be involved in resolving conflicts."

After the subjects came to their respective conclusions and dismissed the information that didn't rationally make sense, the reward circuits in their brains lit up—like rats getting little pellets for pushing a lever or addicts getting a sweet, sweet fix. Westen said, "Essentially, it appears as if partisans twirl the cognitive kaleidoscope until they get the conclusions they want, and then they get massively reinforced for it, with the elimination of negative emotional states and activation of positive ones."

In *Mistakes Were Made (but Not by Me): Why We Justify Foolish Beliefs, Bad Decisions, and Hurtful Acts*, psychologists Carol Tavris and Elliot Aronson write, "Self-justification not only minimizes our mistakes and bad decisions; it is also the reason that everyone can see a hypocrite in action except a hypocrite. It allows us to create a distinction between our moral lapses and someone else's and to blur the discrepancy between our actions and our moral convictions."

And just as everyone can see a hypocrite in action except a hypocrite, everyone can see a lousy apology in action except the lousy apologizer. (What's more, in the case of an apology that doesn't come at all, the person who refuses to apologize likely feels that they don't need to. In fact, they think you probably owe *them* an apology.)

Tavris and Aronson note that self-justification isn't entirely bad. Without it, they note, "we would agonize in the aftermath of almost every decision: Did we do the right thing, marry the right person, buy the right house, choose the best car, enter the right career?" The problem comes when we refuse to see how self-justification can be harmful. "[M]indless self-justification, like quicksand, can draw us deeper into disaster," they write. "It blocks our ability to even see our errors, let alone correct them."

She Blinded Me with Science

Tavris and Aronson also note, "The brain is designed with blind spots, optical and psychological, and one of its cleverest tricks is to confer on us the comforting delusion that we, personally, do not have any." It's like Blindspot Inception.

Dissonance theory is essentially a theory of blind spots. Tavris and Aronson again: "Drivers cannot avoid having blind spots in their field of vision, but good drivers are aware of them; they know they had better be careful backing up and changing lanes if they don't want to crash into fire hydrants and other cars." Telling ourselves that *other people* have blind spots but we ourselves don't leads to rigidity and inflexibility and self-righteousness. The Other Guy, which is what Bruce Banner calls the Incredible Hulk, is the irrational, rage-filled, uncontrollable one. Yet Bruce Banner is the Hulk, and the Hulk is Bruce Banner. (Did we just BLOW YOUR MIND?)

We at SorryWatch believe that when we insist that blind spots—which, again, *everyone has*—are inherently evil and irredeemable, and when we refuse to give someone else the chance to learn about and work around their blind spots, we will never be able to forgive anyone. And SorryWatch thinks that people should be able to earn forgiveness. Granted, not all people deserve to be forgiven. Not everyone is obligated to forgive. But "One strike and you're out" isn't fair. It's not a good rule of play. (A quick addendum: When someone tells you that you have a blind spot about race, gender, or religion, do not demand that someone of that race, gender, or religion explain things to you. Ask someone in your own community.)

Blind spots are a big reason we can instantly home in on the magic buzzer-triggering words in other people's bad apologies—"How dare that guy say 'Sorry if . . .'!" "Look at that big 'but' in that schmuck's apology!" "Oh, she did *not* just use the passive voice!"—yet we don't recognize our own bad apologies as they're coming out of our mouths or frantically typing fingertips. We genuinely don't see what we're doing wrong when we're the ones who are doing it.

Justify My Love

In a seminal study called "Victim and Perpetrator Accounts of Interpersonal Conflict: Autobiographical Narratives About Anger," published in the *Journal of Personality and Social Psychology* in 1990, psychologists Roy F. Baumeister, Arlene Stillwell, and Sara R. Wotman showed just how hard our brains work to justify our own behavior and blame others for theirs. Baumeister asked sixty-three people to share a true story from their past in which they were a victim and another story in which they were the perpetrator. Somehow, when people told stories in which they were the victim, they depicted incidences of terrible betrayal and harm and hurtfulness that had a long-lasting impact on the person telling the story. Often the incident they talked about was "the last straw," the moment at which the victim had finally had enough of a toxic person's behavior. Their stories almost never noted whether the person who victimized them ever apologized, or tried to.

But when the subjects told stories in which *they* were the perpetrator, they presented whatever they did as a single, isolated event without lasting implications. "The same people see things differently depending on whether they participate as perpetrators or victims," Baumeister and his colleagues conclude. "Our results indicate that perpetrators and victims construct events quite differently, but they do not appear to be aware of these discrepancies. . . . Perhaps if people were more able to realize the interpretive discrepancies, they would be less prone to become angry."

Baumeister and company note that the research has implications for the study of historical conflicts. Children in Northern states, for instance, tend to learn about the Civil War as a long-ago event that ended the evil institution of Southern slavery, while children in the South tend to learn that the Civil War (or the War of Northern Aggression) was an attack on the South's culture and way of life, with a lasting impact. These tellings of the story help Northern white people feel superior and perhaps that any lingering racism can be blamed on white Southerners, while white Southerners' telling of the story helps them maintain "an acute sense of grievance." (Again, we're all the hero in our own story.)

Western histories of the Crusades often talk about them as a religious attempt to regain the Holy Land; Muslim accounts stress the burning of villages and massacres of women and children. "Even if both sides agree that a wrong was committed," the study concludes, "the perpetra-tor will be inclined to close the incident and forget about it long before the victim is ready to do so. Indeed, the victims' efforts to sustain the memory may be regarded by the perpetrators as unnecessarily vindic-tive." Victims often see a given offense as the culmination of a bunch of other offenses; perpetrators often see an offense as a single moment and the victims' response as an overreaction.

If we were participating in this study, we'd pick a victim story in which we were crushed, *désolée*—such as the time in which a certain editor in chief asked to see a book proposal of Marjorie's, then promptly ripped off the central conceit, assigned a piece to another writer, printed it in his magazine, and refused to return Marjorie's phone calls and emails. Marjorie's perp story would likely be about a time that she did some-thing objectionable but understandable—such as the time she snarled, *"Why must you make my life harder?"* at her kindergarten-aged offspring, who was repeatedly calling for a snuggle in bed while Marjorie was en-gaged in cleaning up the profuse middle-of-the-night projectile vomit filling the crib of her sobbing younger offspring. Marjorie would be sure to tell you she felt terrible, but also be sure to tell you that after wee off-spring was cleaned up and sheets were changed, she apologized to the older kid, read her a story, hugged her, and gave her water, at which point all was forgiven. So Marjorie wasn't *that* bad. Not like, y'know, that putrescent editor in chief.

Incidentally, Baumeister's study provides a great illustration of why we suggest being very, very careful about offering explanations for your behavior when you apologize for it. (Marjorie's example is an exception to the rule: BECAUSE VOMIT. Vomit trumps almost everything.) Bau-meister showed that perpetrators tended to offer reasons for why they . . . well, perpetrated, but the reasons were actually justifications. They had *excellent reasons* for doing whatever they did that caused pain. Such as: "I only lied to protect him from the truth, which would have hurt him." "I took the bracelet only because it was originally mine and she just kept not giving it back even though I asked." "Whatever I did, I did with cause. Too bad the victim just insanely flew off the handle like that and wouldn't listen to reason." Of course, when the very same storytellers shared anecdotes in which they were the victims, they themselves never flew off the handle unless they were *driven* to it, and they never failed to listen to reason because the perpetrators in their stories were *utterly unreasonable.*

Further, the perpetrators tended to minimize their wrongdoing, if they admitted wrongdoing at all. They didn't do it . . . but if they *did* do it, they were justified in doing it. And if they weren't (entirely) justified in doing it, they simply couldn't help it. And if they maybe could have helped it but did it anyway, it was a single moment in time with a positive outcome and perfect tidy resolution. Everyone has moved on! Everything is forgiven! It was all for the best! It was but a tiny, evanescent moment of darkness in a lifetime of sunny positivity!

And yet, in none of Baumeister's sixty-three victim stories did the victim think the perpetrator's behavior "could not be helped." Remember, in this study the victims and perpetrators are the exact same people. They just see incidents completely differently depending on which hat they're wearing when they're telling a story of being victimized or doing the victimizing.

Come On, Come On, That's Just the Way It Is

Another powerful way our brain conspires to make us resist apologizing (or to apologize poorly) is the Just World bias.

The Just World bias (a.k.a. Just World fallacy, a.k.a. Just World hypothesis) is a cousin of "We are good. But we did a bad thing. How do we reconcile this contradiction?" It's cognitive dissonance on steroids. The logical fallacy goes like this: The world is fair and just. Good is rewarded and evil is punished. You reap what you sow. Justice and fairness are what most religions promise and what our institutions promise. That's why, in a democracy, we submit to the legal and judicial systems we've all agreed on, right?

But when the world is demonstrably unfair, it can shake our sense of how things are supposed to work. When we encounter evidence of police violence and political corruption—when we are confronted with poverty, homelessness, addiction, inequalities in schooling, mental illness, inaccessibility of resources—we consciously or unconsciously blame the victim. The world is just, so if they experience injustice, they must have done something to cause that injustice. They brought it on themselves.

Make no mistake: we're hardwired to seek fairness. Even animals are angered by unfairness. Capuchin monkeys performing tasks for rewards of cucumber chunks will get upset if they see that other monkeys are doing the same tasks and getting better rewards—for example, grapes. OMG, *grapes!* Grapes are *way* better than cucumber chunks! The outraged monkeys go on strike: they won't work for cucumber chunks any longer, once they know that other monkeys are getting grapes. *SCREECH! I WOULD RATHER HAVE NOTHING AT ALL THAN BE TREATED THIS WAY! SCREECH!* They won't accept the inequity, the disrespect.

We'd be upset ourselves, even though SorryWatch, in truth, often prefers cucumber to grapes. (Much depends on the type and freshness of grape.) But, like us—and like wolves and dogs, who will also go on strike when they see their fellows getting better treatment for buzzer-pressing tasks—capuchin monkeys are social animals who value fairness. The desire to be treated fairly comes from ancient, prehuman impulses.

But to have to fight for fairness every time there's an indignity (*SCREECH!*) is exhausting. It adds up. And there's not a lot of motivation to seek true fairness if you're the monkey that gets the grapes.

The notion of Just World bias derives in large part from the research of Melvin J. Lerner at the University of Waterloo, in Ontario. During Lerner's education as a social psychologist, he observed the way mentally ill patients were treated by health-care providers. Even the most generous-spirited professionals seemed on some level to hold patients responsible for their own suffering. He also observed his own students belittling poor people; they seemed to scorn disadvantaged patients without seeming terribly aware of or interested in the social constructs and failures that cause poverty.

So, in 1965, Lerner designed an experiment to test the notion that humans blame victimized people for their own victimization. Seventy-two women were recruited to watch another woman seemingly get a series of electric shocks. At first the witnesses were upset at what they saw. But as the experiment went on, the viewers began to have a lower opinion of the victim. The more she seemed to suffer, the lower their opinion of her fell. When they were told that the victim would receive compensation for her suffering in the study, however, their opinion of her rose. ("Ah, so she wasn't really weak and pathetic; she was getting *paid* for this. We like her more now.")

In another study, Lerner presented male subjects with two identical profiles; the only difference was that the study participants were told that one of the men had won the lottery. The participants overwhelmingly felt that the lottery winner was a harder worker than the non-winner. This makes zero logical sense, of course. But people really want to believe that goodness is rewarded and evil is punished.

Not incidentally, fervently believing that the world is just tends to correlate with both authoritarianism and privilege. People who have power, and people who believe that order must be kept with an iron fist, are generally more likely to believe that the world is fair. But we all experience some degree of Just World bias. More recent studies have shown that observers tend to feel that victims of domestic violence, illnesses, rape—even random traffic accidents—"brought it on themselves." After all, Why didn't she leave him? Was he a smoker? What was she wearing? Why didn't he look more carefully when he stepped into the crosswalk? Thought processes like these offer the reassurance that whatever it was won't happen to *us*.

Wouldn't It Be Nice?

What does all this have to do with apologies? If you think someone is responsible for their own suffering, you're way less likely to want to apologize to them. If you're *compelled* to apologize to them—by a parent or employer, or by social media criticism—you're likely to apologize badly, because you think, consciously or not, that whatever you did to them, they deserved.

We believe that if you're not sorry, don't apologize. Because you'll just mess things up further. But if a person or group tells you that you've harmed them, do them and yourself the courtesy of listening to their reasoning and considering whether your own biases and presuppositions about the world are preventing you from realizing you have a blind spot. Or more than one.

Why the Long Face?

Let's turn from the world of psychology to the world of sociology: not only are non-apologizers and bad apologizers sometimes unaware of their own Just World bias, they may not be aware of their own overarching need to protect their face.

Mid-century sociologist Erving Goffman coined the term "face" to mean the image of the self that people want to project. Our face is constantly being threatened by external forces, and we're perpetually anxious about how we'll look to others. Face is a moving target, a mask that changes depending on the group we're in and the social interactions we're involved in. Loss of face is hurtful and humiliating to us. In general, politeness is an attempt to allow everyone in an interaction to maintain their face. To keep face, we're motivated by pride (which helps us see ourselves as deserving of the things we want), by dignity (which makes us feel competent in social interactions), and by honor (our sense of duty toward the world we inhabit).

Apologizing is inherently a threat to one's face. When we apologize, we have to swallow our pride, subsume our dignity to the needs of the person we're apologizing to, and maintain honor even as we resent having to fulfill our duty to others in a way that isn't fun for us. We apologize badly in a feeble attempt to protect our face. (*Such* a mistake, because a good apology is a thing to take pride in.)

For lovers of vintage television, "face" might be deemed "hand." In a *Seinfeld* episode called "The Pez Dispenser," George Costanza is worried that the woman he's dating, Noel, has more status and dominance in the relationship than he does. He wails to Jerry, "I'm very uncomfortable! I have no power. Why should she have the upper hand? Once in my life I would like the upper hand. I have no hand! No hand at all! She has the hand! I have no hand!" Because George feels he lacks hand, he doesn't want to tell Noel that his friends were responsible for breaking her concentration at her piano recital. (Jerry's antics with a Pez dispenser had made Elaine crack up.) Elaine wants to apologize to Noel, but George convinces her not to, because Noel already has hand. But when Noel hears Elaine laugh her giant honking laugh at another event, she recognizes it from the recital and promptly breaks up with George. He protests, "But I have hand!" Just before slamming the door, Noel snaps, "And you're gonna need it."

The moral: An apology is perceived as a loss of hand/face, but when done well, it can save a relationship. Being determined to have hand/save face makes people lie, refrain from apologizing, and risk losing more face when the truth comes out and the Pez/shit hits the fan.

Vulnerable, Oh, So Vulnerable

In a TED Talk that's been viewed over 52 million times, Brené Brown talks about the importance of vulnerability. She talks about how terrifying parenting can be but says that, as parents, our job isn't to try to make our children perfect. "Our job is to look and say, 'You know what? You're imperfect, and you're wired for struggle, but you are worthy of love and belonging.' That's our job."

Exactly. When we're more concerned that our kids "show well"—making sure they look good to others, rack up accomplishments we can brag about, make the tennis team, and get into the fanciest possible college—than that they're good people, we are not helping them. Because we're showing them that we care more about our own needs and ego than we do about making the world better. Instead, we should be looking at the way their and our actions have an impact on others and focus on helping them build the world we all want to live in.

When we're willing to be vulnerable, when we "practice gratitude and joy in those moments of terror," in Brené Brown's words, and when we apologize for wrongdoing, we can stop catastrophizing and feel gratitude for being alive. SorryWatch would add that, in a kinder world, we'd feel gratitude for the opportunity to admit we've screwed up and have the chance to learn from our mistakes. It's a lot easier to do this in a world where everyone is at least trying to give others the benefit of the doubt.

Having secure self-esteem, an honest ability to assess our own strengths and weaknesses and the confidence to know that we're capable of doing better, is a lot healthier than having fragile self-esteem, which relies only on the approval of others and values *looking* good over *being* good. People with fragile self-esteem have a hard time apologizing, because they have a hard time being in that one-down position: they're all about face rather than acknowledging and engaging with what's behind the mask.

It's Not My Fault

When stories began proliferating in 2020 about a toxic work climate at Ellen DeGeneres's talk show, with racist, bullying, and serially sexually harassing producers holding sway, as well as stories from both famous and not-famous people about DeGeneres herself being a jerk, DeGeneres apologized. But she apologized poorly, twice. One apology was private, the other public. In an internal memo to staff, DeGeneres said that the show was supposed to be "a place of happiness—no one would ever raise their voice, and everyone would be treated with respect." This already raises a red flag. There is no place in which no one *ever* raises their voice. (*SCREECH!*) That's not realistic in a workplace. But it *is* realistic to expect that everyone be treated with respect. It's telling that DeGeneres equated something impossible with something essential.

DeGeneres went on, "Obviously, something changed, and I am disappointed to learn that this has not been the case. And for that, I am sorry. Anyone who knows me knows it's the opposite of what I believe and what I hoped for our show."

Oh, boy, is this ever a Bad Apology Bingo card. Where to begin? DeGeneres stresses intention over impact. She says, "Something changed," which is far too nebulous and nonspecific. It's the apology equivalent of Oscar Isaac in that *Star Wars* movie saying, "Somehow, Palpatine has returned." (How did the *dead emperor* come back? Is the plot of this movie not even going to put in a *modicum* of work to support this narrative? Marjorie is STILL BITTER.)

Moving on: "Disappointed" describes Ellen's own feelings, not the feelings of her staffers who were harmed. The latter are what's important here. Her wishy-washy "This has not been the case" lacks ownership and doesn't take responsibility. It suggests that her staff let her down. She doesn't address her own role in the awfulness—or the accusations that describe her own conduct—at all. The less we say about "anyone who knows me," the better. We *don't* know you. We only know what we see on TV and read in the papers.

DeGeneres also said that, with the show's growing success, she had "not been able to stay on top of everything and relied on others." It's all their fault! All those people claiming to have mean encounters with her? Shhhh.

In September of that year, DeGeneres apologized on air. "As you may have heard this summer, there were allegations of a toxic work environment at our show" is not a promising start. "There were allegations" is again, not specific, doesn't say who did what, doesn't mention the stories about her own behavior. And "allegations" is a weasel word, centering (possibly wrongful!) accusations rather than facts. "I learned that things happened here that never should have happened"—"things"!—makes it sound like she was stunned, an outside observer at her own show, rather than an integral part of the climate there. "I am so sorry to the people who were affected" doesn't help in the specificity department, and "affected" is an awfully wispy word for dozens of former employees saying that producers allegedly groped production assistants, grabbed penises, and offered to perform oral sex on an underling in the bathroom at a company party.

"Being known as the 'Be Kind' Lady is a tricky position to be in," she went on. "So let me give you some advice. If anyone is thinking of changing their title or giving yourself a nickname, do not go with the Be Kind Lady." Ha ha, so funny! Calling yourself kind means you actually have to be kind, or people get upset! Sillies!

DeGeneres said that "articles in the press and on social media" claimed that she was not who she appeared to be on TV. "The truth is, I am that person," she said. "I am also a lot of other things. Sometimes I get sad, I get mad, I get anxious, I get impatient. And I am working on all that. I am a work in progress." Great, but anxiety and sadness are not at issue here. Cruelty is. We are all a lot of things, we are all works in progress, but we do not all (allegedly) foster an environment in which unwilling dicks were fondled in the office. DeGeneres continued, "If I've ever let someone down, if I've ever hurt their feelings, I am so sorry for that." If, if, if, if, if. Come for the apology for hurt feelings, stay for the apology for dick groping! Oh, wait, there is no apology for the dick groping. (Just to be clear, no one has said Ellen herself groped any dicks. Her male producers were the subject of those complaints. New *Time* magazine cover: "Yep, I'm No Dick Groper.")

Ellen's apology episode, which opened the show's eighteenth season, got huge ratings—her highest ratings in four years, in fact. But after tuning in to watch the apology, viewers abandoned the show in droves. Over the next six months, it lost 43 percent of its audience. (The *New York Times* snarkily noted that losing over a million viewers meant DeGeneres was no longer in competition with Dr. Phil; now her ratings were comparable to those of Steve Wilkos, Jerry Springer's former security guard.) The show ended in May 2022.

We'd argue that the lousy apology was a big part of why audiences fled. Could DeGeneres have recovered from eighty-three stories of creating a climate that fostered abuse? Hard to say. The production company fired three producers, but clearly that wasn't enough. What if Ellen had talked about her role in the muck, as a *participant*, rather than someone who had no idea what was going on? What if she talked in detail about deliberately refusing to acknowledge her blind spots, not asking for help, lashing out at others because of her own fragile self-esteem and anger issues? What if she detailed extensive procedures the show had put in place to ensure that the workplace would be entirely different and problems could be reported without fear of reprisal or firing? Maybe a monologue like this could have helped her to be, in one of Brené Brown's favorite words, authentic, which in turn might have satisfied her audience. But her apology was utterly unbelievable and shirked all true responsibility. So much for the "Be Kind" Lady.

A good apology requires us to be vulnerable rather than just saying, "I'm a vulnerable person." You have to own what you did and speak its name. Tell us what you need to face in yourself. Ass coverage is not the right play here. If the thing you're selling in a talk show is yourself, your charm, your realness, your kindness, your next-doorness, and we see in your apology that you're really not who you say you are, why should anyone buy what you're selling?

Meanwhile, compare DeGeneres's apology to John F. Kennedy's statement about the Bay of Pigs fiasco. Did he blame the people around him who did stuff he didn't know about? Or bluff by saying nothing happened? ("What you're seeing and what you're reading is not what's happening," as another president said to a gathering of war veterans.) Did Kennedy insist that authorizing the invasion of Cuba in 1961 was actually the right thing to do? ("It was a perfect call," as another president said about a call to pressure a foreign leader to investigate a political opponent, allegedly in exchange for aid.) Only a week after the failed invasion, Kennedy gave a speech to the American Newspaper Publishers Association at the Waldorf Astoria hotel. He said, "This Administration intends to be candid about its errors; for as a wise man once said: 'An error does not become a mistake until you refuse to correct it.' We intend to accept full responsibility for our errors; and we expect you to point them out when we miss them. Without debate, without criticism, no Administration and no country can succeed—and no republic can survive."

Ellen, take note.

Now, Do You Really Wanna Ride the Fence?

The combo of dissonance theory, Just World bias, and our insistence on protecting our worldview means that many people don't see systemic inequities, or don't believe what they do see, or discount what they see as the fault of the person who is hurt, or shrug off injustice with "That's just the way it is."

People sometimes resist apologizing for racism, sexism, homophobia, antisemitism, Islamophobia, fatphobia, classism, transphobia, and more because they simply don't believe those isms and phobias exist. Or if they *do* exist, any kind of actual bias resulting from said isms and phobias ended long ago. Or you know what? They *definitely* do exist, but they definitely do not exist *in me*. Because that would be totally impossible. Everyone who knows me knows I am not a racist! Everyone who knows me knows what is in my heart! Everyone who knows me knows I don't have a homophobic bone in my body, not even the tiny bones like the ossicles in the middle ear or the vestigial ones like the coccyx! I don't care if you're brown, yellow, green, purple, or Martian! (Though I might care a *tiny* bit more if you're brown and bring down my property values, but that's because of your *taste level*, not your brownness.)

And look, I support the rights of *all* people; I just think some people should not be allowed to use bathrooms. I support the rights of all people; I just think some people are causing my health insurance premiums to go up with their disgusting face-stuffing adiposity. I can't be sexist: I have daughters! I can't be homophobic: I know A Gay! Also, and I really hate to say this, but these people demanding apologies are too pushy, too loud, too aggressive, too unwilling to wait for justice to fall upon them like a gentle summer rain shower, as it surely will if they wait a little longer—and why do they have to be so *in our faces* about it, anyway?

Again: If we don't think Those People really deserve our apologies, and we apologize to them anyway, we're gonna apologize poorly. If we turn any criticism of our conduct into an opportunity to wail about our own oppression, we are NOT DOING GOOD LISTENING, as they say in pre-K before they put us in the Consequences Chair. Our first reaction when called out is often to deny or gaslight. Or when denial is impossible because there were witnesses, or the evidence is right there in that email or in that Holocaust joke you made during the staff meeting, you better sit with the criticism before firing off a response—be that in person, in an email, in a phone call, or in a tweet.

I Apologize a Trillion Times

Sometimes someone from your distant past will pop up like a weed, sliding into your DMs or texting or emailing to apologize for a long-ago sin. Sometimes such apologies are heartfelt, specific, thoughtful, and welcome. Sometimes they're pro forma, poorly considered, a giddy burst of apology enthusiasm from someone clearly beginning the process of recovery. Most apologies that clonk into your life like a dropped barbell are not good apologies. The person isn't really wrestling with what they did or how you felt about it at the time or now. They're apologizing because it's a recovery movement precept, part of their process, a condition of becoming whole. It's about them, not you. They're just "doing the steps," like someone on a treadmill at the gym.

SorryWatch is very much in favor of a good Step 4, making "a searching and fearless moral inventory." But we also believe in thinking hard about whether and how someone really wants to hear from you. If you think they do, please ponder exactly how you'll approach in a nonthreatening, noninvasive manner. Their needs, not yours, must remain paramount. Why, exactly, do you owe this person an apology? Are you really ready to wrestle with how you wronged them? You darn well better have parsed that before you reach out. Do not just blame your addiction! Be sure you've also considered how you might make amends. And do not ask to be forgiven. You're not owed forgiveness. You earn it.

A vile trend of late is to apologize by telling the other person how horrible you are. Three real examples: A writer (let's call her Charlotte, though this is not her name) was caught plagiarizing the work of another writer (let's call her Emily) and sent the latter an email saying, "I'm so sorry! You can punch me in my very punchable face!" A party guest (let's call them Jordan) drank way too much and threw up on the host's rug and sent the host a note the next day: "I invite you to come to my house and vomit on a piece of furniture of your choice!" And an apartment dweller (let's call her Amelia) misplaced her keys and leaned on her next-door neighbor's buzzer at 2 a.m., then wailed upon being let in, "I'm a terrible person! I deserve to die in a fire!" Then there's Paula Deen's more combative "If there's anyone out there that has never said something that they wished they could take back . . . if you're out there, please pick up that stone and throw it so hard at my head that it kills me. Please."

Being self-lacerating this way, encouraging the put-upon person to ponder violence against the offender, is a way (conscious or not) to make the hurt party feel guilty. Planting the image of punching, ralphing upon, or barbecuing the person makes the sinned-against feel like a sinner. It demands that the listener say, "No, no, you're fine!," even if they don't want to. And it's a jokey way to minimize the bad thing the person ought to be apologizing sincerely for.

When we apologize, we should keep in mind the advice of (yes, again) Brené Brown, who suggests we view our *behaviors*, not our essential *selves*, as lousy. "Shame is a focus on self, guilt is a focus on behavior," she says in that TED Talk. "Shame is 'I am bad.' Guilt is 'I did something bad.'"

When an apology focuses on *what we did* (e.g., leaned on the buzzer at 2 a.m.), rather than *who we are* (e.g., a terrible person who deserves to die in a fire), we tend to apologize better. Why? Because we're focusing on how our actions harmed the person we're apologizing to, not on the fact that they hate us because we suck. The former centers their pain; the latter centers yours. The former is "I'm sorry, I made a mistake"; the latter is "I'm sorry, I *am* a mistake." When our apology is a hyperbolic wail of self-hatred, it puts the listener, the person we're purportedly apologizing to, into another rotten position. Which sucks for them. (As Alanis Morissette put it, "It's not fair, to deny me / Of the cross I bear that you gave to me.") It's not fair to put the harmed party in the position of saying, "C'mon, you're not so bad," especially if they're not ready to move on.

You know how RuPaul constantly says, "If you can't love yourself, how in the hell you gonna love someone else?" (Half of SorryWatch lives with a child who is addicted to *Drag Race*.) That sentiment works for apologies too. We have to love ourselves enough to deal with our own mistakes and flaws; they're not the sum total of who we are. When we know we're worthy of love, we can afford to turn a harsh eye on our conduct and take the risk of apologizing well.

Shut Up, Just Shut Up, Shut Up. Shut Up. Shut It Up, Just Shut Up, Shut Up.

Certain perfectly good words become triggers when they show up in an apology.

Take the word "feel." Maggie Balistreri's *Evasion-English Dictionary* illustrates its dangers:

> *"I can't believe I let it happen. I feel responsible."*

> *"You have every reason to be angry with me. I feel so guilty."*

> *"Man, it looks like you're doing all the work yourself. I feel so lazy and unproductive."*

Hmm. What if we replaced *"feel"* in these examples with *"am"*? Isn't it immediately clear why the use of "feel" is so maddening? That one word turns each example into a demand. It turns the speaker (a.k.a. the jerk) into the victim (a.k.a. the person owed an apology). What a wacky linguistic thing: Saying "I *feel* responsible" is the equivalent of saying "I'm *not* responsible."

And how about the word "it"? Balistreri explains, "Evasive agents bemoan the consequences of their own actions." To wit:

> *"It was so thoughtless. I know it hurt you."*

> *"You know me. I'm not abusive—that is not who I am as a person. It was so out of character."*

> *"That kind of behavior—it went too far. It shouldn't have gotten so heated."*

As Balistreri puts it, "Agents don't lose agency simply by suppressing themselves from their narrative." What would happen if "it" were replaced with, gee, we don't know, "I"????? Suddenly, ownership is taken! Specificity occurs! A much better subject has shown up at the virtual door of the sentence!

Coldhearted Snake

An apology from a narcissistic personality is rarely satisfying.

Take the apology from David "Son of Sam" Berkowitz, who in 1993 apologized for his serial-killing ways back in the summer of 1977. "I did take some lives and I'm very sorry for that," he said. He merely wanted "to bring chaos to the city . . . bringing the city of New York to its knees and so forth." And so forth.

Then there was Kevin Spacey's apology on Twitter after fellow actor

Anthony Rapp accused him of attempted sexual assault when the latter was fourteen.

> *I have a lot of respect for Anthony Rapp as an actor. I'm beyond horrified to hear his story. I honestly do not remember the encounter, it would have been over 30 years ago. But if I did behave then as he describes, I owe him the sincerest apology for what would have been deeply inappropriate drunken behavior, and I am sorry for the feelings he describes having carried with him all these years.*
>
> *This story has encouraged me to address other things about my life. I know that there are stories out there about me and that some have been fueled by the fact that I have been so protective of my privacy. As those closest to me know, in my life I have had relationships with both men and women. I have loved and had romantic encounters with men throughout my life, and I choose now to live as a gay man. I want to deal with this honestly and openly and that starts with examining my own behavior.*

That's terrible. The first sentence shakes its head like a Mariah Carey meme, smiling sweetly and murmuring, "I don't know her." To paraphrase and to turn subtext into text, SorryWatch will translate Assholese into English:

> *I respect this adult man—what was the name again?—as an artist, because I am generous of spirit. Now it is my sad duty to say I have no idea what Anton is talking about. But if it happened, I was drunk. I apologize for Anatole's emotional state rather than for my own actions, which, as I mentioned, I don't recall. I am unaware that the phrase "the feelings he describes" seems intended to distance me even further from Andre's sad psyche. I'm also unaware that "carried with him all these years" is redolent of "Jesus, get over*

it already." I'm certainly not implying that Antwerp is unable to move on from something that happened 30 years ago, because that would imply that there was something to move on from. Also, look over here, bright shiny object, I am taking this opportunity to come out. I am now lumping together an accusation of sexual assault and the idea of my privacy not being respected, and these two things are totally equivalent. Dragging me out of the closet like this is so rude of that other actor—his name slips my mind—but I'm going to be noble about it. People will probably accuse me of linking homosexuality with child sexual assault, but, wow, that would be horrible, and that's on them.

You needn't be a celebrity to be a narcissistic bad-apologizing schmuck. A 2010 meta-study found that American college students were 40 percent less empathetic than students of the 1970s to 1990s, and narcissism and self-absorption seem to be on the rise. The study's author, Sara Konrath at the University of Michigan's Institute for Social Research, suggests that more research is needed about why this is so, but the change *might* be attributable to factors such as our dense info-dump climate, violent video games having a negative impact on our ability to empathize, and/or the rise in social media messing with how we communicate. We feel that it's a bit lazy to blame the Age of the Selfie for a decline in empathy. But we're also willing to acknowledge that, whatever the reasons, some of the Youth of Today have a sense of entitlement that keeps them from apologizing well.

America, America

A further cause of bad apologies: living in a culture that insists on looking forward, one that discourages musings about the mistakes of the past. We have short memories. We see how there are plenty of second chances in American lives. For certain people of a certain class and hue, especially.

Other countries are less stingy with apologies. Aaron Lazare wrote in his essential *On Apology*, "Japanese apologies are more likely to include expressions of self-denigration and submission than do English apologies. For example, they often contain modifiers that can be translated 'humbly,' 'in humility,' 'profusely,' 'abjectly,' and 'unconditionally.'" Lazare wrote that American apologies seem to prize sincerity, while Japanese apologies strive for humility. Japanese apology culture is more wary of explanations than American apology culture because the former sees explanations as non-humble, more like excuses. We Americans love to mock Japanese, Canadian, and British folks for apologizing too much, but one might argue that we Americans do not apologize enough.

The distancing effects of social media can harm apologies too. The lack of shared real-life space makes it easier to dehumanize others. Online, we can cause hurt in an instant, and affect—the way we look and sound—is harder to read. Jokes fall flat. Misunderstandings fester. When our friend says something hurtful to us across the table at a diner, it's easier to say, "Wait, what did you mean by that?" When we're sitting together, face-to-face (f2f, we said back in the dawn of the World Wide Web), we can read each other's body language and hear each other's tone, and if we feel hurt during a conversation, we can deal with it right there, looking into each other's eyes, both of us hoping for an authentic, open exchange. But these days few of us spend a lot of time in the village green, attending community board meetings, living a life with tons of human contact and commitment to our neighbors. Suffering from pandemic PTSD, we may be even less likely to communicate well . . . or choose empathy.

ACTION ITEMS

☐ **Apologizing? Put the recipient's feelings above your own.** If you can't do that, don't apologize.

☐ **Received an apology you're not happy with?** Feel free to tell the other person *why* you're not happy. (If you want a relationship with them, do this as patiently as you can.) Use this book to explain why specific phrases and sentiments in the apology are less than satisfying.

☐ **Have you been told your apologies suck?** Molly Howes, PhD, author of *A Good Apology: Four Steps to Make Things Right*, suggests using a practice script when someone is mad at you. Try: "I've got a pretty good idea of what's going on, but I think there might be more I should know about how what I did affected you," or "I truly want to understand what happened," or "I'll do my best just to listen."

☐ **When you get an apology you think is lousy, ask yourself: Are there mitigating factors I don't know about?** For instance, is there more to this person's story I don't know? Is the apologizer autistic? (One of us has an autistic kid: this child means well, but they're sometimes awkward and miss social cues.) Might we be able to hash through our feelings together in a grown-up, non-performative, vulnerable way?

Thirteen Words That Don't Belong in an Apology

Obviously

Regrettable

Already

Dialogue

Alleged

Positivity

Jesus

Journey

Self-discovery

If

But

Context

Unfortunate

BAD APOLOGY BINGO CARD #2

sorry you feel that way	if I offended	it was a different time	believe the worst	cannot know for sure
I feel bad	rumors	do not recall	I'm only human	now I realize
believed it was consensual	matter of perspective	**FREE SQUARE**	I know my heart ❤	grow as a person
I regret	one moment in time	out of context	strived to	duly
for the good	anyone who knows me	what I believe	who I am	my character

CHAPTER 5

"I'M SORRY I CHASED YOU WITH A BOOGER": TEACHING CHILDREN TO APOLOGIZE

It has come to our attention that some of our readers may have children. Congratulations on that. Some of you may have *been* children. (Some of you may be children right now. Hi!) Apologies from little kids can be so charming, touching, and funny, and SorryWatch adores their apology notes. Take Riley here:

> dear ciara I'm sorry. I chased you with a booger on my finger i put it here so you can get me back love Riley.

This is an excellent apology. Riley uses the word "sorry," apologizes *to* Ciara rather than to the public or a third party, and makes amends by providing a payback opportunity. (You can see a photo of the actual note and actual booger on our website. Though we don't know why you'd want to.) Notice how Riley did *not* write "dear ms johnson I regret if I disturbed the class love Riley." There's no "if." Riley knows the booger chasing was wrong and does not pretend it wasn't. And Riley saved that booger for Ciara. Now *that's* restitution. We like to think that Ciara will not get Riley back with the booger, because she's better than that. But she clearly has permission.

Here is another excellent apology, this one from a young fellow named Jack.

> *This Ben and Jerry's card is for the people who cleaned up the throwup of a kid on Friday the 28th. I don't know their names but I thank them alot and I'm sorry again for throwing up. And hope you enjoy your Ice cream.*
>
> *From*
> *Jack. AKA the kid that puked right next to the bathroom*

Again, the kid in question states precisely what he's apologizing for (he's sorry for his puke, not for "the puke that occurred," or for "the regrettable vomnado situation"). He shows he understands the impact (someone had to clean up his mouthpoop) and he tries to make amends. It's particularly lovely that Jack wants to atone for something he clearly couldn't help; the location of the hurl indicates that in all probability he was heading for the bathroom and didn't quite make it.

Does it matter if Jack's parents rather than Jack paid for the Ben & Jerry's card or told Jack to write the letter? It does not. Jack wrote the letter. The letter is clearly in Jack's own words. Applause for Jack's parents for handling this perfectly. Parents understand that vomit happens. It is not a joy, but it is a price we pay for life on this earth. It can happen anywhere. (Disneyland and Walt Disney World used to use "protein spill" as code for "vomit or other bodily fluid requiring cleanup"; the current term is supposedly "Code V." You're welcome.) Cleaning up vomit is never fun, *especially* when the vomit did not come from your child, so a gift card is a nice gesture and an apology is essential.

Through diligent research, SorryWatch has learned that Jack's regurgitation situation occurred at Powell's Books in Portland, Oregon, and that the apology arrived via U.S. mail in an envelope addressed to "Attention Barf Cleaners." (SorryWatch is good at forensic apology work.) Bravo for Jack, bravo for the good humor shown by the Powell's employee who shared this online, and bravo for whatever role Jack's parents played in this saga.

The Land of Bad Examples

How do you become the kind of parent, grandparent, or guardian who raises a Riley or a Jack? How can you help create a culture—in your kid's classroom, say, or religious institution or soccer club or theater camp or roller derby league—that values good apologies?

To get there, let's first look at the way many parents *don't* teach their children well. As you know from much of this book, bad apologies are, sadly, more common than good ones. And as adults go, so go our children. We begin by discussing things to avoid when teaching kids how to apologize. Things to avoid and things to smite. Don't worry, soon we'll get to the stuff you *should* do.

Most bad ways to teach kids about apology are implicit rather than explicit. Nobody ever *says*, "Apologize for what you did, and then I'll yell at you." But in practice, that's often what happens. We teach kids to fear or resent apologizing because it results in being yelled at. Why even bother? We know from our own experiences that apologizing is scary; how about building a foundation in which the first response to taking responsibility is not to unleash a tirade?

This is exactly like a mistake beginning dog owners often make when they call the dog and the dog doesn't come. In fact, the idiot puppy continues scampering around heedlessly. The owner calls and calls AND CALLS, and finally the dog comes. The owner, infuriated by all the earlier romping and frisking, grabs the dog's collar and says "BAD DOG! BAD, BAD DOG!" This teaches the dog not to come: the large creatures just grab you and yell at you! Why even bother?

A parallel pitfall: lecturing a kid after their apology. Don't do that. Say "Thank you." Or "I accept your apology." Or "That helps me feel better." Or all three. If you need to explain why the thing they broke meant a lot to you or why that word hurts people's feelings or why you're gloomy about calling a plumber because of what they flushed down the toilet, do it *before* the apology. (SorryWatch was shown an apology from a boy who flushed an entire bagel down a school toilet. "I didn't know it would be this bad," he observed in his note to the principal. Philosophical!) If the child apologizes for something that requires more action on your or their part, respond to the apology with "I hear you—now what do you think we need to do about this?" And let them lead you through the course of action, as much as they're able to at whatever age they are. (If they suggest a Ben & Jerry's gift card as a good course of action, and you can afford a Ben & Jerry's gift card, lots of people like Ben & Jerry's gift cards. They even have lactose-free ice cream now.)

The most common bad apology role model is the parent who never apologizes. In Susan's maternal great-grandparents' generation, if it turned out one kid had been punished for something another kid had done, there was no apology from the punishing adult. What was said was, "Well, you did *something* else I didn't catch you at, so let the whipping be for that." Did that make the unjustly punished one feel better? No. That's why we're still complaining about it three generations later. Don't be old-fashioned like that.

Marjorie grew up with one parent who often yelled and another parent who served up a daunting Pelosi-like "I'm very disappointed in you" face. Her brother Andy responded by blaming his friend Kenny for everything from pee on the toilet seat to failure to clean up toys. He did this reflexively, even if Kenny had not been over for days. In Marjorie's family, "Kenny did it" is still a saying used for any refusal to take responsibility. Did someone Photoshop your child's face onto a stock photo of a pole-vaulter as part of a scheme to gain admission into a fancy college?

Did someone use your Venmo to pay for illicit activities? Did someone say to use explosives to get that dead whale off the beach? Kenny did it.

Kate Rossmanith, author of *Small Wrongs: How We Really Say Sorry in Love, Life and Law*, recalls her parents' stormy relationship and the fact that she never knew how reconciliation took place. "My parents' fights shook the rooms, and my sister, brother and I would stay close, finding places to take cover. Although they were not physically violent . . . there was shouting, doors slamming, crying, and sometimes stuff was smashed and broken. The fall-out lasted days." Her mother repeatedly told her three kids to pack because they were leaving, and the kids packed, but then the promised departure never happened. "After each argument, we three would wake up one morning a few days later to find our mother and father joking together in the kitchen, him pulling her to him and kissing her playfully on the forehead," she writes. "Our world was restored. We were confused: *how* had love returned?" How indeed? Her parents never said. "My parents never sat us down and explained to us what had occurred and why," she writes. "We never witnessed them making peace, saying sorry. For my mother and father, the jokes in the kitchen over breakfast erased the cataclysmic event. It was as if it had never happened."

Maybe *You* Were a Brat, but Not Every Kid Is a Manipulative Little Snot

Another irrational mistake adults occasionally make when compelling children to apologize is to ascribe more craftiness to the kid than the kid actually possesses. When SorryWatch's friend Felicity was a fourth grader at St. Gemma's, she did *something* that really upset Sister Bernadette, who demanded that Felicity apologize in front of the assembled school. Felicity didn't know what she had done. She still doesn't know. She will never know. Sister Bernadette hissed, "*You know exactly what you did,*" and refused to say more.

"I was sobbing—I was eight years old—and deeply embarrassed and ashamed and could barely say anything," Felicity told us. "But she had a painfully tight grip on my arm and forced me to utter an incoherent apology, the gist of which was that I didn't know what I'd done but I was sorry. This memory is still extremely upsetting to me sixty-four years later. Sometimes it makes me cry! So, yeah, traumatic."

If Sister Bernadette were here, we'd inform her gently that if a kid doesn't know what they did wrong, how can they keep from doing it again?

Sometimes Adults Can Be Manipulative Big Snots

It's also wrong to use an apology as a way to manipulate a kid. This can happen when a child is made to apologize to another family member. Sometimes SorryWatch is in favor of that. You *will* apologize to your sister for breaking her plastic horse's leg. You *will* apologize to your brother for spitting on his dinosaur. You *will* apologize to your cousin for saying diaper babies aren't allowed to play tag.

But when children are repeatedly made to apologize to their parents, that's not a good situation. When you make kids abase themselves all the time, you push them out of the family circle and make them grovel to get back in. Or partway back in. That's inhumane.

One example of this kind of unhealthy situation comes from a book about psychotherapy, Deborah Anna Luepnitz's *Schopenhauer's Porcupines: Intimacy and Its Dilemmas; Five Stories of Psychotherapy*. She describes a patient, "Dave," who recalled his father "punishing him by making him stand up at the dinner table and apologiz[e] for making a mess." Repeatedly. That's bullying.

It's reminiscent of a regular family meal scene described by the Ukrainian Jewish writer Irène Némirovsky in her autobiographical novel *The Wine of Solitude*. There were always "reasons" to make the child

Irène apologize for ruining everything. Thus, at a family lunch where she had been criticized for having her mouth open, and for knocking over a glass, she had to kiss her mother's cheek and say "I'm sorry, Mama." The young Némirovsky was filled with rage and revulsion as she went through this ritual, and that met with more criticism: "Please, for heaven's sake, don't bother. I don't want an apology that comes from your lips but not from your heart. Go away." This is like the fourth-grade teacher described by psychologist Harriet Lerner, who glares at misbehaving kids until they apologize, and then responds, "If you were really sorry, you wouldn't have done it."

These were not good lessons on how to apologize. These were lessons in how to humiliate and reject a child in front of an audience.

It's important that children see their apologies accepted. Kate Rossmanith recalls childhood attempts to placate her critical parents with apology. "I learnt to see myself as a chronic wrongdoer even when I wasn't. And there was no pardon either. If, after a transgression, or perceived transgression, I approached Dad and whispered, 'Sorry', there were pursed lips and stoniness. The consequence of even the smallest error was exile."

There is one kind of apology we're certain *is* good for the whole class to witness, and that is the apology from a teacher who has belittled a student. One classic form this takes is a teacher's accusation that a student who's done good work is a plagiarist. This is most likely to happen to a kid who hasn't been a great student—and when they finally do something impressive, they're not rewarded, they're attacked. If the teacher has (ugh) made the accusation publicly, the apology should be public. If the teacher made the accusation privately, the apology should be private. Regardless, it needs to happen.

Sometimes excellent students deserve apologies too. In *You'll Never Believe What Happened to Lacey*, Amber Ruffin and sister Lacey Lamar describe Lacey's experience in fifth grade. Lacey, a devoted artist, was thrilled to learn that they'd be getting a teacher just for art. She hoped the art teacher would be impressed with a life-size pastel of Leif Erikson she had finished the previous week, which was hanging by the chalkboard. The new teacher walked in, saw the pastel, and asked the class if the teacher had done it. "I did!" said Lacey. "That's a lie. There's no way you drew this," said the new art teacher, who then tore the picture off the wall, ripped it in half, crumpled the halves, and threw them in the wastebasket. Lacey got up and walked out, went home, and told her mother. Who walked Lacey back to school and had a talk with the principal and the art teacher. The art teacher then apologized to Lacey in front of the class.

A colleague of Susan's had to do a similar thing with a younger child. The teacher was telling the class about famous U.S. landmarks such as the Grand Canyon and Mount Rushmore. Many times the kid (let's call him Jordan) would pipe up, "I went there!" Finally the teacher said gently, "Jordan has a good imagination!" Jordan, not incidentally, was the only Black kid in the class. After school, Jordan asked his mother, "Did we really go to those places?" Before arriving in California, the family had taken a cross-country road trip, visiting many landmarks. Susan's colleague was not happy when she learned why her son was doubting his own memory. The next day she walked into class and confronted the teacher, who did not want to have that conversation in front of the kids. She assured the teacher Jordan was truthful when he said he'd seen those landmarks. "I was *polite*!" said the teacher defensively. "These kids know what 'Jordan has a good imagination' means. You called him a liar," said Susan's colleague, and required the teacher to apologize to Jordan in front of the class. Again, this is an apology that needs to be public.

Whose Side Are You On?

Another example of adults using apology against kids in a manipulative way comes from a friend of Susan's, an outgoing and charming person who confessed that she had doubts about apologies. Weren't they just ways to push people around?

It seems that during this friend's interesting childhood, it often happened that her Dramatic Mother would complain tragically to her Important and Busy Father about some alleged rudeness or mischief from the kid. The father would descend from intellectual heights (or return from glamorous travels) and, upon hearing the mother's plaints, would order his daughter to apologize to her mother. Susan's friend remembers apologies as ways in which one parent sought to bond with the other at her expense. Today, it's hard for her not to view apologies as calculating, Machiavellian ploys she wants nothing to do with. The apologies she grew up with celebrated the alliance between mother and father and pushed the child away.

Theater of Cruelty

The above bad examples give us some easy things to avoid. Don't demand apologies when you're in a state of rage. Never use apologies to humiliate kids or to pit family members against each other. And here's an important one in some situations: Ask yourself if there really needs to be an audience—other than the one being apologized to.

It's true that one of the best ways to learn something is to watch *someone else* being taught. This is called the "model-rival method," and it's been used by Professor Irene Pepperberg to teach African gray parrots to speak English *with comprehension*. Rather than teach the famous Alex and other parrots directly, Pepperberg will teach a graduate student and let the parrot observe. But Pepperberg demonstrates a teaching process with the grad student, not a humiliation process. (Yes, Alex did learn to say "I'm sorry" when people were irritated. Not by being taught, but by observing what people said to other people. But he was a parrot, so we're not sure he was sincere.) This technique transfers well to other creatures, including humans.

Does the kid need to apologize in front of the assembly, the class, the family collective? Really? Why? You *know* that makes it harder. Don't sacrifice the feelings of the apologizing kid just to provide an example for the other kids. Because, remember, you won't just be teaching them about apology; you'll be teaching them about *bullying by adults*.

Something else you might be accidentally teaching kids is that you don't care about justice. When adults make kids stop fighting and refuse to listen to the history of the fight, they're signaling that they don't care who did what, that children's griefs and pride are unimportant. ("Cease squabbling," Susan's father sometimes instructed. Susan and her sister did not feel respected. Also, they continued squabbling.)

If you tell kids to call it off and shake hands, you may be letting a bully off easy. You may be telling a picked-on kid that they can't hope for protection. You may be missing a chance to sort out a genuine misunderstanding.

Susan remembers relatives wading into a cluster of quarreling kids, telling them to quit it, and informing the entire scrum that they weren't interested in hearing about who struck John. But kids are interested in fairness. This is true from a very young age. Psychologists at Boston College, Boston University, and the University of Michigan have spent years studying the way the desire for fairness guides children's behavior. They constructed a game: Two kids who don't know each other sit together. One gets one Skittle and the other gets four Skittles. One of the two kids gets to decide if this situation is okay. If the decider says it is, both kids get to keep their allotted candy. If the decider says it isn't, neither kid gets any candy. You'd expect the kid who got only one Skittle to reject this scenario, and they did. But most of the kids who got four Skittles *also* rejected the scenario. "Getting nothing seems better than getting more than a peer, even a child whom they have just met," the authors wrote in *Scientific American*. And in a paired experiment, kids wanted to intervene when one kid they didn't know seemed to be refusing to share candy with another kid they didn't know. The bystanders were willing to give up some of their own candy if researchers told them that was the cost of ensuring that fairness was done. Other studies have shown that kids as young as twelve months expect to see resources divided equally between two participants in an experiment.

Don't we want to live in a world that teaches kids, as they grow up, that fairness and justice are valued and expected? Taking responsibility and apologizing well are part of building that world.

What About Forgiveness?

There's a reason SorryWatch often repeats the phrase "Apologies are mandatory; forgiveness is not." It applies to kids as well as to adults, yet adults often insist on mandating forgiveness to kids. Quite a few Sorry-Watch readers sent us a blog post by an elementary school teacher who taught her students how to apologize. She made a poster listing four steps. The first step is saying, "I'm sorry for . . . ," with excellent instructions on being specific. Don't say, "I'm sorry I was rude." Say: "I'm sorry I said your drawing looks like cat vomit." (SorryWatch is paraphrasing here.)

The second step is saying, "This is wrong because . . ." Then you say why it was hurtful (to the other person—not because the teacher got mad). Also great! The third step is saying, "In the future, I will . . ." This may be something like, "In the future I will not call anybody names." Applause!

But the fourth step is saying, "Will you forgive me?" And we regretfully must say we strongly disagree with this step. (We regret having to call out the teacher, whose intentions are clearly good. We do not regret disagreeing with her. Nor do we apologize for disagreeing with her. See how that works?) Asking for forgiveness dumps a burden on the kid being apologized to. As we noted earlier in the book, forgiveness is a gift to be granted. You don't get to ask for a gift. You react to a gift with surprise and delight. No matter the occasion, you should never behave as if a gift is expected. What are you, some kind of Veruca Salt?

Think about what will happen when the kid in this classroom duti-fully recites, "Will you forgive me?" If this is happening in front of the whole class, all eyes will swivel from the kid apologizing over to the other kid. What will they say? Will they do the right thing?

This teacher does give kids the chance to take their apologies "out-side," so the whole class isn't necessarily watching. But it's still a question waiting for an answer. Better not to have a question. Have the kid say, "I hope you forgive me," or "I hope we can be friends again," but don't put the other kid on the spot.

Consider this 1768 apology from twelve-year-old Charles FitzGerald (later Rear Admiral FitzGerald and 1st Baron Lecale):

> *My dear Mama, I am very sorry that I have given you so much grief. I dun a great many things very improper and beneath a gentleman and below my rank. I am very sorry for my ill behavior. I have disobeyed you and Mr. Ogilvie Mama wich to be chure wass very improper. I own I am vastly distrest. I hope you will be so good as to forgive me. i give you my word and honour my dear Mama that I will never do such a thing again.*

On the negative side, Charles is a total snob. (To be fair, Charles lived in an era of noblesse oblige, during which rich and fancy people were expected to be honorable simply because they were rich and fancy, not because they were human. People with privilege were obligated, be-cause of their stations, to behave nobly toward their lessers. Presumably Mr. Ogilvie was Charles's lesser because he was the hired help or a non-titled working person, and Mama is not quite Charles's inferior—she is, after all, Mama—but she is a woman. And, well, you know.)

Another negative aspect is that Charles is not specific about the great many bad things he did. On the positive side, note that Charles says he hopes Mama will forgive him but does not demand that she do so. Very correct, Charles.

Kiss and Make Up?

In the same vein as the mandatory forgiveness demand is the mysterious demand some adults make that kids kiss each other after an apology. Adults probably do this because they find it INCREDIBLY ADORABLE when little angels kiss. But unless both parties are in the habit of ready and enthusiastic kissing, it lends an icky note of insincerity and creepitude to the proceedings. People are entitled to bodily autonomy, whatever their age. No one should ever have to kiss anyone, ever.

And making kids kiss adults might be worse. Remember Irène Némirovsky's revulsion at being made to kiss her mother after apologizing for being an inadequate meal companion? Just, ew. As for kissing any other grown-up: Nope. Kids should not be obligated to kiss or hug anyone, not even Great Bubbe or Cousin Freddie Who We Only See Every Few Years (Meaning the Child Has No Idea Who Cousin Freddie Is). Have you seen those videos in which a teacher lets each child in their class choose their own kind of morning greeting? The kid can choose a hug, a wave, a high five, a dap, a fist bump, or a little dance. Cute! And it offers each kid agency and control at a time in their lives when kids don't really have much of either. It models the idea that a kid should have choices over their own body and who touches it and how. This is good. It's also good when it comes to apologies. You have to say the words "I'm sorry"; you do not have to make physical contact.

Our friend Wendy recalls an outrage that took place in second grade and still rankles. Wendy's lunch was missing. The assistant principal, Mrs. Taylor (notice that Wendy has not forgotten this name . . . and it has been decades; Mrs. Taylor, we hope you're happy), announced that she and Wendy would search all the lockers for it. Wendy was skeptical that this would produce the missing lunch. "What I said was 'This is silly.' What she heard was 'This is stupid.'"

The principal said, "You hurt Mrs. Taylor's feelings. You upset her," and ordered Wendy to apologize. "I had to kiss her horrible powdered cheek and smell her perfume," recalls Wendy, still revolted.

The Piranha Is Very Sorry

Kisses can be problematic in so many ways. At a day care for babies and toddlers that Susan and her spouse took their first child to, there was a Biter. (Not Marjorie's daughter Josie. Different biter. There are often Biters.) This Biter was a staggeringly cute toddler, dressed in winsome ruffles. One day when Susan showed up, the Biter was being encouraged to make nice with a kid she had bitten. These were tiny kids, not yet big talkers. The Biter couldn't say, "I'm sorry I bit you." She was told to give the other kid a hug and a kiss, which she was happy to do. But the other child was horrified by the sight of the Biter lurching toward her, arms wide, lips parted. . . . You get the picture.

How to Do It Right

Obviously, those are mistakes you won't make. Right? So let's talk about good ways to teach kids to apologize. It's simple. We didn't say it's easy, because it does take some practice.

When we teach kids to apologize, we need to remember that apologizing is an act that is not intrinsically fun. If you don't remember that, the kid will probably remind you. Isolate the act of apology from bad things. Keep it separate from lectures and punishment, and *praise* the child for doing it, even if you had to drag it out of them. Truthfully tell them that they've now done something many adults are too . . . immature, or whatever . . . to do. Tell them apologies are acts of strength, because they are. Tell them you understand how difficult this is, because you do. (Later, you can perhaps share a story of your own difficulties apologizing. Back when you were a child yourself and clung to "Kenny did it" or, um, last week, when you rolled your eyes during the staff meeting. Because Jordan's comment was really, really stupid. But you should have kept the eye roll on the inside of your brain, not on the outside of your face. Because Jordan saw it and called you on it, after which you should not have said, "I did not," when you absolutely, totally did. And you should have privately apologized to Jordan after the meeting instead of avoiding Jordan for days.)

And just as with bad apologies, examples are powerful. You need to walk the walk yourself. Let your kid see and hear you apologize to them, to your spouse, to the waitress, to the friend you interrupted mid-story, to the cat when you tripped over him, to Kenny. If kids grow up around people who apologize when appropriate, apologizing won't seem like some mysterious torture you dreamed up BECAUSE YOU'RE MEAN AND YOU HATE THEM.

I'm Just a Soul Whose Intentions Are Good

Kids often have a very hard time understanding that "I didn't MEAN to!" isn't a free pass. They still have to apologize for breaking the window, stepping on someone's hand, or spilling the entire container of homemade mango kombucha—in the living room, where IT'S NOT EVEN SUPPOSED TO BE. They may also have to put their birthday money toward fixing the window and learn how to clean up kombucha in the living room.

Kids often need reassurance that adults understand that they didn't intend those things to happen. But the things did happen. And the kids still have to do their best to make things right again.

It's as if there were two offenses: breaking the window, and planning to break the window. Kids who didn't plan to break the window focus on the fact that they didn't plan to break it, and not the fact that they did break it. It's especially upsetting for kids who were trying to do good things—show another kid how to hit a fungo, demonstrate a new dance move, cheer a sibling up on a rainy day with an impromptu picnic (in the living room, where kombucha is NEVER supposed to be).

You know, maybe it's not that it's harder for kids to understand that "I didn't mean to" doesn't get you out of jail free. Maybe it's just that adults have more *sophisticated* ways of saying, "I didn't mean to." Like saying, "My remarks were taken out of context!" "It was not my intent to offend anyone!" "My friends know I'm not homophobic!" "My comedy is being censored by social justice warriors!" (To quote the kid in the vintage Partnership for a Drug-Free America ad, "I learned it by watching you!")

"These Cashews! Wait, I Got That Wrong"

When teaching kids to apologize, there may need to be more emphasis on understanding *why* an apology is called for, because kids are young and they don't know everything yet. In our lives, we learn things at different rates. Apology lessons have to be age-appropriate, and they shouldn't assume kids already know things they have no way of knowing.

A certain sixth grader in Georgia was old enough to understand the joke of surprising people with a cry of "Deez nuts!" If you're not familiar with this prank, which comes from Dr. Dre's 1992 album, *The Chronic*, you might need the sixth grader to explain to you that getting someone to say something to which you reply, "Deez nuts!" (translation: "These testicles!") is *incredibly funny* and shows a *sophisticated historical knowledge of musical culture.*

The same knowledgeable sixth grader in Georgia was *not* old enough to understand why it was *not* a good idea to accept a dare from his idiot friends to call 911 and holler, "Deez nuts!" He understood it was rude; he was not knowledgeable enough to realize that 911 could track the call down and tell his parents about it.

His parents made him write an apology. They escorted him to the police department's 911 center to deliver it. And read it aloud.

> *Dear Emergency Dispacher,*
>
>   *Last night I called and said "Deez Nuts." I know this was stupid but I was not listening to myself but I knew it was wrong. Please forgive me for what I said. I know there will be consequences for my actions and I will not complaine about them. . . . What happened was that me and my friends we're talking and I got dared to call you. I would get nothing out of it and only get in trouble for it. In the end I got in trouble for it and this is a letter for you. I am sorry for what I did and hope that you can forgive me.*

By this time he seems to have known: stupid. But he doesn't seem to have known: why stupid.

It's the parents' job to make the why clear.

Look, here is an example of a British child whose parents did that, and the fact that they did is clear in the kid's apology. (The British child did not say, "Deez Nuts," but they did prank 999, which is the emergency services number in the UK. Prank calls are very tempting, even if kids today do not understand why Prince Albert was in the can or why they should let him out.)

To ever it concers I pressed 999 and I am so so sorry.
    Why I should not press 999 only if it's an emensey.

1. Because you will get a fine
2. You will get really told off by the people on the phone
3. It could stop someone else that needs help

    I so sorry and I under stand how serius it was, I promise that I will never ever do it again. I am very, very sorry.

We don't know whether the East Midlands Ambulance Service responded to the child or whether they merely tweeted the letter. (Ah, social media.) But we do know that the Georgia dispatchers loved getting the sixth grader's apology. They gave the family a tour of the dispatch center so the kid could understand the lifesaving work they do and the help they provide to desperate people. And why they don't need idiot kids tying up the lines to shout about nuts. Excellent. We think he understood then.

But it would have been excellent if his parents had also made it clear to him. Apologies should not be about getting caught and dutifully muttering, "I'm sorry." It's on parents to explain why the thing the kid is apologizing for was wrong, how the kid's actions affected others, and how we want society to function. Yes, that's important.

Jordan Doesn't Know Other People Have Feelings Too

What about very little kids who may not understand or actually empathize with others that much yet? They gotta fake it till they make it. It's important to go through the motions. You, the grown-up, explain the whys and hows and wherefores. The little kid only has to say the two words "I'm sorry." (And not blame Kenny.) As the kid ages, the kid starts internalizing the lessons you're reinforcing; their apologies get more nuanced; the responsibilities of kindness and citizenship begin to shift from you to the kid. If you're consistent and you model the behavior you want to see, we promise: eventually the lessons will sink in. Someday.

And remember: if the kid is apologizing to another kid, there's a benefit for the other kid . . . even if *your* kid doesn't truly feel the remorse they should. It's not all about your kid, you know.

Marjorie's mother used to say, "Ontogeny recapitulates phylogeny," referring to a scientific theory about how traits that show up in different stages of an embryo are repetitions of the ancestry. This is apparently not exactly correct, scientifically. (Sorry, Mom.) But what Marjorie's mom meant was that you learn the things you're supposed to do, the actions, the words, and eventually the meaning behind them becomes internalized as well.

You know the expression "The brain is a muscle"? Stanford University psychologist Carol Dweck has written a lot about how kids who see intelligence as a fixed trait (something you have or you don't) are more fearful of failure and more likely to shy away from challenges than kids who think intelligence is malleable (something you can develop). Apology skills are something we can all develop. We can all get better at them. Kids and grown-ups.

And again: no one has to forgive. Teach your kid not to follow up an apology with "We're good, right?" They have to be gracious if they've wronged someone, but the other kid is under no obligation to accept their apology and shouldn't be asked to do so. If your kid is on the receiving end of an apology, ask them not whether they were wronged but whether they think the apology was sincere. If the other kid screwed up but is willing to own that fact, teaching your kid to hang on to resentments isn't doing them any favors. When Jordan left his backpack in the aisle after being told that backpacks do not belong in the aisle, and your kid trips and Jordan apologizes and actually seems to understand that leaving the backpack in the aisle was wrong and caused pain, your kid should be encouraged to accept the apology and move on.

Teaching your kid to recognize gaslighting, on the other hand, is a valuable skill to take into adulthood. When Jordan deliberately tripped your kid and then said, "Sorry but it was an accident and I thought you saw my leg sticking out and you should really be more careful," your kid is under no obligation to accept that apology.

Maybe start with teaching your kid to say, "Thank you for the apology." And no more. Those words don't mean "I forgive you." And if the other kid is a cretin, encourage your kid to stay away if possible and expand their friend circle. Mean girls and jerky boys often make themselves known very early on.

The Apology Collective

There's a concept in K–8 education called the "Responsive Classroom," which focuses on social-emotional learning as much as it does book learning. The approach has four cornerstones: academics, positive community, effective management, and developmental awareness. The idea is to create a healthy school climate as well as an academically successful one. Even if you're not an educator—though let's face it, if you're a parent or caregiver, you are an educator—it's fun to search online for signs from Responsive Classrooms, which frequently model good community approaches to apologizing for little kids.

A sign about consequences, for instance, tells kids: "You break it, you fix it! If you break it or hurt someone's feelings, you need to make it better!" When a sign like that is on the wall of a classroom, and school staff make sure that those words aren't just words but rather an expected and encouraged course of action, kids know that they're in a place where kindness and apology mean something. Another sign describes the "Apology of Action" associated with "You break it, you fix it": If you call someone an ugly name, work on saying nice things about them. If you made fun of someone's work, tell them what you like about it. If you shoved your friend, draw an "I'm sorry" picture. Is this reductive? Of course! These are signs for little kids! It's up to the adults in their lives to model and draw out how to weave the advice into the kids' daily lives. Consider the sign offering "Our Classroom Promises": "We will make choices that help us do our best learning. We will be kind and take care of each other. We will do our best and keep trying, even when things get tough."

Good advice for grown-ups to live by too.

We All Thank You

When SorryWatch's pal Michele was ten or eleven, she was asked to babysit for some neighbor kids. The parents said she could eat anything she wanted. After the little ones were in bed, Michele had some ice cream. A day or so later, Michele's mother told her that she'd talked to the neighbors and learned that the freezer door had been left ajar. All the frozen food had melted or had to be thrown out.

Now, Michele's parents had always said that if she did anything wrong, she should just tell them, and she wouldn't get in trouble. They kept their word. If Michele told her parents what she'd done, she wasn't punished. Even in the case of that unfortunate slingshot incident. So Michele, armed with faith in honesty, raced over to the neighbor's to apologize. "I thought I closed the freezer door, but I must not have closed it all the way. I'm *really* sorry." Impressed, the neighbors answered, "That's a very grown-up thing to say. A lot of adults wouldn't apologize like that." A compliment Michele remembers to this day.

Teaching children how to apologize well and how to accept apologies gracefully contributes to children's overall happiness and sense of security and helps make the world better. We hope your children—and ours—become good people and that goodness emanates from them all their days.

ACTION ITEMS

❑ **Avoid secondhand apologies.** If your kid is old enough to have words, don't apologize *for them* instead of having them apologize *for themselves.* "Jordan's sorry they kicked Julio and they won't do it again"? NO. Use your words, Jordan.

❑ **Explain the steps to your kid and correct them when they're evasive.** Start young. It'll be easier in the long run.

❑ **Six apology steps for kids** (maybe don't teach them the word "sexpartite" until you trust them to use it responsibly):

1. **SAY "I'm sorry" or "I apologize."** Luckily, little kids don't usually have the vocabulary to futz around with dodges like "I rue the unfortunate events" or "What a pity that happened to Bodger's teddy bear. Sad!" And they should apologize *to* the person who was hurt or upset.

2. **FOR what they did.** Specifically, "for calling you a big sucky liar," not "for calling you names."

3. **ACKNOWLEDGE the effect.** "Barbie's never going to get those heels on again."

4. **EXPLAIN why they did it.** Optional. This may be hard for kids, who sometimes have no idea why they do things. Still: "I thought it would be funny if it was raining fruit punch, and I didn't realize you'd get sticky and have to take a bath and change your clothes." Just be sure, as your kids get older, that they understand the difference between an explanation and an excuse. It's often better to avoid the former if the kid tends to start sliding into the latter.

5. **Tell the person harmed WHY THEY'RE SAFE NOW.** A.k.a. "I'll never do it again."

6. **HOW will you make it up to them?** "I'm going to help sew Bodger's legs back on." "You can have my Barbie." "Here's the booger. Feel free to chase me with it."

Easy peasy, right? Wrong. It's hard for grown-ups and it's hard for kids. But we can learn to do it well—and so can they.

Seven Great Children's Books About Saying "I'm Sorry"

Lilly's Purple Plastic Purse by Kevin Henkes

Oh No, George! by Chris Haughton

Horrible Bear! by Ame Dyckman, illustrated by Zachariah OHora

I Am Extremely Absolutely Boiling by Lauren Child

Sometimes I'm Bombaloo by Rachel Vail, illustrated by Yumi Heo

David Gets in Trouble by David Shannon

Harriet, You'll Drive Me Wild! by Mem Fox, illustrated by Marla Frazee

BAD APOLOGY BINGO CARD #3
SULLEN TEEN EDITION!

but she	just happened	never said	but you said	although
but everyone else	sorry, but	but they	but what about	first of all . . .
sorry if	I meant	**FREE SQUARE**	misunderstood	unfortunate
as a child	unfair	sorry that you	not my fault	big yikes
as a family	intend	look forward	but go off	punished

CHAPTER 6

"SORRY, OUR POLICY IS THAT WE ARE NEVER AT FAULT": THE ODIOUSNESS THAT IS CORPORATE

Beyond human psychology, sociology, and a generational failure to model good apologies, *even more* factors contribute to the preponderance of putrid apologies on this planet. Let us now turn to the *institutions* that contribute to the likelihood that a given apology will be vomitous. Why are corporations, hospitals, lawyers, insurers, and police departments so often determinedly, bullheadedly, infuriatingly wrong about how apologies work?

Physician (and Also Ye Who Adviseth the Physician), Heal Thyself

Marjorie showed up a few minutes early for a doctor's appointment, as is her wont. It was her first time seeing this doctor. She waited. And waited. And waited. She did not want to leave without being seen, because you know how far in advance those people are booked. After nearly three hours, Marjorie was called into an exam room. She waited another forty minutes there, twiddling her thumbs in a backless paper gown. Finally the doctor swanned in and launched into the "What brought you in today?" speech. Marjorie responded, in a hint as broad as the side of a barn, "Hey, is the wait to see you always that long?" The doc responded, "I was just on vacation, so things are kind of backed up." Marjorie further hinted, "I waited over three hours." The doc reiterated, "Well, I was away, so this isn't typical." Marjorie was too cowardly to keep pursuing the words "I'm sorry I made you wait over three hours." (She is very fierce about the need for apologies when she is at a keyboard but more chickenshit when face-to-face, as well as backless-gown-to-white-coat.)

After the appointment, though, she emailed the doctor with her request for an apology. No response. She then emailed the hospital system and got some form of "We regret . . ." statement, as well as the acknowledgment that her comments would be passed along to the doctor in question. Her only recourse after that was to tell everyone she knows on this planet not to see this doctor—who has excellent reviews as a clinician—unless they have a spare three hours and hate apologies. (And don't get Marjorie started about the geneticist who left a MESSAGE on her ANSWERING MACHINE on a FRIDAY AFTERNOON when Marjorie was PREGNANT telling her she was a CARRIER for a POTENTIALLY FATAL GENETIC DISEASE. Fortunately, Marjorie remembered enough about recessive genes from a high school biology class about Gregor Mendel and his pea plants to stave off utter panic, and her husband was tested and was not a carrier, and *whew!* BUT STILL . . . No apology from that doc, practice, or hospital system either.)

The lack of apology from these folks—but particularly the doctors, who each had *three chances* to say the words "I'm sorry" (once in person, once in email, and once after receiving notification from their employers of Marjorie's distress)—is galling. And many of us have similar stories of doctors refusing to apologize or offering up wishy-washy, nonspecific, unsatisfying, "We regret . . ."-type statements.

What's Up with You, Doc?

There are several possible reasons doctors are crappy apologizers: they're incredibly busy and harried in this era of managed care; they're human beings like the rest of us and apologies, as we've learned, are difficult for human beings; they don't view patients' complaints as valid; and they're used to wielding power over a parade of nearly faceless patients in identical breezy gowns, which may corrupt their ability to say they're sorry, since, as we learned in chapter 4, people who hold authoritarian views are less likely to apologize for their wrongdoings.

But we'd say there are two primary reasons doctors are such lousy apologizers. Most were never taught to apologize in medical school, and they've been given the terrible (and not evidence-based! medicine is supposed to be evidence-based!) advice to not apologize for fear of lawsuits.

Let's address the fear of lawsuits first. According to the 2006 Harvard hospital system report *When Things Go Wrong: Responding to Adverse Events*, there's very little evidence to show that good apologies increase the risk of malpractice suits. "In fact," the report notes, "experience in malpractice cases indicates just the opposite: that the failure to communicate openly, take responsibility, and apologize contributes to patients' anger. Some malpractice lawyers contend that two-thirds of malpractice suits stem from a failure to take responsibility, apologize, and communicate openly."

Yes, there are studies by business and law professors showing that apologies *do* increase the risk of lawsuits. But most of these studies don't distinguish between good and bad apologies. And we know from our own experiences—and we're sure you do, too—that bad apologies are so infuriating, they make us vindictive. The kinds of apologies that lawyers often suggest—the kinds that don't take any responsibility and rely on the passive voice and vague, impersonal statements of regret—do not satisfy patients yearning for authentic apology. We want to sue just *reading* about them.

While thirty-nine states and the District of Columbia have medical apology laws that prevent doctors' and hospitals' apologies from being used against them in court, we argue that the way such laws are written does more harm than good. Many of these laws protect only statements of sympathy; statements that take responsibility can still be used against doctors in court. What good is that?

Patient Presents with Complaints of Disrespect

Furthermore, a well-designed 2019 study in the *Stanford Law Review* involving a regression analysis of eight years of insurance company data found that medical apology laws, as they currently exist, don't help surgeons and actually *hurt* non-surgeons. Yes, non-surgeons were both more likely to pay and likely to pay more *because of apology laws*! In their analysis, the paper's authors say their work "illustrates the importance of knowing what to say and when to say it, and apology laws provide training on neither of these points." We agree. And "if an apology law protects only statements of sympathy, physicians may not be able to fully explain the nature of a particular medical error. If this is the case, then patients may not perceive an apology as sincere, which may provoke rather than assuage anger." See? So much evidence that bad apologies piss people off!

A far better idea to achieve the *goals* of apology laws would be individual disclosure programs written by folks who work at and feel connected to each hospital, and training in physician-patient communications for doctors and administrators so that when "adverse events" do occur, doctors and their colleagues can talk about what happened, explain, and apologize in a way that doesn't infuriate patients and their families further. When you apologize well, you're likely to avoid having to go to court at all, forestalling stress for doctors and patients and families alike, and refraining from contributing to spiraling health-care costs.

The Harvard hospital report suggests four steps to full communication:

1. *Tell the patient and family what happened.*

2. *Take responsibility.*

3. *Apologize.*

4. *Explain what will be done to prevent future events.*

Easy peasy! Completely in line with SorryWatch's view that a good apology includes all those parts! One study—quoted by Professor Jennifer K. Robbennolt at the University of Illinois College of Law in her superb (and very readable by people who do not speak academic jargonese) 2008 paper "Apologies and Medical Error"—found that over 90 percent of people who filed malpractice suits did so because they wanted to prevent the same thing from happening to someone else, wanted an explanation for what had happened, and/or wanted the doctor to understand the impact of their actions. Among surgery patients in a different study who'd experienced medical errors and filed malpractice suits, yet felt that their lawsuits were preventable, 40 percent said that if they'd received both an explanation *and* an apology, they would not have sued. In only 15 percent of those cases did the patients get an apology, and in only 13 percent of cases did patients say that the surgeon took responsibility.

When an apology is paired with an offer of fair compensation for physical and/or emotional harm *without being prompted by the patient*, doctors and patients alike feel unburdened, relieved, more at peace. Ultimately, good apologies forestall more expensive lawsuits, save hospitals money, help doctors become better communicators, and improve doctor-patient relationships.

And there must be compensation for physical or emotional harm. Professor Robbennolt quotes Bishop Desmond Tutu: "If you take my pen and say you are sorry, but don't give me the pen back, nothing has happened." The medical equivalent, according to Nancy Berlinger, author of the 2005 book *After Harm: Medical Error and the Ethics of Forgiveness*, is "if a physician apologizes to an injured patient, if a physician genuinely feels remorse for having injured the patient, if a physician acknowledges that the mistake was her fault, but there are no provisions for fairly compensating the patient for the cost of medical care and lost wages resulting from the injury and no provisions for helping this physician to avoid injuring other patients, nothing has happened."

Recompense, in this view, is an inherent part of the apology process. And when you make an offer without being asked and without going to court, patients are satisfied with a much smaller offer (to say nothing of the legal costs saved) than they'd have sued for.

Okay, Here's a Wild Idea

Fortunately, policies incorporating disclosure, taking responsibility, apologizing, and explaining future steps to prevent similar incidents—as well as offering compensation—are in place at a number of hospitals already. They work. For instance, the Harvard report notes, the Veterans Affairs Medical Center in Lexington, Kentucky, implemented a policy in 1997 of disclosing errors to patients and/or their families and offering compensation. Before they started this program, the Lexington VAMC had among the highest malpractice payments of VAMCs of its size. But after implementing the policy, the Lexington VAMC's malpractice payments dropped to among *the lowest 25 percent in its peer group.*

In 2002, the University of Michigan began its disclosure and apology policy. Attorney fees plummeted by two-thirds and lawsuits also decreased radically. In 2017 the *BMJ* (formerly the *British Medical Journal*) looked at communication and resolution programs at two academic medical centers and four community hospitals. In the centers and hospitals using these programs, the number of legal actions was incredibly low. In 929 separate cases, only 5.1 percent led to claims or lawsuits. And among the claims made, many were settled without lawsuits and/or were for modest sums as medical claims go (the median payout was $75,000, which is not even enough for a greasy personal injury lawyer to brag about in a local TV commercial).

The results were initially reported in the journal *Health Affairs*. Lead author Michelle M. Mello, professor at both Stanford School of Medicine and Stanford Law School (overachiever), noted, "Our findings suggest that communication and resolution programs will not lead to higher liability costs when hospitals adhere to their commitment to offer compensation proactively." The study also noted that explaining *why* adverse events occurred—something many lawyers counsel against and many doctors and hospital administrators avoid like the plague—can defuse patients' anger.

Patients' rage when they don't get the apologies they want can be all-consuming. A 1996 survey called "How Do Patients Want Physicians to Handle Mistakes?: A Survey of Internal Medicine Patients in an Academic Setting" in the *Archives of Internal Medicine* found that 98 percent (98 percent!) of patients wanted acknowledgment of errors doctors and hospitals made, even minor errors. Patients were far more likely to consider litigation if doctors didn't disclose those error(s). In a 1994 survey in the British journal the *Lancet*, 227 patients and relatives who were suing for malpractice said they wanted more honesty, "an appreciation of the severity of the trauma they had suffered, and assurances that lessons had been learned from their experiences." Mello says that hospital payouts are more due to that anger than to medical issues.

There's a nonprofit called Sorry Works! dedicated to medical disclosure training and advocacy, founded by a guy named Doug Wojcieszak, whose big brother Jim died as a result of medical errors back in 1998. Jim had been admitted to the hospital after a heart attack, but the hospital mixed up his chart and took no action, leaving him languishing in bed for two days. As a direct result, Jim required open-heart surgery, during which he died. The Wojcieszak family sued for malpractice, saying that not only had Jim died unnecessarily but the hospital had also tried to cover up its errors. The family won. "But even after money exchanged hands and liability waivers signed, the hospital lawyers couldn't (or wouldn't) apologize, explain the mistakes that happened, and discuss how the hospital's processes would be corrected so it wouldn't happen to the next patient and family," Wojcieszak wrote. "It was a maddening process."

In 2001, Doug read about the program at the Lexington VA hospital. He was working in public policy and PR then and wanted to spread the message that apologies can forestall lawsuits and help families like his be less furious. Sorry Works! now offers disclosure training for hospitals and reviews of disclosure policies for people considering making large donations to health systems, hospitals, and nursing homes.

It also offers case studies of good apologies in action. One such study involved a thirty-two-year-old man who visited a rural Hawaiian ER in 2013, complaining of a sore throat. He was diagnosed with an abscess in his tonsils and referred to an ENT. But before he could go to the ENT, the ER doctor decided to evaluate his condition further, using sedation without an anesthesiologist present. The doctor used too much sedative, and the young man died. He left a wife and three small kids. The man's widow received a $4.2 million settlement from the federal government— the health center was a federally qualified community nonprofit—but the center went further.

It implemented major changes to its procedures. A new ER director and a new full-time chief compliance officer came on board and publicly outlined the safety changes the health center would be making as a result of the tragedy. The hospital's leadership apologized to the young widow publicly and privately; hugs were exchanged.

At the press conference, the widow said, "I don't hate or judge. I just hope that the [health center] does make everything better for other families." Wojcieszak writes in his characteristic informal style, "There was no gag order . . . no take your money but we won't admit fault . . . none of that." He concluded, "If your organization made a mistake there should be a real apology, a meeting with the patient/family, hug and cry with them if it feels right, a fair settlement, and show the patient/family what changes have been made so the mistakes will not be repeated. It's how we would all want to be treated if something bad happened to us."

The Case of Apology Laws vs. "Oh, Come On, Just Say You're Freaking Sorry for God's Sake"

Remember that Stanford paper that eviscerated America's apology laws? Its authors nonetheless believe—fervently—in the power of apology. They write, "While the results undermine the conclusion that apology laws are effective at accomplishing the liability cost reduction task for which they were passed, our results do *not* undermine the other, verified benefits of apologies. Apologies remain an important part of our social fabric, and the specific inability of apology laws to reduce litigation against physicians does not change this fact." Amen. They, too, advocate for hospital-specific apology programs and physician training in how to apologize well.

Conveniently, hospitals don't even have to develop such programs themselves! The U.S. Department of Health and Human Services' Agency for Healthcare Research and Quality (this is a mouthful; welcome to government work) has developed the Communication and Optimal

Resolution (CANDOR) Toolkit, which is a prebuilt primer on disclosure work funded by a multimillion-dollar grant initiative. It's even cheap for states to incorporate. CANDOR, everybody! Way better than half-assed ass-covering apology laws!

Physician Sara Manning Peskin wrote a piece for the *New York Times* in 2018 wistfully noting that Sweden's and New Zealand's federal apology policies work way better than the United States' policies currently do. Doctors in these exotic foreign lands are actually expected to help patients request compensation after a mistake as part of their jobs. Meanwhile, she says, in America "we can say, 'I'm sorry this happened,' but not 'I'm sorry I did this to you.'" As we have established, everyone hates that.

Peskin herself, despite being a doctor, failed to elicit an apology for a mistake from her own doctor. Her doctor had missed a complication; nothing truly terrible happened, but it was a mistake. When Peskin finally saw the doctor, she said, "I know it wasn't intentional, but I'm disappointed I wasn't told to come in." Peskin's doctor replied, "I can't turn back time." Peskin kept trying to engage her in discussion, but the doctor only repeated, "I can't turn back time." After this failed attempt at discussion, the doctor put a note in Peskin's file saying "she is unhappy with her care" and removed herself from being Peskin's doctor.

Peskin's story isn't surprising. That 1994 *Lancet* piece we cited earlier in the chapter included doctors who had been harmed by medical error themselves. And, sure enough, even doctors didn't experience the apology behavior they wanted from fellow doctors. The survey found that only a third of physician and non-physician respondents received an explanation or apology for what had happened to them.

Not to be reductive here, but to be reductive here: Good apologies good, bad apology laws bad.

Teaching Doctors to Apologize—It's Doable!

Apologizing is healing for doctors as well as patients. *To Err Is Human: Building a Safer Health System*, a seminal 1999 report from the U.S. Institute of Medicine, found that health-care workers, just like families, feel guilty after medical mistakes. Families feel they failed the patient and worry that doctors will be vindictive if they ask for too much information or an apology. Health-care workers clam up or slink away because they're afraid for their patient—not one *wants* to harm a patient!—as well as for their own hides. Feeling like they have to put a positive spin on everything takes a terrible toll on clinicians.

Fortunately, things are slowly changing. Jennifer K. Robbennolt notes that at Mount Sinai School of Medicine and several other medical schools, residents are being trained in how to apologize.

In his magnificent memoir *When Breath Becomes Air*, the late surgeon Paul Kalanithi discusses how his cancer diagnosis humanized him; his time as a patient and his awareness of his own limited life span made him a better doctor and a better person. Teaching medical residents at Stanford, he talked about the importance of apologizing and taking responsibility for errors. Not every student got it. He writes of one young man:

> He was a talented surgeon, but he could not admit when he'd made a mistake. I sat with him one day in the lounge as he begged me to help him save his career.
>
> "All you have to do," I said, "is look me in the eye and say, 'I'm sorry. What happened was my fault, and I won't let it happen again.'"
>
> "But it was the nurse who—"
>
> "No. You have to be able to say it and mean it. Try again."
>
> "But—"
>
> "No. Say it."
>
> This went on for an hour before I knew he was doomed.

Unlike this guy, most surgeons do want to learn. (Yep, even surgeons. Generally considered the assholes of the medical profession, even by other doctors. On Marjorie's recent pediatric ER visit with a kid who has a medical condition that causes frequent shoulder dislocations, the sweet physician's assistant recommended some orthopedic surgeons. He answered Marjorie's question, "Which one is the nicest?" with "Uh, well, you know, they're *surgeons*.")

Marjorie recently enjoyed a thread on Reddit titled "Which medical specialty has the biggest jerks?" Surgeons (general, orthopedic, and neuro) overwhelmingly won this informal poll. One respondent said, "The only person who has ever thrown something metal at me was a neurosurgeon." (A neurosurgeon immediately responded, "You deserved it.") Marjorie's father was a psychiatrist who used to tell an old med school joke: "What's the difference between God and a neurosurgeon? God knows he's not a neurosurgeon."

All that said, one study found that although 90 percent of surgeons had zero training in disclosure skills, when they received training, 93 percent of them called it a "very good or excellent educational experience." So offering doctors continuing education in disclosures and apologizing is clearly welcome, even by surgeons. Reaching med students before they have the chance to apologize badly or fail to apologize at all, however, is clearly the best strategy.

At Georgia Health Sciences University, first-year med students receive training in apologies as part of the curriculum. Three instructors reported on the results in a 2011 paper in the *Journal of Family Medicine*. They studied 384 students and found that students' confidence in providing effective apologies increased with training, as did their comfort in disclosing errors to a faculty member or patient. The students gained new respect for the importance of apologies in a medical setting, and 74 percent found the training helpful. (Additional tidbit: apologies by female students were rated considerably higher in effectiveness than apologies by male students. But are women med students better at apologizing, or are apology recipients more open to apologies from women? Unclear! The issue does "warrant further consideration.") At other schools, the authors note, pilot programs are also teaching students the art of apology. The students role-play with actors playing patients and learn the nuances of how to disclose and discuss errors.

It's Not Just About the Lawsuits

The Harvard hospital system paper notes, in unusually plainspoken language, "We are making a moral argument here, not a business case or an evidence-based clinical guideline." It continues, "We are committed to full disclosure because it is the right thing to do. The patient and family have the right to know what happened. In addition, honest communication promotes trust between the patient and provider, so that the primary focus of the clinician-patient relationship remains patient care." And other families in the future will benefit too.

Patients don't want to feel gaslit. They don't want to be given the runaround or to hit a wall of silence when seeking answers. And doctors don't want to feel unsupported by their institutions, don't want to feel helpless in the face of inevitable human mistakes, don't want to feel ashamed. When a bad thing happens, it is human nature to want something good to come out of it. Apologies, including taking concrete steps to prevent a recurrence of the error, can be that good something.

The Business of Good Apologies

In the canyons of commerce, apologies have real impact too. Businesses, like health-care systems, have to create an environment that makes it safe for employees to admit errors and then work collaboratively to fix them. Harvard Business School professor Amy C. Edmondson—writing this chapter, huh, we are suddenly aware of how many apology experts are female—discovered that inclusive, collaborative bosses were good for business. In a series of studies beginning in 1999 and continuing today, she's found that leaders who express appreciation for others' work in cross-disciplinary teams create more cohesive workplaces. More cohesive teams, oddly, make more mistakes.

Or do they? Nope. They *report* more mistakes. They do so because they feel able to talk about problems and confident that others will work with them to fix what went wrong. Edmondson invented the term "psychological safety" to refer to an environment in which people feel it's okay to ask questions and take risks—which leads to more successful performance.

Physicians apologize poorly when they're terrified of getting in trouble. Businesses apologize poorly because they're afraid of disappointing stockholders and losing market share and turning off customers. CEOs may evade apologizing because they don't want to look weak to the next corporate board that might hire them. Many businesses' first response to a mistake is to deny, deny, deny. When they finally apologize, it's bad, because they've already tried a cover-up as a strategy. Workplaces like these frequently aren't a safe environment for people to face errors head-on and address them in an open, honest, solution-oriented way rather than in a way that is akin to a cat kicking sand over a poop.

We all recognize crappy corporate apologies. And yet, executives just keep excreting them.

A Tale of Two Airlines

One of the very worst corporate responses to a crisis in recent memory involved United Airlines and the horrifying video of a sixty-nine-year-old Asian American doctor being dragged down the aisle by the arms—screaming, face bloody, glasses askew—of an overbooked United plane to make room for members of a flight crew. The doctor wound up with a concussion, a broken nose, and two missing teeth. United offered several terrible responses to the incident . . . only a month after CEO Oscar Munoz was named 2017's Communicator of the Year by *PRWeek*. "Munoz has shown himself to be a smart, dedicated, and excellent leader who understands the value of communications," *PRWeek* said. Too soon!

The violence against Dr. David Dao on United Express Flight 3411 occurred just two weeks after another awful (if less bloody) incident in which United barred two teenage girls wearing leggings from a flight. They were left sobbing at the gate. United repeatedly defended the gate agent on Twitter, saying first that the airline had the right to prevent anyone "inappropriately dressed" from getting on a plane, then saying that the girls were ticketed as relatives of someone who worked for United and "there is a dress code for pass travelers as they are representing UA when they fly." (Maybe it's time to revisit that dress code, certainly when it is applied to minors?)

Two weeks after that, Dao was dragged from his flight by aviation police that United called in. Around four hours later, United issued its first official statement: "Flight 3411 from Chicago to Louisville was overbooked. After our team looked for volunteers, one customer refused to leave the aircraft voluntarily and law enforcement was asked to come to the gate. We apologize for the overbook situation. Further details on the removed customer should be directed to authorities." Sorry about the overbooking; too bad about the uncooperative asshole! Tell it to the cops, not us! (Notice the passive voice of "law enforcement was asked to come to the gate." By ZOMBIES?)

United's response went over poorly—can't imagine why—and shortly after noon the next day CEO Munoz tweeted, "This is an upsetting event to all of us here at United. I apologize for having to reaccomodate these customers. Our team is moving with a sense of urgency to work with the authorities and conduct our own detailed review of what happened. We are also reaching out to this passenger to talk directly to him and further address and resolve this situation." Still terrible! No apology. "Situation." "Re-accomodate." "These customers." (We're concerned only about that one elderly, sobbing, bleeding customer.) And while we're sure it was "an upsetting event to all of us here at United," we can only imagine how upsetting it was for Dr. Dao. In fact, we have to imagine, since Munoz didn't mention the beatdown at all.

Munoz made it worse (again! a truly impressive feat!) with a letter to United staff on Monday night that was leaked to the press.

> Dear Team, Like you, I was upset to see and hear about what happened last night aboard United Express Flight 3411 headed from Chicago to Louisville. While the facts and circumstances are still evolving, especially with respect to why this customer defied Chicago Aviation Security Officers the way he did, to give you a clearer picture of what transpired, I've included below a recap from the preliminary reports filed by our employees.
>
> As you will read, this situation was unfortunately compounded when one of the passengers we politely asked to deplane refused and it became necessary to contact Chicago Aviation Security Officers to help. Our employees followed established procedures for dealing with situations like this.
>
> While I deeply regret this situation arose, I also emphatically stand behind all of you, and I want to commend you for continuing to go above and beyond to ensure we fly right. I do, however, believe there are lessons we can learn from this experience, and we are taking a close look at the circumstances surrounding this incident.
>
> Treating our customers and each other with respect and dignity is at the core of who we are, and we must always remember this no matter how challenging the situation.

"While I deeply regret this situation arose"? Nice lack of responsibility taking. So regrettable, the dragging that somehow occurred, without any action on United's part, that merely *arose*, like Venus rising from the ocean froth in her seashell. Munoz still hadn't apologized, even privately to his own people, who likely also found the national fury and relentless social media mockery aimed at them dismaying. Maybe the phrase "treating our customers with respect and dignity" was a poor choice of words, given what everyone saw with their own human eyeballs? Plus saying that the customer "defied" the cops? Sadly noting that the customer was "politely asked to deplane"? Meaning that if he'd only cooperated, the cops United called on him wouldn't have had to beat the daylights out of him? He was asking for it? Unmentioned is the fact that he paid for his ticket, and while overbooking may be an ugly fact of modern life, being "politely asked to deplane" doesn't change the fact that it's abhorrent to buy a seat and then not be guaranteed the right to use it.

Munoz helpfully appended a timeline of events. It included the fact that customers were offered a thousand bucks (which is practically Dr. Evil's ONE MILLION DOLLARS) to deplane; that "when we approached one of these passengers to explain apologetically that he was being denied boarding, he raised his voice and refused to comply with crew member instructions" (WE ASKED NICELY! HE RAISED HIS VOICE! HE DESERVED SMACKERY!); he "became more and more disruptive and belligerent" (JAIL FOR HIM! JAIL FOR ONE THOUSAND YEARS!); that United was "left with no choice" but to call the cops because the elderly man "repeatedly declined to leave" (HULK SMASH!) and he persisted in "running back onto the aircraft in defiance of both our crew and security officials" (THAT BLOODY ELDERLY ASSHOLE WOULD NOT STAY DOWN!).

Somehow this memo made matters worse! Soon a parody Twitter account showed up called "United Overbooks," consisting of corporate apologies for overbooking accompanied by gifs of elderly people being pushed down flights of stairs and Andre the Giant putting Johnny Carson in a choke hold.

Within hours, Munoz issued yet another statement:

> *The truly horrific event that occurred on this flight has elicited many responses from all of us: outrage, anger, disappointment. I share all of those sentiments, and one above all: my deepest apologies for what happened. Like you, I continue to be disturbed by what happened on this flight and I deeply apologize to the customer forcibly removed and to all the customers aboard. No one should ever be mistreated this way.*
>
> *I want you to know that we take full responsibility and we will work to make it right.*
>
> *It's never too late to do the right thing. I have committed to our customers and our employees that we are going to fix what's broken so this never happens again. This will include a thorough review of crew movement, our policies for incentivizing volunteers in these situations, how we handle oversold situations and an examination of how we partner with airport authorities and local law enforcement. We'll communicate the results of our review by April 30th.*
>
> *I promise you we will do better.*

First use of the word "apologize," but no mention of what "the truly horrific event that occurred" was. And again no causal verb action: Munoz says, "We take full responsibility," but he never says what United *did*. Once more, the event just *materialized*, spontaneously, like a dance party on a subway platform after a Robyn concert. Munoz was "disturbed by what happened" (again, specificity is lacking). Fortunately, United is working on "incentivizing volunteers" in ways that don't involve brute force.

There were more statements. United's stock price plunged. Americans were assured that "this horrible situation has provided a harsh learning experience." (For whom? we wonder.) Munoz took an apology trip to *Good Morning America* and talked about how he felt "shame." (Again, good apologies focus on what the victim feels, not what the offender feels.) United finally apologized publicly to Dr. Dao. Refunds were offered to customers on the flight.

At last United made a commitment to real change: not involving law enforcement "unless it is a matter of safety and security," reevaluating "crew movement" (which presumably means the policies around booting paying customers in favor of flight crews), revamping training programs so that "our values—not just systems—will guide everything we do." United also stated that Munoz and the company called Dr. Dao "on numerous occasions to express our heartfelt and deepest apologies." Dr. Dao's lawyer said at a press conference held by the family that this was false. So, great start in living your values there, United!

Apologies Above All

Compare and contrast this aviation-related customer service debacle with that of JetBlue on Valentine's Day of 2007. Thanks to an ice storm at JFK airport, 139 of 156 JetBlue flights were grounded. The airline gambled, wrongly, on a weather report saying that the ice was likely to turn to rain, and continued to load passengers onto planes. Some wound up stuck on the runway for six hours. Delayed flights begat delayed flights, with domino effects all over the country, and JFK didn't catch up to normalcy for six whole days—a lifetime in the travel business—affecting over 130,000 JetBlue customers.

After those six days, the company took out full-page ads in New York City, Boston, and DC newspapers, reading, in part:

We are sorry and embarrassed. But most of all, we are deeply sorry. Last week was the worst operational week in JetBlue's seven year history. [...]

Words cannot express how truly sorry we are for the anxiety, frustration and inconvenience that we caused. [...] We know we failed to deliver on this promise last week.

We are committed to you, our valued customers, and are taking immediate corrective steps to regain your confidence in us. We have begun putting a comprehensive plan in place to provide better and more timely information to you, more tools and resources for our crewmembers and improved procedures for handling operational difficulties in the future. [...]

Most importantly, we have published the JetBlue Airways Customer Bill of Rights—our official commitment to you of how we will handle operational interruptions going forward—including details of compensation. [...]

You deserved better—a lot better—from us last week. [...]

The letter was signed by the airline's CEO.

Why is this apology so much better than United's? First off, *it leads with the apology.* It doesn't dwell on the CEO's or the company's emotions or "regret"; it keeps a tight focus on the customer's feelings of rage and betrayal. Phrases like "we know we failed," "you deserved better—a lot better—from us," and "truly sorry for the anxiety, frustration and inconvenience that we caused" take ownership—something United never truly did—and feel empathetic rather than evasive. The letter looks ahead to the actions it's taking to ensure that this won't happen again and offers reparations by bringing up compensation immediately. Unlike United's squirmy, evasive, corporatespeak-laden responses, JetBlue addressed its customers in conversational language. So much less infuriating, right?

The Capitalist Elephant in the Room

There's a problem, however, inherent in both these apologies. Guess what? It's capitalism!

We may swear up and down that we'll never fly a given airline again, but if it gets us to our destination when we want to get there and it's the cheapest or more direct option, what are we gonna do? The airlines know this. And while they're concerned with keeping shareholders happy, they know that people ultimately vote with their pocketbooks. Factor in the incentive of frequent flier miles, and, frankly, outrage over a bad misstep—even the beating up of an elderly man—doesn't have a lot of long-term impact.

Another problem: people have short memories. Only a couple of years after the ice storm incident, JetBlue was back in the news for the story of the flight attendant yelling, "I'm done!" as the plane was taxiing to a stop, deploying the evacuation slide, grabbing two beers, and sliding off the plane. (Cue the memes!) Funny. But security experts pointed out that the incident revealed a number of JetBlue security failings. The airline also made headlines in 2021 for making its first political donation after the January 6 attack on the U.S. Capitol to Congresswoman Nicole Malliotakis, one of the lawmakers who called the 2020 election results illegitimate. She happened to also sit on the House panel that oversees aviation. A coincidence, surely. United, meanwhile, made approving headlines in 2021 for announcing that it had launched a flight academy with a diversity initiative to train five thousand new pilots by 2030, half of them women or people of color. So how much does a corporate apology really matter?

Sometimes, honestly, not much. When companies are more beholden to shareholders than to the public, or when the company does the calculus and decides that apologizing poorly or not at all will work out as well or better for them than apologizing well and making meaningful changes—annoying changes like addressing workplace culture, creating better working conditions, allowing workers to unionize, offering reparations to employees and customers who were harmed, creating a genuinely more diverse and tolerant company, etc.—why the heck should businesses do the work or shoulder the expense of apologizing meaningfully and doing better?

And for some companies that cultivate a faux punk rock or no-snowflakes image, refusing to apologize is good for the brand. Which further shows that corporations are not people, no matter what politicians say. For people, good apologies are both mandatory and life-changing. For companies, apologies are primarily about commerce. And that's one reason we may not receive the satisfying, affirming apologies from companies that we seek.

If Corporations Are Persons, Are They People Persons?

Let's say a bit more about corporations not being people. It's often said that if a corporation *really* were a person, it'd be a person who's a psychopath. We'd go further. A corporation can be demonically possessed. A corporation can become a zombie. A corporation can take up with a bad boyfriend (by which we mean a management consultant). A corporation can have religious beliefs. But the truth is that it's *not* the corporation but rather its top executive or executives who can have religious beliefs. A company may have a CEO who announces one day, "We at Engulf & Devour are all about disruption." The next day the CEO announces she's leaving for another company. Her successor then announces, "E&D is all about family." Then next month, maybe after the new CEO is taken away in handcuffs, E&D announces that it is pivoting! To the music! E&D is all about the music!

One example is the time in 1981 when the Lucasfilm legal department decided to go after *Mad* magazine for Mort Drucker's "The Empire

Strikes Out" parody of *The Empire Strikes Back*. Cease, they demanded. Desist. Or face the wrath of Lucasfilm. Unrepentant, the magazine responded with a copy of a letter they'd gotten a month earlier, a letter from George Lucas likening Drucker to da Vinci and asking to buy the original artwork of the parody. We hope somebody apologized to somebody in there somewhere, but our point remains: a corporation is not ... of one mind. So if HR promises you one thing, get it in writing before you go to Payroll.

If Corporations Are Only Pretending to Be People, Why Not Pretend to Be *Good* People?

Sometimes, though, companies apologizing well and making changes matter a lot. We just saw how that's true across the board in the medical field. Here's a corporate example. This case—one that's still taught in business schools and public relations programs around the country over forty years after it happened—is the story of the Tylenol poisonings of 1982.

A mass murderer—one who was never found—somehow laced bottles of Extra-Strength Tylenol in the Chicago suburbs with lethal doses of cyanide. Seven people died in three days. The entire country was terrified.

Johnson & Johnson, the maker of Tylenol, acted quickly. Its chair, James E. Burke, put together a seven-member strategy team and told them their first priority was "How do we protect the people?" and the second was "How do we save the product?" Even before it was clear whether there were more than two tainted bottles, J&J voluntarily recalled all 31 million bottles in circulation, in both stores and hospitals. A national recall was a new concept in 1982. The cost to the company was over $100 million, which is over $290 million today. They went from 34 percent of the market to 0 percent overnight. Burke reached out to the heads of every national news network (in an era when many more people watched the nightly news), giving them daily updates and allowing them to sit in on internal meetings. "The lawyers hated the fact that I was doing it," Burke said later in an interview, "because they didn't know what our obligations were legally." The company set up a hotline for consumers and sent telexes (an early form of fax) to doctors' officers warning them to alert patients not to use Tylenol. Crisis management, PR, branding, and ad executives predicted that the company was doomed. "I don't think they can ever sell another product under that name," legendary adman Jerry Della Femina told the *New York Times*. "There may be an advertising person who thinks he can solve this and if they find him, I want to hire him, because then I want him to turn our water cooler into a wine cooler."

But only two months later J&J reintroduced the product in a new form, with new packaging, making it more difficult to hack: plastic around the bottle's cap, foil over the top of the bottle itself, and capsules made of gel instead of powder. Within a year, Tylenol had not only regained but surpassed its lost market share. And, of course, safer packaging still exists today.

We can't find evidence that J&J apologized. (The closest we could get: when asked at a press conference whether he was sorry the company hadn't acted more quickly, Burke said yes.) We'd argue that in this case it doesn't matter whether the chief executive said the words "I'm sorry" or "I apologize." His actions were the apology. The company did everything right and took a huge financial hit in response to a terrorist act not of their making.

Generally speaking, the best business apologies involve both words and actions; one or the other alone isn't enough. Research seems to show that when they're personally affected by a company's wrongdoing, customers seem to prefer a good apology to an apology-free payout. A cleverly constructed 2009 study in the UK found that when businesses tell disgruntled customers that they're sorry, those customers feel more satisfied than customers who are bribed (um, sorry, "who receive financial compensation"). The study offered eBay users who left negative or neutral feedback either an apology ("We are very sorry and want to apologise"—with an *s* because England), or 5 euros in exchange for withdrawing the feedback. Around 45 percent of participants withdrew their feedback after the apology, but only 23 percent withdrew their feedback for compensation.

Menstrual Mess-Up Amends (Say That Ten Times Fast)

And if a company apologizes well, offers recompense, takes action to fix the situation, *and* shows a sense of humor, better still! Take the case of OB tampons. In 2010, after a combo of supply chain interruptions and a dumb business decision, Johnson & Johnson decided to withdraw OB Ultra from the market. Unfortunately, they'd underestimated their supersized tampon's popularity. (Marjorie's personal fave, btw. Heavy-flow queens, unite!) Customers freaked when they couldn't find the product on drugstore shelves. Enterprising jerks began offering individual boxes on eBay for a hundred bucks. Enraged consumers called for a boycott of OB.

Johnson & Johnson (them again! . . . but then again, they own everything) realized pretty quickly that it had screwed up and worked to fix things. The company put the product back into production and got it back on shelves four months later. J&J sent apology notes to consumers and offered coupons right and left. And then there was the aforementioned use of humor.

J&J sent over 65,000 tampon buyers a "personal" email with a link to a YouTube video containing their first names. (The online "your name in a song" thing is ubiquitous now; it wasn't then.) An unthreateningly hot white guy in a meadow overlooking the ocean huskily whispered your name—let's say, "Marjorieeeeee"—and blew a handful of rose petals at you. Suddenly the rose petals re-formed into the letters of your name! The man launched into a power ballad, playing a glossy white piano. "I know we went away," he sang soulfully, "and let you down," he added, looking *down* for emphasis. "We're so sorry! So sorry! Write your name across the sky—cue the airplane guy!" And then "Marjorie" appeared in skywriting. "We're double sorry, triple sorry," he sang soulfully, ripping one sleeve to reveal a "sorry" tattoo on one unthreateningly slightly muscular pale shoulder, then ripping off the other sleeve to reveal a matching "Marjorie" tattoo. Then he released a white dove into the air, where it fluttered next to a hot-air balloon—suddenly it's sunset; don't ask—with your name on it. "You deserve the best and more," the unthreateningly hot white guy sang into our eyes. "So take this coupon to the store."

And then: coupon.

People with periods emailed the link hither and yon. The ad offered the vibe of the "Look at me, I'm on a horse" deodorant guy, but with smaller pecs and more personalization. Fifteen years later, OB Ultra remains on shelves. Well done, OB.

So: companies can apologize well if they care to. It's just not always worth it for them to care to. This isn't a moral flaw on their part; they're not human beings. It's just business.

Woop Woop: That's the Sound of the Police Refusing to Apologize

Police forces differ from companies when it comes to apologies in at least one crucial respect: Companies often recognize that they *should* apologize to consumers, yet consciously decide it's not worthwhile for them to apologize. Police forces largely feel they shouldn't apologize, period.

Concern about police apologies and accountability aren't new. Back in 1982, when the *Los Angeles Times* reported that twelve out of fifteen people to die in police choke holds were Black, LA police chief Daryl Gates responded that he was seeking research to confirm his "hunch" that Black people's veins and arteries "do not open as fast as they do in normal people."

Gates refused to apologize for saying this, believing that he was showing "great sensitivity." "I have absolutely no apology to make at all for what I was thinking," he said at a police commission hearing. "But I very deeply want to apologize for the manner in which I expressed it . . . my reference to 'normal people' was unfortunate—very unfortunate— and was meant only to apply to the normal functioning of blood traveling through arteries to the brain." He added, "I was pursuing what I believed to be a compassionate course." Naturally.

The Police and the Public See the World Very Differently

Feeling misunderstood is common among police officers. According to a nationwide Pew study, more than 80 percent of officers surveyed feel that people don't understand the risks of police work. (The same percentage of the public says that, yeah, they do.) When it comes to police officers killing Black people, 67 percent of the police but only 39 percent of the public describe these encounters as "isolated incidents" rather than signs of a systemic problem. Unsurprisingly, 72 percent of white officers, but less than half of all Black officers, see such killings as isolated incidents. And 92 percent of white officers but only 29 percent of Black officers say that the United States has achieved equal rights between Black and white people; among the public, about half (48 percent), including 57 percent of white people but only 12 percent of Black people, believe that the country has made the necessary changes to give Black people in America equal rights.

When it comes to protests against police brutality, the Pew study found, only 35 percent of police officers believe that demonstrations against police are motivated even a little bit by a desire to make cops answerable to the public. Meanwhile, 65 percent of the public feels that accountability is a motive for police protests. And when you look only at white survey respondents, further stark divisions appear: just 27 percent of white officers believe that protesters are motivated by a desire for accountability, while 63 percent of white non-police respondents say this. This poll was taken in 2017, before the killings of George Floyd and Breonna Taylor became national news and before the Defund the Police and Black Lives Matter movements had truly taken hold. We imagine that the differences between white officers and the public are even greater now.

Some police forces are trying to reckon with history. In 2016, Terrence M. Cunningham, the chief of police in Wellesley, Massachusetts, said at the International Association of Chiefs of Police convention: "Events over the past several years have caused many to question the actions of our officers and has [sic] tragically undermined the trust that the public must and should have in their police departments." Already, there's a lack of personalization in his statement: "Events . . . have caused many to question" is pretty tortured syntax, and "tragically" seems to refer to what has happened to the police, not to the people who have died at their hands. "The history of the law enforcement profession is replete with examples of bravery, self-sacrifice, and service to the community," Cunningham continued, calling police work "a noble profession." Again, this isn't likely to sit well with people who are not positively disposed toward the police. Cunningham went on, "At the same time, it is also clear that the history of policing has also had darker periods," and mentioned laws that "have required police officers to perform many unpalatable tasks . . . [and] while this is no longer the case, this dark side of our shared history has created a multigenerational—almost inherited—mistrust between many communities of color and their law enforcement agencies." No. Cunningham blames lawmakers, not police themselves, and calling police mistrust "inherited" is like calling it genetic, caused by DNA rather than lived experience. Cunningham continued, "While we obviously cannot change the past, it is clear that we must change the future. . . . For our part, the first step is for law enforcement and the IACP to acknowledge and apologize for the actions of the past and the role that our profession has played in society's historical mistreatment of communities of color." Again, it's all in the past! He concluded, "It is my hope that, by working together, we can break this historic cycle of mistrust and build a better and safer future for us all." His use of "working together" and "cycle of mistrust" makes *both* parties responsible for this strained relationship.

We've already discussed how poor apologies make people angrier than no apology at all.

In 2021, after a Black and Latino lieutenant in the U.S. Army Medical Corps, wearing his uniform, was pulled over by state police in Windsor, Virginia, pepper-sprayed, and threatened with death (when the lieutenant said he was afraid, the officers told him, "You should be," and threatened that he'd "ride the lightning," a reference to the electric chair), town authorities danced around an apology without quite getting there. "The town of Windsor prides itself on its small-town charm and the community-wide respect of its Police Department," an official statement said. "Due to this, we are saddened for events like this to cast our community in a negative light. Rather than deflect criticism, we have addressed these matters with our personnel administratively, we are reaching out to community stakeholders to engage in dialogue, and commit ourselves to additional discussions in the future." Like the "tragically" inclined Wellesley police chief, Windsor is "saddened." At least Windsor is completely up-front in saying its concern is for its own image. Heaven forfend that Windsor be seen "in a negative light" by anyone.

All Good Police Apologies Matter

Research shows that good apologies from police officers are capable of having real impact. In their paper "Reconciling Police and Communities with Apologies, Acknowledgments, or Both: A Controlled Experiment," published in 2020 in the *Annals of the Academy of Political and Social Science*, Thomas C. O'Brien, Tracey L. Meares, and Tom R. Tyler show that "police leaders should combine acknowledgement of responsibility for the mistrust with an apology if they want to enlist the cooperation of people who are least likely to trust the police."

O'Brien (a psychologist at the University of Illinois at Urbana-Champaign), Meares, and Tyler (both Yale Law School professors) found that police leaders often mention "mistrust" of police when they make public statements after an act of police harm against civilians in their communities. The scholars looked at the results of avoiding versus acknowledging responsibility for that mistrust, and the results of issuing or not issuing an apology for their actions. Among the people least likely to trust police, evidence strongly suggests that combining acknowledgment of responsibility and an act of apology works best.

Collecting data from 678 Black Americans, the authors found that a "consensual authority-community relationship" can prevent distrust of and anger toward police from skyrocketing. "In a community where people feel that authorities ensure their security, want to help them, and do so through fair processes, people feel more secure," they note. "Sincerity is central to the process of reconciliation. Communities must perceive that initiatives to build trust are sincere; otherwise they may backfire and reduce legitimacy." Good public apologies are hugely helpful in the trust-building process. And the denial of the problem "further distances communities from authorities, making it more difficult for them to benefit from community cooperation."

Sadly, a good police apology is hard to find. (Hint: If it uses the phrase "bad apples," it is not a good apology.)

A Lovely if Belated Police Apology

But here's an excellent one mentioned in passing by O'Brien, Meares, and Tyler: In 2013, at the First Baptist Church in Montgomery, Alabama, the city's police chief apologized to Representative John Lewis for the Montgomery Police Department's enforcement of "unjust laws" and failure to protect the Freedom Riders back in 1961. Chief Kevin Murphy took off his badge, saying, "This symbol of authority, which used to be a symbol of oppression, needs to be a symbol of reconciliation." Handing the badge to Lewis, he said, "This is a token of appreciation, Congressman, because you changed this city, you changed this state, you changed this country, and you changed the world, and for that we are truly grateful." Lewis was moved to tears. (Before taking the badge, he hesitated: "Do you have another one?")

Lewis said later that day, "I've been arrested and jailed about 40 times, and never has a police officer offered to apologize. And when I started crying, I was crying tears of gratitude, and I guess that we had come to this point: even when I think about it today, for a young police officer— a young, white police officer; the chief in Montgomery, Alabama, who had not even been born fifty-two years ago when this all took place— to give me his badge, and he took it off of his lapel . . . I've been keeping it in my pocket all day."

Murphy walked the walk, too, working to change the institutional culture of MPD. Shortly after he took the top job in 2011, he instituted a mandatory class for the entire force called "Policing in a Historic City" that analyzes the police department's actions during the civil rights era. "It's an educational effort to show our officers, especially the very young ones—some were born in 1991 and are now wearing a badge—that we can't repeat the mistakes of the past," he told Rachel Maddow.

Murphy's apology wasn't perfect. He told Maddow, "It's a new day. . . . People are working together more now than they ever have in the history of our country, than in the history of our state, and certainly in the history of our city, and we need to continue to move forward." As we note elsewhere in this book, "move forward" is not a phrase for the person apologizing to say; only the person victimized gets to decide when it's time to move forward. But if Murphy's apology was good enough for Congressman Lewis, it's good enough for us to cite. A potent apology doesn't erase the past; it doesn't magically fix America's long-standing civil rights failures. But it can help us look forward meaningfully by not insisting that everything's all better now so let's let bygones be bygones.

Murphy may have paid a price for his apology. The mayor ousted him the next year, after twenty-eight years on the force and only three as chief. Many Black residents felt that it was because of his words to John Lewis. Fortunately, Murphy was immediately hired by the Montgomery County Sheriff's Office, where he still works as of this writing.

Cracks in the Blue Wall Sometimes Let the Light In

Another belated—but not quite as belated—police apology comes from Kansas City, where Ryan Stokes was killed by police in 2013. The official story was that Stokes was accused of theft, there was an armed standoff, and the police were forced to shoot him in the chest.

Later the story changed. A drunk person had accused Stokes of stealing his iPhone . . . but only after first accusing someone else. Later, when the drunk man was sober, he said that in truth he'd never seen anyone else with his phone and had probably dropped it.

It turned out Stokes hadn't been armed. In fact he'd been surrendering to Officer Daniel Straub when Officer William Thompson shot him in the back.

It took a while for that information to come out. In the meantime, the Board of Police Commissioners gave Officer Thompson a commendation. The truth only came out because Officer Straub testified about Stokes's death in a civil suit brought by Stokes's grieving mother, Narene. Four years later, Thompson's commendation was rescinded.

Narene Stokes's lawsuit did not succeed (an appeal is pending as we write this). Although Stokes wasn't armed, the court said, it was reasonable for Thompson to *think* he was. A KCPD spokesperson said, "The result of the events is terribly tragic for the family members and all involved. We are sorry for the pain that Mr. Stokes' family experienced." Not an apology, not even a bad one.

Two years later, in 2019, Straub was pushed out of the force. The KCPD and Straub have different ideas about why. Straub thinks his testimony in the civil suit had something to do with it. After he lost his job, he reached out to Narene Stokes to apologize to her. "I am truly sorry for what happened to Ryan," he told her. (Remember, he isn't the cop who shot her son.) Stokes and Straub talked. She was "flabbergasted" and moved to get his apology. "I couldn't believe it."

Straub told local station KCUR that he needed to apologize to Narene Stokes as part of the integrity of being a law enforcement officer. "I feel there's something greater that is missing from police departments across the country. That missing trait is empathy, and the ability to see the good in everyone . . . no matter who they are."

It's telling that Straub didn't reach out to Mrs. Stokes while he was still on the force—and that his personal apology was so much better than the official one.

More Reasons for our Perpetual Search for Good Police Apologies

It's no shock that we have trouble finding examples of good law enforcement apologies. In addition to the factors already discussed, several additional ones harm police departments' ability to apologize well. According to a 2016 study, when police engage with people they view as disrespectful of them, they view engagement as a threat to their (usually) masculine identity; police violence is actually a way to address that identity threat. Another study found that being perceived as racist, or being perceived as acting out of illegitimate motives, in fact motivates officers to use violence. This is a vicious cycle, and not the kind Terrence M. Cunningham mentioned in his speech to the IAPC. It's not that Black people *inherit* distrust in the cops; it's that cops keep *earning* distrust through racist acts they repeatedly refuse to acknowledge as racist . . . or apologize for.

Think about the words of the Cherokee County Sheriff's Office in Georgia after a white man went on a shooting spree at three Asian-owned massage parlors in 2021, killing six Asian women at a time when Asians were being widely blamed for Covid-19 and violence against Asian Americans was skyrocketing. The sheriff's office official said that the shooter was having "a really bad day." The shooter had a "sex addiction" and his act was motivated by the desire to help others with sex addictions, so it was not a hate crime. He was just "kind of at the end of his rope."

When bad PR occurred after this press conference was held and the statements that had been made by the official were the cause of distress—see, we can use bad-apology syntax, too—the sheriff's office issued a statement. The official's words were "the subject of much debate and anger." Just the words! Not the sentiments behind them! "In as much as his words were taken or construed as insensitive or inappropriate, they were not intended to disrespect the victims," the statement assured the public. We needed to understand that the official "had a difficult task" and it was "one of the hardest in his 28 years in law enforcement"! HE WAS HAVING A BAD DAY TOO! We should appreciate that this is such a sensitive, supportive bunch of sheriffs—always checking out if a coworker or perp is struggling!

Another factor standing in the way of good law enforcement apologies is that charges against cops are often dismissed before they get anywhere near a courtroom . . . and even after an internal conviction. Why apologize if there's no consequence for your actions?

For example, in New York City, even if a trial judge finds that NYPD cops abuse their authority, even if a civilian complaint review board investigates charges and finds the allegations of victims of police violence to be substantiated, even when a police department judge rules on internal NYPD charges against officers after examining evidence and listening to believable witness testimony, the city's police commissioner gets the last word. If he doesn't believe the officers should be punished, they won't be. In one 2017 example cited by the independent journalism outlet *The City*, three plainclothes detectives were chasing a suspect in East Harlem. Without a warrant, they pushed their way into an apartment looking for the suspect. One resident said the police pinned her frightened autistic brother against a wall. They did find and arrest the subject. A trial judge determined that they'd entered the apartment illegally and found them guilty of abuse of authority. But New York City's police commissioner threw out the judge's verdict, claiming that the tenant had let the officers in voluntarily. The fact that one of the three officers had had three unauthorized-force charges against him in a year—one for using a prohibited choke hold, one for using a nightstick as a club, and one unspecified use of physical force—was irrelevant. Within a month, the cop in question was promoted to detective.

Finally, cops are rarely convicted of manslaughter or murder. A study by Philip M. Stinson, a Bowling Green State University criminologist, looked at the data for 1,400 officers arrested for violent crimes commit-ted while on duty. Only 50 percent of those arrested for manslaughter or murder were convicted, compared to 70 percent of civilians charged with these crimes. And when police who are charged with fatal shootings are convicted, it's usually for lesser charges. So why would they apologize for actions unlikely to result in convictions?

How to Win Safer Streets and Better Police Apologies

Tons of evidence shows that when people in authority are viewed as being part of the community in which they serve, they're more likely to be trusted. They're more able to do their jobs. They're more likely to receive cooperation, buy-in, and participation from those among whom they live and work. Right now, police are widely perceived to be using their power unjustly. The nonprofit Sentencing Project has found that Black people are far more likely to be arrested for drug-related offenses, even though they aren't more likely than white people to use or sell drugs. Black defendants are also far more likely to receive a longer sen-tence than white people for the same crime. They're also far more likely to be stopped for "investigative" reasons—meaning the officer has nearly infinite discretion in why they've stopped a given person—than white people.

Police officers are also being asked to do jobs that they haven't been adequately trained for. Research shows that nine out of ten calls to the police are for nonviolent incidents. What if people who were better trained in de-escalation were called instead? What if taxpayer money shifted toward funding social services that work to ameliorate systemic problems like mental illness, addiction, and homelessness? Why not take a two-pronged approach, not only training officers to recognize the sys-temic biases under which we all operate and to apologize well for their actions, but also working to ensure that police officers aren't *put* in the position of having to apologize—and failing at it—quite so often in the first place? Wouldn't that help promote real justice?

SorryWatch Regrets the Error

Journalists tend to "regret the error" rather than apologize. Regretting the error is a reflex, a phrase used for accidental misspellings and huge moral mistakes alike, a rhetorical tradition grown out of the long history of writing as if one were omniscient.

When in journalism one is shown to be flawed, one has the institution speak for the individual. 'Twas ever thus. The tone is formal. The phrase feels more ritualistic than heartfelt. If there is self-examination, the reader and/or viewer does not generally learn about it.

Most journalists have been taught to believe in the notion of being neutral, being above the story: a beautiful cloud of non-bias hovering over mere mortals who do things like *take sides* and *have beliefs*. Media folks tend not to recognize the impossibility—and, indeed, the undesirability—of being truly without opinions. Some media organizations won't let a writer who has spoken of being a victim of harassment or sexual assault cover stories that deal with harassment or sexual assault. (Hey, guys, nearly all of us women have experienced harassment or sexual assault!) Some outlets insist on quoting "both sides," even when one side has a long history of lying or misrepresentation. (Also, some insist on using terms like "misrepresentation" when they should say "lying.") Giving equal airing to all perspectives isn't desirable when some perspectives are, say, grounded in science denial. Sources shouldn't be quoted as if they're unbiased if they clearly have a perspective that informs their actions. This is why medical journals demand that contributors reveal who has given them money for research.

News outlets: they're just like us! Our first reaction as individuals to being called out is to become defensive. We want to defend our work. "I know the intense pressures that reporters, editors and engagement teams are under to keep the audience informed and also to drive traffic to your content," wrote Doris Truong, director of training and diversity at the Poynter Institute. "I have been the person who wrote the news alert, then pushed the button that sent breaking news to millions of devices. But we have to do better."

Doing better means understanding—and making clear to readers—that sources have their own agendas. Doing better means turning to different sources rather than the same ones all the time. It means not printing statements from powerful people and institutions as if they were facts. It means providing context. It means understanding that different kinds of prejudice present in different ways.

When journalists make generalizations, or fail to provide historical background, or engage in victim blaming, we have to own it. (We, Susan and Marjorie, count ourselves among the journalists.) We have a choice to spotlight victims of crimes or perpetrators; when we implicitly or explicitly disparage a crime victim's fashion choices, career, or state of inebriation, we engage in editorial behavior that warrants an apology. Media moves fast, but we still have to pause to apologize when we get it wrong. Taking the opportunity to educate readers as well as to acknowledge our own failings is vital. Everyone deserves to know how the sausage is made.

Forgive Me, Congregants, for I Have Sinned

What are the barriers to religious institutions and clergy apologizing well?

As we've noted, powerful institutions tend not to want to give up power. An apology is a surefire giving away of power. It's an admission of wrongdoing. When you claim to speak for God, as some faith leaders (not all!) do, what are you supposed to do, admit that God has erred?

God does not make mistakes! This is of course tied in to the Just World hypothesis: if God is just, the world must be just. If anyone is suffering, there's a reason. They deserved it, or maybe we just don't understand God's plan. If the suffering person is good, they'll find solace in the world to come.

Belief in an all-powerful God is connected to a belief in authoritarianism, another barrier to apologizing well. (In addition, religious leaders are overwhelmingly male, and as we'll see in chapter 10, men tend to think their conduct requires fewer apologies than women do.)

Religious institutions are frequently unaccustomed to being challenged and being transparent. Many denominations of many faiths have stories of sins being swept under the carpet: abuse scandals, theft, ripping babies from their homes and mothers, forcing colonized people to give up their language and culture. Some institutions apologize privately for clergymen's sexual abuse but quietly move them to another house of worship, where they go forth and sin again.

Sometimes, though, religious institutions try to do better. Jesuits in the United States and Canada are currently engaged with an internal battle to address their history of owning and selling slaves. As Ayan Ali, a researcher for the Slavery, History, Memory, and Reconciliation Project of the Jesuit Conference of Canada and the United States, notes, "By foregrounding the voices and perspectives of enslaved people and their descendants, we work to honor and uplift the Black Americans who played a role in the creation of Jesuit institutions and have been excluded from the historical narrative."

In 2017 the order of Jesuits and Jesuit-founded Georgetown University formally repented for slavery. "We express our solemn contrition for our participation in slavery and the benefit our institution received," said Georgetown's president, John J. DeGioia. "We cannot hide from this truth, bury this truth, ignore this truth. Slavery remains the original evil in our republic, an evil that our university was complicit in." Over one hundred descendants of enslaved people attended the ceremony, many in tears. In 2021 the Jesuits vowed to raise $100 million for these descendants and for racial reconciliation initiatives throughout North America. (The descendants' group had asked for $1 billion; the Jesuits countered with the smaller figure and so far have put $15 million in trust and promised to raise the rest within five years.)

"This is an opportunity for Jesuits to begin a very serious process of truth and reconciliation," said Father Timothy Kesicki, president of the Jesuit Conference of Canada and the United States. "Our shameful history of Jesuit slaveholding in the United States has been taken off the dusty shelf, and it can never be put back."

Other institutions are also attempting to apologize for slavery. Some colleges are renaming buildings named for prominent enslavers and creating reparations funds and scholarships for students who have the heritage of those harmed.

All institutions could apologize well and make amends if they chose to. The rules are the same for institutions as for individuals: Say you're sorry, name the thing you did, show you understand its impact, don't make excuses or blame others, make things right to the degree possible, make reparations to the degree possible. If an institution has harmed a specific individual, its representatives need to apologize privately as well as publicly. Sadly, as we've seen, there are multiple mechanisms in place that keep institutions from doing the right thing.

ACTION ITEMS

❏ **Did you screw up?** Think about long-term solutions, not PR-related fixes.

❏ **Are you in charge of a team? Are you a parent? A colleague?** Encourage honest communication with those you work and live with. When someone errs without malice, do not mock them and do not slap them down. Consider the teachable moments.

❑ **Learn to acknowledge and accept your own feelings and your own biases.** When you owe an apology, don't hide behind your authority or institutional role.

❑ **Model good behavior to those in your orbit.** Lead by example. Take responsibility, openly, for your mistakes; apologize freely when you make them.

The Five Worst Corporate Apologies of All Time

Though to be fair, some of the most heinous corporate decision-making fails—Calvin Klein's 1995 amateur porn-style ads featuring a wood-paneled rec room, a leering and disembodied voice, and a lot of *very* young-looking models; Frito-Lay's low-cal olestra chips that caused "anal leakage" throughout the 1990s; Just For Feet's racist 1999 Super Bowl ad featuring a bunch of white-looking people hunting down and drugging a barefoot Kenyan runner—didn't trigger apologies at all.

1. The CEO of BP, after the 2010 Deepwater Horizon explosion that killed eleven workers and caused the largest oil spill in history: "I'm sorry. We're sorry for the massive disruption it's caused their lives. There's no one who wants this over more than I do. I'd like my life back." (Also! "The Gulf of Mexico is a very big ocean. The amount of volume of oil and dispersant we are putting into

it is tiny in relation to the total water volume.") He later apologized for his apology.

2. Pepsi, after the opportunistic, tone-deaf 2017 ad depicting the reality-TV personage Kendall Jenner ending police brutality: "Pepsi was trying to project a global message of unity, peace and understanding. Clearly, we missed the mark and apologize. We are pulling the content and halting any further rollout. We also apologize for putting Kendall Jenner in this position." As *Inc.* pointed out, "Pepsi spent 10 words out of the 40-word statement apologizing to Kendall Jenner."

3. Equifax's CEO, after a massive 2017 data breach affecting 143 million Americans, one the company didn't disclose for three months (coincidentally, we're sure, right after three top executives dumped a ton of stock): "This is clearly a disappointing event for our company, and one that strikes at the heart of who we are and what we do. I apologize to consumers and our business customers for the concern and frustration this causes." Poor Equifax, having to feel disappointment! That is definitely the most painful part of this incident.

4. Henry Ford, facing a libel suit, apologizing to "the Jews" in 1927: Ford's publications the *Dearborn Independent* and *The International Jew* contained stories (in the *Independent*'s case, every week for ninety-one straight weeks) like "How Jews in the U.S. Conceal Their Strength" and "Does Jewish Power Control the World Press?" Under pressure, Ford stated, "Although both publications are my property, it goes without saying that in the multitude of my activities it has been impossible for me to devote

personal attention to their management or to keep informed as to their contents. . . . Had I appreciated even the general nature, to say nothing of the details, of these utterances, I would have forbidden their circulation without a moment's hesitation. . . . I deem it to be my duty as an honorable man to make amends for the wrong done to the Jews as fellow-men and brothers, by asking their forgiveness for the harm that I have unintention-ally committed, by retracting so far as lies within my power the offensive charges laid at their door by these publications, and by giving them the unqualified assurance that henceforth they may look to me for friendship and good will." Weird that he knew nothing about the editorials, given that they carried his byline. And that he apologized right before the filing of a defamation suit by a Jewish farm community organizer.

5. It hasn't happened yet. Sadly, inevitably, there's always a more terrible apology out there.

BAD APOLOGY BINGO CARD #4
CORPORATE EDITION!

more could have been done	any inference	refocus	not racial	what we stand for
disappointed	I am so proud	was seen as	the perception	troubling
became public	this situation	**FREE SQUARE**	came to light	look ahead
commitment to our customers	regarded as	a distraction	inadvertently	may have
regrettable	did not intend	our values	deficiencies	brought to our attention

THE GOVERNMENT FEELS SAD ABOUT HOW THAT ALL WENT DOWN: HOW POLITICAL APOLOGIES GET MADE

We've talked about how individuals and companies apologize; now we'll look at how governments apologize. It's impossible in this book to go as deep as we'd like into historical apologies, or governmental apologies that *should* happen—and, we hope, might still. That's because the world of government injustice is so vast, it feels infinite.

Some governmental apologies are for things that just happened, but some are for long-ago wrongs. Can we apologize for sins that occurred before we were born? Why should we? *How* should we?

Patching Things Up After the Murder in the Cathedral

Hey, who *was* that barefoot guy kneeling in front of that tomb, getting beaten by monks? The king of England, you say? Wow. He must be *really* sorry about Thomas Becket.

The backstory: In 1155, King Henry II appointed his buddy Becket to be archbishop of Canterbury. The two were old friends who'd also spent years wrangling over stuff. (Like the time Henry said to Becket, "Doesn't that ragged old man look cold? Wouldn't it be Christian to give him some warm clothes?" and when Becket agreed, Henry yanked off

Becket's splendid new ministerial cloak and gave it to the old man while the king's retinue laughed heartily.)

As archbishop of Canterbury, Becket started challenging Henry about the power of the crown versus the power of the Church. Exasperated, Henry said something—alas, not on audio—variously given as "Will no one rid me of this turbulent priest?" or "What miserable drones and traitors have I nourished and brought up in my household, who let their lord be treated with such shameful contempt by a low-born cleric?" or "A man who has eaten my bread, who came to my court poor and I have raised him high—now he draws up his heel to kick me in the teeth! He has shamed my kin, shamed my realm: the grief goes to my heart, and no one has avenged me!" (It is not true that Henry exclaimed, "Where's my Roy Cohn?")

On it! Hearing the king's complaint/rant, four knights headed to Canterbury Cathedral, maybe planning to drag Becket back to face the king. Somehow, they killed him. Anyway, dead. Because of what Henry II said. Everyone went crazy, including Henry's not-100-percent-loyal family. Kings can't kill archbishops! Excommunicate Henry! Becket is now a martyred saint! And now we shall call him à Becket, because that's fancy!

The veneration of Becket—sorry, à Becket—made Henry look bad. People were making pilgrimages to à Becket's grave, hailing him as a religious hero who fought against a secular king who meddled in Church business. Henry had to do public penance. On July 12, 1174, he traveled to Canterbury, took off his shoes, donned sackcloth, and walked three miles to the cathedral. There he publicly confessed his guilt in the death of à Becket and allowed himself to be struck with rods by various bishops and eighty monks. He spent the night in vigil by à Becket's tomb. He also did penance at a cathedral in Normandy, barefoot and crownless. He made major concessions to the Church, like sending two hundred knights to the Crusades, letting English churchmen make appeals to Rome, and returning confiscated land to the Canterbury archdiocese. He said he never wanted Becket murdered but admitted that his words caused the murder-y events. (He was taken out of context!)

Was Henry II really sorry, just trying to hold on to his kingdom, or both? We can't say. Regardless, as king, Henry II represented England, not just himself; his agreements bound his nation. His words and actions in the à Becket case are a very early example of a governmental apology in which public amends were made for misuse of power.

Nations on Their Knees

Generally speaking, nations are crap at apology. Even more than the average celebrity or corporation, national governments are *obsessed* with their images. Governments are always looking in the mirror, wanting to be photographed from their good side, hiring highly paid teams to virtually massage and Photoshop everything possible.

Governments avoid apologizing out of pride, fear, and power seeking. Government leaders may avoid apologizing out of ego. Governments often fear setting precedents with apologies. Many of them seek popular support with crude patriotism, and fear apologies will get in the way: they're anxious about alienating supporters by offending *their* national pride. Some citizens want their countries *never* to apologize. They see their government's apologies as a vicarious blow to their pride and patriotism. It's like bellowing "That's not who I am!" on a national level.

We think countries can issue apologies to be proud of, sort of as people can. Countries can and should act like grown-ups—honorably—and citizens can and should take pride when they do.

Carol Tavris and Elliot Aronson's *Mistakes Were Made (but Not by Me)* quotes Lao Tzu, in a translation by Stephen Mitchell:

> *A great nation is like a great man:*
> *When he makes a mistake, he realizes it.*

Having realized it, he admits it.
Having admitted it, he corrects it.
He considers those who point out his faults as his most benevolent teachers.

That does sound like greatness to aspire to.

It Wasn't Me, I Wasn't There

When it comes to apologizing for things that happened in the distant past, you'll sometimes run across arguments that suggest national responsibility is genetic. For instance, in a strange disregard for historical continuity, the late Antonin Scalia (before he was on the Supreme Court—also before he was late) said he had no duty to make redress for slavery, because his father had emigrated from Italy after that time and wasn't involved in racial discrimination, nor did he make any money from it. That's nonsense. Slavery and its impacts are so deeply woven into our country's past that none of us can claim to be free of it. To grab a fast example, Scalia went to Georgetown University, supported in its early days by plantations worked by enslaved people. In 1838, in debt and short of cash, Georgetown sold off 272 enslaved men, women, and children. No amount of crying, "We just got here! We didn't see a thing!" erases the fact that Scalia benefited from slavery's past.

Not everyone is so eager to shrug off responsibility: In 2019 there was a referendum of Georgetown students on assessing themselves a semesterly fee toward reparations to the descendants of the 272. Two-thirds of the students voted for it, but it was then held up by the school's board of directors.

Of course no one who took part in American slavery is alive today. No one who took part in the American Revolution is alive today, either. It makes no logical or moral sense to deny all connection with one set of events while glorying in one's connection to the other. We tend to cele-

brate the parts of our national history that give us joy without acknowledging that we're obligated to apologize for the parts that bring us shame
(and *should* bring us shame).

Apologies to African Americans and Native Americans

The United States has not made redress for the dreadful injustice of slavery. Many people consider Lincoln's second inaugural address, given as
the Civil War was ending, to be an apology. A lot has happened since Lincoln spoke of the offense of people "wringing their bread from the sweat
of other men's faces" and of the possibility that "every drop of blood
drawn with the lash shall be paid by another drawn with the sword." That
was March 1865. In April, Lincoln was assassinated. The famous promise
made by General Sherman and Secretary of War Stanton to give "forty
acres and a mule" to formerly enslaved people had barely begun to happen before President Andrew Johnson overturned it and gave the land
back to planters.

The House of Representatives in 2008 and the Senate in 2009 each
proposed an official apology for slavery, but the House's apology didn't
pass the Senate and the Senate's apology didn't pass the House. And reparations? Ha.

There's nothing preventing individual states from apologizing for
their historic role in this heinous institution, of course. But only half the
eighteen states with enslaved populations have done so. (Mississippi
didn't actually ratify the Thirteenth Amendment, which ended slavery,
until 1995, so . . .)

Never doubt that slavery's repercussions are still felt today. As William Faulkner said, "The past is never dead. It's not even past." Economi-
cally, Black people in America still lag far behind white people. Black
people's wealth is 10 percent that of whites. After years of redlining—the
creation of neighborhood boundaries in which residents were prevented

from getting mortgages (now officially illegal, but an established fact for decades)—African Americans are far less likely than white Americans to own homes. Many Black veterans were prevented from getting benefits under the G.I. Bill. The percentage of Black children living below the poverty line is three times that of white children. Educational opportunities in this country are far from equal: majority-Black public schools are wildly underfunded compared to majority-white public schools. Health disparities are also vast: Black Americans suffer far higher rates of high blood pressure, heart disease, asthma, and diabetes than white Americans. The infant mortality rate for Black Americans is more than twice that of their white counterparts, and Black American women face nearly three times the risk of pregnancy-related deaths as white women.

How Was I Supposed to Know That?

Americans are not taught well about slavery in schools. In 2015 a McGraw-Hill high school geography textbook stated that "the Atlantic Slave Trade between the 1500s and the 1800s brought millions of workers from Africa to the southern United States to work on agricultural plantations." (*Workers.*) In 2010, Texas's social studies curriculum was revamped to remove "slavery" as the central cause of the Civil War; instead, the cause was deemed to be "states' rights." The new curriculum made no mention of the rise of the KKK during Reconstruction or the existence of Jim Crow. Not until 2018 was the curriculum changed; now it gives slavery, secession, and states' rights equal weight as causes of the Civil War. (So, progress, maybe, sort of?)

For generations, slavery was taught in the North as "not as central to the American story but as an unfortunate blemish washed away by the blood of the Civil War," in the words of *Washington Post* education reporter Joe Heim. Students rarely learn that slavery existed in all thirteen original American colonies or that the Northern as well as Southern economy relied on slave labor. It's no wonder that a 2011 Pew Research Center poll found that 48 percent of Americans said the Civil War was mainly about states' rights, compared with 38 percent who said its main cause was slavery. (Nine percent said both factors were equal.)

Growing up in Providence, Rhode Island, Marjorie and her classmates were field-tripped incessantly to Old Slater Mill to be lectured about their state's vital, marvelous role in the industrial revolution. Hooray, water-powered textile spinning. Yet somehow no one ever thought to teach her and her peers that their state controlled between 60 and 90 percent of the eighteenth-century American slave trade. (In *The Notorious Triangle: Rhode Island and the African Slave Trade, 1700–1807*, historian Jay Coughtry observed that from the early eighteenth to the early nineteenth centuries the American slave trade might better have been called the Rhode Island slave trade.)

Slavery is just one of the many things America needs to apologize to Black people for. Among the other things is the Tulsa Race Massacre. Too few Americans even know about it. Tulsa itself didn't begin teaching about it in public schools until 2012.

What happened was that on May 31, 1921, a white mob attacked a Black neighborhood in Tulsa using machine guns and firebombs. They killed three hundred people, burned forty blocks, and left eight thousand people homeless. Survivor Buck Colbert Franklin wrote an eyewitness account, now housed in the National Museum of African American History and Culture in Washington, DC: "Lurid flames roared and belched and licked their forked tongues into the air. Smoke ascended the sky in thick, black volumes and amid it all, the planes—now a dozen or more in number—still hummed and darted here and there with the agility of natural birds of the air." *Planes.*

The neighborhood in question, Greenwood, also known as the Black Wall Street, had become prosperous. Native Americans and African Americans had discovered oil on land previously thought worthless, and white people were furious. "The side-walks were literally covered with burning turpentine balls," he wrote. "I knew all too well where they came from, and I knew all too well why every burning building first caught from the top." Private planes, owned by white citizens, were strafing the neighborhood. "I paused and waited for an opportune time to escape," he wrote. " 'Where oh where is our splendid fire department with its half dozen stations?' I asked myself. 'Is the city in conspiracy with the mob?' "

Aid was not forthcoming. "For fully forty-eight hours, the fires raged and burned everything in its path and it left nothing but ashes and burned safes and trunks and the like where once stood beautiful homes and business houses," Franklin wrote. "And so proud, rich, black Tulsa was destroyed by fire—that is its buildings and property; but its spirit was neither killed nor daunted."

No one was ever convicted of participating in the massacre, supposedly triggered by white word of mouth about a young Black boy sexually threatening a white woman. (In actuality, Franklin said, the Black boy had accidentally stepped on a white girl's foot in a crowded downtown elevator.) A grand jury blamed the Black community for what happened to them. No one was compensated for lost property.

In the intervening years, there's been a lot of official somber regretting about Tulsa, but little true apologizing. Governor Frank Keating, Mayor M. Susan Savage, state representative Don Ross, and Tulsa police chief Chuck Jordan have all apologized, some better than others, but there have still been no reparations, an essential part of a good apology. In 2001 the Oklahoma Commission to Study the Tulsa Race Riot of 1921 (please stop calling it the Tulsa Race Riot; it was not a riot) recommended reparations for survivors and their descendants, the establishment of a scholarship fund, the creation of an economic development enterprise zone in Greenwood, and the building of a memorial. Today the memorial exists. The Oklahoma Legislature has refused to pay any reparations, saying that to do so is "constitutionally prohibited." Survivors tried to sue in U.S. federal court, but the government said that the statute of limitations on reparations had expired. Attempts in Congress to repeal that statute of limitations keep failing.

Tulsa is not unique. We won't go into the 1919 massacre in Elaine, Arkansas, or the 1920 massacre in Ocoee, Florida, or others. We will mention the city of San Jose, California's 2021 resolution of apology for the 1887 burning down of their Chinatown. "An apology for grievous injustices cannot erase the past, but admission of the historic wrongdoings committed can aid us in solving the critical problems of racial discrimination facing America today," the resolution says. Connie Young Yu, whose grandfather fled Chinatown, said the apology gave her an "enormous sense of reconciliation and a sense of peace. This is beyond an apology. It is taking responsibility, which is a beautiful thing to me." It also acknowledges that bias and prejudice aren't all in the past. "This reconciliation . . . serves as a reminder to continue striving for an inclusive society," said the mayor.

I Was Always Told We Came in Peace

Would you like to hear about the United States government apologizing to Indigenous Americans and paying reparations for enslaving them, seizing Native land, corralling Native peoples into reservations? So would we. The impacts of these long-ago American governmental actions are still powerfully felt today, as seen in the vast health disparities and higher poverty rates in Native communities.

After World War II, President Harry Truman established the Indian Claims Commission, purportedly as a way to thank Native Americans for their wartime service. The commission promised to reimburse tribal nations for their land and eventually paid out $818,172,606.64 for 546 separate cases. But many tribal nations wanted land, not money. Others had to give up their federally recognized status to get any money at all. Some have gotten apologies from both national and local authorities; most haven't. There have been individual suits, individual verdicts, and individual payouts to different tribal nations, making it hard to generalize about the state of reparations today.

In 2000, Kevin Gover (Pawnee), assistant secretary for Indian affairs, gave an apology for the actions of that inimical agency, the Bureau of Indian Affairs:

> Let us begin by expressing our profound sorrow for what this agency has done in the past. Just like you, when we think of these misdeeds and their tragic consequences, our hearts break and our grief is as pure and complete as yours. We desperately wish we could change history. . . . Never again will this agency stand silent when hate and violence are committed against Indians. Never again will we allow policy to proceed from the assumption that Indians possess less human genius than the other races. Never again will we be complicit in the theft of Indian property. Never again will we appoint false leaders who serve purposes other than those of the tribes. Never again will we allow unflattering and stereotypical images of Indian people to deface the halls of government or lead the American people to shallow and ignorant beliefs about Indians. Never again will we attack your religions, your languages, your rituals, or any of your tribal ways. Never again will we seize your children, nor teach them to be ashamed of who they are. Never again.

That's a revised version of the speech Gover originally wrote for President Bill Clinton to deliver while visiting the Black Hills in 1999. That visit didn't happen . . . something to do with the Lakota Sioux wanting the Black Hills *back*. The Supreme Court had ruled in 1980 that the Black Hills had been stolen by the United States, which should pay the Lakota $106 million for them. The Lakota refused the money. Again: they want the Black Hills *back*. The money, still sitting in a bank and earning interest, is up to $1.2 billion. Anyway, Gover revised the speech for Clinton into a BIA speech and delivered it himself. It's pretty good, but he should have cut the "our grief is as pure and complete as yours." It's not.

There has only been one official apology from Congress to Native Americans. It happened in 2010 (TWO THOUSAND AND TEN) and was hidden in a completely unrelated bill, the Defense Appropriations Act of 2010 (H.R. 3326). It's on page 45 (FORTY-FIVE) if you want to look, and it is pretty terse. See Section 8113: "APOLOGY TO NATIVE PEOPLES OF THE UNITED STATES."

H.R. 3326 "commends and honors Native Peoples for the thousands of years that they have stewarded and protected this land" (aw, how highfalutin and noble) and "apologizes on behalf of the people of the United States to all Native Peoples for the many instances of violence, maltreatment, and neglect inflicted on Native Peoples by citizens of the United States." (Note that just the citizens are mentioned, not the government. So much for taking responsibility.) H.R. 3326 then "expresses its regret for the ramifications of former wrongs and its commitment to build on the positive relationships of the past and present to move toward a brighter future where all the people of this land live reconciled as brothers and sisters, and harmoniously steward and protect this land together." We regret the ramifications! Whatever they are! Now let's move toward a brighter future! (Bad Apology Bingo!) This isn't even great for page 45 of a completely unrelated appropriations bill.

But then, the DISCLAIMER, and you'd better believe the word DISCLAIMER is all in caps, just like the word APOLOGY. "Nothing in this section . . . authorizes or supports any claim against the United States; or serves as a settlement of any claim against the United States." Bummer. But, hey, it "urges the President to acknowledge the wrongs of the United States against Indian tribes."

President Barack Obama took Congress up on this urging in 2010.

But not publicly, not even out loud. Robert T. Coulter, Citizen Potawatomi Nation member and executive director of the Indian Law Resource Center, noted the "overwhelming silence" about the signing of the resolution. "There were no public announcements, there were no press conferences, there was no national attention, much less international," he said. Also, there was no apology for the little-discussed enslavement of millions of Native Americans (as many as 5 million). Andrés Reséndez, professor at UC Davis and author of *The Other Slavery: The Uncovered Story of Indian Enslavement in America*, notes that "in contrast to the enslavement of Africans, which included a large percentage of adult males, the majority of enslaved Native Americans were women and children."

The two great outstanding sins of this country are its treatment of Native Americans and its treatment of Black Americans from slavery onward. Will we move toward true apologies, acknowledgment, and redress for these? It's unlikely to happen soon and it won't be easy, but it's not impossible. Alas, the smaller the wrongdoing, the more imaginable the redress.

An Excellent Out-Loud Apology

Perhaps tellingly, this next apology is to a relatively narrow audience. (Narrow, at least, compared to ALL THE BLACK PEOPLE and ALL THE INDIGENOUS PEOPLE.) It's President Bill Clinton's apology for the Tuskegee experiment. From 1932 to 1972, the United States government enrolled six hundred Black men in a study of syphilis without obtaining proper consent and without treating them ethically (or, indeed, medically). They were told they were being treated for "bad blood" and were given free meals, free medical exams—though not proper medical *treatment*—and free burials (those, they got). Not long after the study began, penicillin was shown to be the best treatment for the disease. But the government's scientists never gave it to the men, 399 of whom had syphilis; they also never offered them the option of quitting the study. They just observed the disease progress.

Two men blew the whistle on the Tuskegee Syphilis Study, nearly forty years after it began: Bill Jenkins (a Black statistician in the United States Public Health Service in Washington, DC, who discovered the study and tried without much success to call journalists' attention to it—his efforts still haven't gotten the attention they deserve) and Peter Buxtun (a white epidemiologist who learned about the experiment from coworkers and leaked it to the *New York Times*). In 1974 the U.S. government offered victims a $10 million settlement and lifetime medical benefits and burial services. In 1975 these benefits were offered to victims' wives, widows, and kids. Twenty years after that, survivors and their families also began receiving health benefits. The last survivor died in 2004, the last widow in 2009. Today, according to the CDC, there are eleven offspring still receiving medical and health benefits.

The financial reparations aren't commensurate with the wrong committed. Clinton's apology in 1997, however, was good. He spoke to the survivors and families at the behest of Dr. David Satcher, the director of the Centers for Disease Control and Prevention, and members of the Congressional Black Caucus. Here's what he said:

> The United States government did something that was wrong—deeply, profoundly, morally wrong. It was an outrage to our commitment to integrity and equality for all our citizens.
>
> To the survivors, to the wives and family members, the children and the grandchildren, I say what you know: No power on Earth can give you back the lives lost, the pain suffered, the years of internal torment and anguish. What was done cannot be undone. But we can end the silence. We can stop turning our heads away. We can look at you in the eye and finally say on behalf of the American

people, what the United States government did was shameful, and I am sorry.

The American people are sorry—for the loss, for the years of hurt. You did nothing wrong, but you were grievously wronged. I apologize and I am sorry that this apology has been so long in coming.

To Macon County, to Tuskegee, to the doctors who have been wrongly associated with the events there, you have our apology, as well. To our African American citizens, I am sorry that your federal government orchestrated a study so clearly racist. That can never be allowed to happen again. It is against everything our country stands for and what we must stand against is what it was.

During his apology, Clinton made concrete promises to the survivors and families; he seems to have honored them. He vowed to build a memorial (the Tuskegee History Center opened in 1998), strengthen researchers bioethics' training (this seems to be happening in part through a presidential grant to establish the National Center for Bioethics in Research and Health Care at Tuskegee University), and create postdoctoral fellowships for African American bioethicists (we can't find any federally funded postdoc programs that specifically mention the Tuskegee Study, but there are internships at the CDC focused on public health ethics, open to both undergrads and grad students, selected by the National Center for Bioethics in Research and Health Care).

A 2018 study found that harm from the Tuskegee experiment extended far beyond those enrolled: "We find that the disclosure of the study in 1972 is correlated with increases in medical mistrust and mortality and decreases in both outpatient and inpatient physician interactions for older black men. Our estimates imply life expectancy at age forty-five for black men fell by up to 1.5 years in response to the disclosure. . . ." By increasing suspicion of medical interventions like vaccines, the Tuskegee study may still be killing people today.

What Does a True Patriot Care for Facts?

Some government leaders are simply anti-apology. In 1988, Vice President George H. W. Bush declared, "I will never apologize for the United States of America, ever. I don't care what the facts are." This declaration might or might not have referred to the fact that the month before, a U.S. Navy cruiser had shot down an Iranian passenger plane, Iran Air Flight 655, destroying 290 souls. No one thought the Navy *wanted* to shoot down a passenger flight, and everyone knew they *did*. Bush's remark shows a shocking schoolyard bully attitude. In the end, "regrets" were expressed. When asked whether the regrets constituted an apology, then-president Reagan said, "Yes." SorryWatch says, "Gaah."

Again: regret is not apology.

In a similar vein, Mitt Romney, running for president, wrote a book titled *No Apology: The Case for American Greatness*, and accused President Obama of having gone on an "apology tour" to other countries. Other Republicans chimed in, declaiming that Obama went around telling people in other lands how sorry he was that America sucked. Those who examined the claim said this wasn't true; Obama said things like, "There have been times where America has shown arrogance" and "Our country still struggles with the legacies of slavery and segregation, the past treatment of Native Americans." He did not apologize for America. Though that might have been a good thing. To reiterate: a good apology is a sign of strength, not weakness.

A Nation Turns Its Rueful Eyes to You

A country can apologize directly to another country—"Sorry we shot down your passenger plane." A country can apologize to some of its citizens—"We apologize for saying you didn't exist and for selling the land you lived on." A country can apologize for events in the distant past—

"Sorry we treated your ancestors badly." It can apologize for events in the recent past—"We apologize for bombing your field hospital."

Legal scholar Martha Minow says when nations discuss how to respond to past evils, they "lurch among rhetorics of history (truth), theology (forgiveness), justice (punishment, compensation, and deterrence), therapy (healing), art (commemoration and disturbance), and education (learning lessons)." Many of these rhetorics do not lead to apologies, let alone good ones. For example, Brian Weiner says theological rhetoric "may . . . frame political misdeeds as sins and cast individuals in the roles of guilty or innocent. To apologize is to admit wrongdoing." People are apt to think, *I didn't do that! That is* exactly *the kind of thing I do not do! How dare you apologize in my name?*

Not being guilty is different from not being responsible. Weiner says that a good national apology can be a government declaring that it has changed, one that "has become the type of government that extends justice to those it has victimized in the past." That doesn't apply to the Iran Air Flight 655 case. There were extensive investigations of what led to the mistake, but the belligerent and careless captain of the Navy cruiser later got the Legion of Merit for his service. When the person who did the bad thing is praised and rewarded, it hardly makes his colleagues anxious about repeating the mistake.

Things Were Different When Our Predecessors Apparently Made That Thing Happen

Let's compare two governments' apologies for similar offenses: the U.S. government's apology for incarcerating its Japanese Americans citizens and the Canadian government's apology to Japanese Canadians for similar offenses. Two notes on terminology: both Japanese Americans and Japanese Canadians can be referred to as Nikkei—Japanese emigrants and their descendants. And the U.S./Canadian treatment of the Nikkei during World War II is commonly referred to as "internment," but Densho, an organization which documents those events, argues that "detainment" or "incarceration" fit the facts better.

Ronald Reagan resisted plans to apologize and make reparations to Japanese Americans who had been incarcerated during World War II. He came up with various reasons not to, most bizarrely the idea that the incarceration *didn't happen*. He told his friend Thomas H. Kean, governor of New Jersey, that he'd never believed the Nikkei were forced into camps. He figured they'd gone to camps "on their own volition." (What the what? The best we can come up with is that Reagan chose to think that Nikkei wanted to be locked up to be safe from mobs? We may be assigning too much rationality to Reagan's thinking.)

The events of the internment weren't taught in any of the public schools we attended. Except for one history class—which strayed from the California state curriculum—in which the driver's ed teacher came in to tell Susan's class about how he and his family were incarcerated. Our children also weren't taught about this in their schools. Many non-Japanese Americans didn't learn this shameful history at all until *Star Trek*'s George Takei started telling his family's story.

We hope you're better educated than we were. We hope you were taught that after the bombing of Pearl Harbor, 110,000 Japanese Americans were herded up and sent to camps, where they were kept under armed guard for the rest of the war. Their property was seized. Many lost their homes and businesses or sold them at a great loss. It didn't matter if you were a U.S. citizen, as most were; there was *nothing you could do* to prove loyalty. The camps were mostly on the West Coast but also in Utah, Colorado, Wyoming, Texas, and other places.

Ballet dancer Sono Osato, whose mother was white and whose father was Japanese American, wasn't saved from prejudice by her fame. She'd been the first American and the youngest person to dance with the Ballets Russes. She danced at the American Ballet Theater. She originated the role of Ivy Smith in *On the Town*. But after the bombing of Pearl Harbor, she wasn't allowed to tour with her company. She wasn't allowed to dance under her own name. (She began using her mother's maiden name, Fitzgerald.) Her father was incarcerated as an enemy alien, even as her brother fought for the Allies with the 442nd Regiment in Italy.

In 1942, when George Takei was five, his family was rounded up from their Los Angeles home and incarcerated in the Santa Anita horse stables, then sent to an Arkansas camp surrounded by barbed wire (little George thought the barbed wire was to keep dinosaurs out), and finally to another camp in California. It didn't matter that his mother had been born in America or that his parents were productive, tax-paying citizens. When the family was released in 1945, his parents' dry cleaning business was gone, as were their bank accounts and house. They wound up homeless, living on LA's Skid Row for five years.

People who objected to this kind of unconstitutional, irrational, and cruel treatment were ignored. A relative of Susan's, then in a Los Angeles high school, recalled that the school's indignant student body, in protest of the government's actions, unanimously elected a Nisei (second-generation Nikkei) kid as student body president. The kid and his family were sent to the camps anyway.

In charge of this effort was General John DeWitt, an ambitious racist who wanted to intern even more Japanese Americans, as well as Italian Americans and German Americans. He told President Roosevelt that the fact that no sabotage by Nikkei had ever been discovered was "a disturbing and confirming indication that such action *will* be taken." (They haven't done anything? That proves they're planning *something big*!)

Follow the Racism

When DeWitt wasn't allowed to incarcerate Italian Americans and German Americans, he slapped strict curfews on them. This didn't last long, in part because there were many Italian Americans in the fishing industry and canned fish was needed to feed the troops. Also, though this wasn't stated, they were white. (DeWitt had nothing to do with bribing Peru with armaments to arrest thousands of Peruvian Nikkei and ship them to the United States to be declared "illegal aliens" and then sent to incarceration camps. No, that was the OSS.)

In another seldom-noted motive, Nikkei farmers tended to be exceptionally good, *successful* farmers, using methods brought from Japan. Many non-Nikkei farmers hated this. Before the war, these other farmers throughout the American West lobbied for "alien land laws" to keep Nikkei from owning farmland. According to scholars like crop scientist Sarah Taber, some of the first calls to incarcerate Nikkei farmers came from the California farm lobby. Within hours after Pearl Harbor, they sent a representative to Washington to argue for their interests. He told the *Saturday Evening Post*, "We're charged with wanting to get rid of the J—— for selfish reasons. We might as well be honest. . . . It's a question of whether the white man lives on the Pacific Coast or the brown men. They came into this valley to work, and they stayed to take over."

The result of detaining so many of the best farmers on the West Coast? Produce shortages. Hence the need for Victory Gardens, families' home gardens that were needed to supplement their rations. A third of the fruits and vegetables Americans consumed during the war came from Victory Gardens.

Despite all this, some thirty-three thousand Japanese American men served in World War II. Except for a few fluent Japanese speakers assigned to military intelligence, they weren't allowed to serve in the Pacific Theater, though German Americans and Italian Americans served in Europe. Over fourteen thousand Nikkei fought in Europe in the 442nd Regiment, including Sono Osato's brother. The 442nd, known as the "Go for Broke" boys, became the most decorated unit for its size in Army history. Its soldiers took part in the liberation of France, the rescue of the

"Lost Battalion," and the liberation of Dachau. They were brave and they were used recklessly. Many of the 442nd's officers felt that higher-ups were treating their troops as cannon fodder. On one occasion division commander General John E. Dahlquist ordered the 442nd mustered for an awards ceremony. He was annoyed when only eighteen out of the four hundred men who'd been assigned to the 442nd's K Company appeared. He told the officer in charge, a Lieutenant Colonel Miller, that he wanted *all* the men present. "That's all of K Company left, sir," Miller answered.

In December 1945, there was a ceremony honoring Kazuo Masuda of the 442nd, killed in action in Italy. Masuda was posthumously awarded the Distinguished Service Cross by General Joseph Stilwell. Stilwell was tired, and asked Captain Ronald Reagan of the 1st Motion Picture Unit to say a few words. It is unclear what Captain Reagan said, although this became significant later. (Keep this in mind.)

The ceremony was on the porch of the Masuda family farmhouse in Talbert, Orange County. While the Masudas were incarcerated, another family had moved onto their land and into their house. When the camps opened up in 1945, Kazuo Masuda's sister Mary went to Talbert to check out the situation. She had to stay with friends. She got a threatening call—"Go back to the concentration camp, because Japanese Americans aren't welcome in Orange County"—and an intimidating visit from four or five men calling themselves "Native Sons of the Golden West," who also told her to go back to the camp. ("Native Sons"? Were they Indians? We don't think so.) The Masuda family returned to their home and farm anyway. The War Relocation Authority publicized the award ceremony to send a message that anti-Japanese American activity had to stop.

A "Setback" to Fundamental American Principles

Between 1948 and 1955, some former detainees were compensated for property loss under the Japanese-American Evacuation Claims Act, but not for spending years locked up for imaginary disloyalty. In 1976, President Gerald Ford figured the Bicentennial was a good time to revoke Executive Order 9066, under which the Nikkei were incarcerated. "An honest reckoning . . . must include a recognition of our national mistakes as well as our national achievements," he said. He called the incarceration a setback to fundamental American principles and said there should be a promise "that this kind of action shall never again be repeated."

In 1980, President Jimmy Carter set up the Commission on Wartime Relocation and Internment of Civilians to look into the matter further. They spent a few years hearing hundreds of witnesses. In 1984 they made recommendations to the Reagan administration. They found there'd been "misconduct of justice" due to "race prejudice, war hysteria, and a failure of political leadership." (Nothing about farm yields, unless that falls under "race prejudice.")

There were differing views among Nikkei about the value of pursuing redress. "We came out of these camps with a sense of shame and guilt, of having been considered betrayers of our country," John Tateishi, one of the leaders pushing for redress, told NPR. Most Nikkei families had never spoken about the experience. "There were no complaints, no big rallies or demands for justice because it was not the Japanese way." As time passed, though, many took inspiration from successes of the civil rights movement. While many older Nikkei wanted to forget the whole experience, others were motivated on behalf of younger generations. "There is a saying in Japanese culture, 'kodomo no tame ni,' which means, 'for the sake of the children.' And for us running this campaign, that had much to do with it," Tateishi said. "It's the legacy we're handing down to them and to the nation to say that, 'You can make this mistake, but you also have to correct it—and by correcting it, hopefully not repeat it again.' "

The legislation crafted in response to the commission's findings was called H.R. 442, after the "Go for Broke" unit. It suggested a government apology, a trust fund, and $20,000 stipends to each detained person. Reagan did not like those recommendations. He did not like the idea of reparations or of apology. He found support for his dislike. Some people, like North Carolina senator Jesse Helms, made an argument that Americans who weren't born "when Pearl Harbor was virtually destroyed and our fleet was lying on the bottom" shouldn't have to pay for redress. Helms said he might propose an amendment to block appropriations for redress until Japan compensated the families of Pearl Harbor victims. Congressman Norm Mineta of California pointed out the stupidity (our word) of this: "This bill has nothing to do with the nation or people of Japan. It deals with how the U.S. government treats its own citizens." In a monkey wrench–hurling spirit, Wyoming senator Malcolm Wallop claimed to be considering adding an amendment saying, "No funds shall be appropriated under this title until the U.S. Government has also fairly compensated the descendants of the victims of the Trail of Tears."

Wallop wasn't actually seeking justice for Trail of Tears descendants. We think he was saying, "Don't give them justice because then everyone will want justice, and *you know* you don't want to compensate the Indians." He hoped to derail the bill. But there was a good idea hiding in his mischief. Everyone *should* want (and get) justice.

How Will I Look if I Apologize?

Reagan told staff that financial reparations would make him look like the "big-spending liberals" he had campaigned against. He said Ford's 1976 proclamation was plenty. His attorney general, Edwin Meese, didn't want to establish "a bad precedent for other groups who feel that they have suffered injustices."

Meanwhile, after H.R. 442 was introduced, Prime Minister Yasuhiro

Nakasone of Japan criticized the Reagan administration for not getting it passed immediately. He said passing it would be good for U.S.-Japan relations. Reagan and his staff found that insulting and didn't like the pressure. Privately, Reagan wanted to let Nakasone know he "did not make legislation at the whim of the Japanese Diet." Those are the "national security concerns" Reagan sometimes used as an excuse for not endorsing H.R. 442.

The bill went from the House to the Senate, where the Alaska delegation inserted a rider about compensating Aleutian Islanders (more on them later). It was while the bill was flopping around in the Senate that Reagan told Governor Thomas Kean he'd always thought Japanese Americans went to the camps by choice. Maybe this whole thing was merely a Democratic plot to make him look bad! Governor Kean tipped off a redress activist and former detainee, Grant Ujifusa, about Reagan's doubts. Ujifusa, redress strategy chair of the Japanese American Citizens League, wrote to Reagan and sent him letters from other detainees along with photos and petitions, assuring him that "we did not voluntarily leave our homes, our neighborhoods, and our work." We think he did not use the word "duh." Ujifusa mentioned the 1945 posthumous ceremony for Kazuo Masuda at which then-captain Reagan had spoken. Masuda's sister, June Masuda Goto, also wrote, praising Reagan's "heroic words" of the time.

Here things become interestingly murky. Political scientist Timothy P. Maga, drawing on declassified materials at the Ronald Reagan Library, wrote in 1998, "After more than forty years, the Reagan story took on quite a few versions. They varied from Reagan being present at the military ceremony to leading it in prayer. His exact words uttered at this ceremony also grew in eloquence and significance as his role there became a matter of concern to anyone interested in redress."

At some point a glorious version was "discovered" that became

Reagan's favorite. He liked the idea that he had said it and bragged about it to a friend, Representative Mervyn Dymally of California, director of the Congressional Black Caucus and a tireless supporter of redress:

> *The real American is the man who calls it a fair exchange to lay down his life in order that American ideals may go on living. And judging by such a test, Sgt. Masuda was a better American than any of us here today. Blood that has soaked into the sands of a beach is all one color. America stands unique in the world, the only country not founded on race, but on a way—an ideal. Not in spite of, but because of our polyglot background, we have had all the strength in the world. That is the American way.*

Reagan still wanted to veto the bill but was persuaded that the political fallout would be bad for the Republican Party. The Senate passed it and he signed it in August 1988. It included the $20,000 stipends to former detainees. The apology he read said, "No payment can make up for those three lost years. So what is most important in this bill has less to do with property than with honor. For here we admit a wrong. Here we reaffirm our commitment as a nation to equal justice under the law." Then he read the supposed Masuda speech from 1945 again.

Where did that speech come from? Was it real, written for General Stilwell and read by Reagan? Did Reagan come up with it on the spot in 1945? Was it written later by people who thought that's sort of what they remembered him saying, or who wished that's what he'd said, or a little of each? If that last possibility is true, did they do such a good job that Reagan agreed to the bill just so he could read a great speech?

We at SorryWatch wish we knew. In any case, the redress to Japanese American detainees did indeed set a powerful precedent. Representative Norm Mineta said the bipartisan passage of the bill was one of his proudest achievements.

History Happened—What Am I Supposed to Do About It?

Canada's approach to their Japanese citizens was different. But also the same. Once again, racism, war hysteria, and greed combined to make an ugly process. Once again, no citizen with Japanese heritage was ever accused of disloyalty. Not one. "From the army point of view, I cannot see that Japanese Canadians constitute the slightest menace to national security," said Major General Kenneth Stuart. Whatever.

Under the War Measures Act, twenty-one thousand Canadian citizens of Japanese descent were rounded up and sent east from British Columbia to miserable accommodations. The government took their houses, farms, businesses, and fishing boats into "protective custody," then sold them "to pay the costs of detaining Japanese Canadians." Since they were housed in detainment camps—many in ghost towns without electricity or running water—or put to work on sugar beet farms in Alberta, the government probably *made money* on that. (The government had done something similar with Ukrainian Canadians during World War I, so they had practice.)

After the war, Japanese Canadians were told they could either move to war-torn Japan—since most had been born in Canada, this was *not* a case of moving "back" to Japan—or settle east of the Rockies. They were definitely not allowed back in British Columbia, where Nikkei had been annoyingly successful at berry farming.

In 1948 their right to vote was restored. Then the geographic restriction was lifted. In 1984, in response to suggestions about redress from then–opposition leader Brian Mulroney, Prime Minister Pierre Trudeau was irked. "I do not see how I can apologize for some historic event to which we . . . were not a party. We can regret that it happened." He asked where such requests would end. "How many other historical wrongs would have to be righted? I do not think it is the purpose of a government to right the past. I cannot rewrite history."

188 Marjorie Ingall & Susan McCarthy

In 1988, a month after Reagan's signing of the U.S. redress bill, Mulroney—now Canada's prime minister—apologized:

> The Government of Canada wrongfully incarcerated, seized the property, and disenfranchised thousands of citizens of Japanese ancestry. Apologies are the only way we can cleanse the past. I speak for members on all sides of the House today in offering to Japanese Canadians the formal and sincere apology of this Parliament for those past injustices against them, against their families, and against their heritage, and our solemn commitment and undertaking to Canadians of every origin that such violations will never again in this country be countenanced or repeated.

The War Measures Act was repealed. Redress payments ($21,000) were made to former detainees, and funds were provided that ultimately produced the Nikkei National Museum & Cultural Centre, an assisted-living facility, a nursing home, and $24 million for a Canadian race relations foundation. The entire package cost $300 million. Those who'd been deported to Japan could get Canadian citizenship back. In a separate action, Canada also created a Truth and Reconciliation Commission as part of an Indian Residential Schools Settlement Agreement.

"The Most Apologized-to Family"

How did the Nikkei feel about this? Anytime you talk about the reactions of 130,000-plus people, you'll get a mix of responses. It's vital to distinguish between what we at SorryWatch call part one of the apology—"We're sorry" or "We apologize"—and the rest of the apology, which is supposed to say *what the apology is for, why it won't happen again,* and *what about reparations?* Without these, it's no apology.

Some who see little value in government apologies are only talking about part one. Playwright and educator Mitch Miyagawa wrote fascinatingly for the Canadian magazine *The Walrus* about this apology.

Miyagawa says he comes from "the most apologized-to family in the country—maybe the world." The Nikkei members of his family received apologies from the Canadian government for incarceration. His mother's second husband was among those who received official apologies for having to pay a racist "Chinese head tax." (Five hundred dollars. *In 1919.*) And his father's second wife, of a Cree First Nation, was one of those apologized to for the institutionalized cruelty and deliberate cultural destruction of residential schools.

Miyagawa's father had been deported from British Columbia, where the family had a flourishing berry farm, to Alberta, where they were forced to labor on other people's sugar beet farms. After the war, forbidden to return to BC, they settled in Alberta, where Miyagawa was born. He says the apology was pointless to his father. "He had already turned the other cheek. *Shikata na gai*, the saying goes—what's done is done."

Just as We Feared, They're Getting Ideas

At a 2008 conference on the twentieth anniversary of redress to the Nikkei detainees, Miyagawa met Roy Miki, a leader in the redress fight who was on the negotiating committee for the National Association of Japanese Canadians. He told Miyagawa that the negotiators hadn't been terribly focused on getting an apology. What they *really* wanted was acknowledgment that "democracy had broken down, and that people had benefited from the internment of Japanese Canadians." What was most vital, Miki said, was protecting people in the future. "The real victim was democracy itself, not the people."

In other words, Miki was less focused on the "formal and sincere apology of this Parliament" than on the "solemn commitment and undertaking . . . that such violations will never again in this country be countenanced or repeated." And the repeal of the War Measures Act. And the museum. And also the race relations foundation.

As Pierre Trudeau had feared, other groups took inspiration from redress. Miyagawa beheld "the hyphenated and dual named of our country: a Japanese-, Chinese-, Indo-, Black, Aboriginal, and Ukrainian-Canadian rainbow behind two long fold-out tables." All these communities had been harmed by the Canadian government. All kept saying "We have to remember, so it will never happen again."

Miyagawa mused, "I'd come to believe that government apologies were more about forgetting than remembering." Reflecting on a 2006 apology from Prime Minister Stephen Harper for the Chinese head tax and the 1923 Chinese Immigration Act, he wrote, "statements like these seem to break our link with history, separating us from who we were and promoting the notion of our moral advancement. They also whitewash the ways in which Canadians still benefit from that past . . ."

He has a point about that apology. Harper apologized for the tax and for the decades-long ban on immigration from China, but the *only* redress was to survivors or their spouses—about twenty people. There is a continued fight for redress to surviving children. Earlier efforts to get funding for a nonprofit foundation to educate Canadians about anti-Chinese discrimination disappeared in political infighting. Not impressive.

Ultimately, Miyagawa declares himself both a cynic and a believer. There's an aspect of government apologies that can be a whitewash. Everything bad is over! All fixed now! That doesn't work if injustice is ongoing. Yet the part of a good apology that acknowledges what happened and says that it was wrong is still valuable. That's what got Mulroney's audience to their feet, cheering. That's what moved Miyagawa's stepmother very deeply when she heard Stephen Harper's apology for the residential schools. It was a long speech, and we'll just quote a bit near the end:

The Government of Canada sincerely apologizes and asks the forgiveness of the Aboriginal peoples of this country for failing them so profoundly.

Nous le regrettons.

We are sorry.

Nimitataynan.

Niminchinowesamin.

Mamiattugut.

Perceptions of Justice and Anxiety About Precedent

Often government compensation is associated with acts no amount of money can make right. A Japanese American who was incarcerated from age five to nine told psychiatrist and author Aaron Lazare that the $20,000 he got was insulting. "The American government stole 4 years of my childhood and has now put a price of $5,000 for each stolen year," he said. "It would have been better to receive no financial settlement." Yet even inadequate payment—and could any amount be adequate?—can demonstrate that a good apology is more than words. Because wouldn't governments love it if they *didn't* have to pay anything? Lazare also quotes Reva Shefer, a seventy-five-year-old Holocaust survivor. She got $400 from the government of Switzerland "as partial reparations for Swiss complicity with the Nazis during World War II." Not much, but she said, "The amount means nothing. I care about the fact of it. . . . [A]fter all these decades, somebody is saying, 'You suffered and we know it.'"

Edwin Meese and Pierre Trudeau both worried about setting a precedent. If we apologize for punching that one guy, then *everyone* we punched will want an apology! This is not a good reason to evade responsibility. But they also weren't wrong about precedents inspiring others. The way we see it, government apologies can have benefits for others not in the class apologized to. Other citizens can take pride in the apology and in the government that makes it. Those who got the apology may be on high alert to protect others from being mistreated as they were. The apology they got may empower them to speak out.

In 2017, when President Donald J. Trump signed the "Muslim ban"—an executive order forbidding the entry into the United States of people from seven majority-Muslim countries—there were widespread outcries and protests from Americans, including many who drew on their families' histories with past government injustices. (That was Susan's mother-in-law protesting at San Francisco International Airport, holding up a picture of Anne Frank.) The Japanese American Citizens League, which had fought for "the triumph that we had hoped for"—the 1988 H.R. 442 Civil Liberties Act apology and redress—filed an amicus brief in an ACLU lawsuit to overturn the ban. "The court has once again deferred to claims of national security need, despite the overwhelming evidence of racial and religious animus as the basis for the policy," they wrote in a statement. Their concern was for the civil rights of all minority groups who might be next. "It is a belief that we have stood for since 1942 and never forgotten."

Yes, apologies *can* create precedents. Good precedents.

Fish and Wildlife Is Sorry for Forcing You to Kill the Wildlife

Okay, remember how we mentioned there was a bit folded into H.R. 442 about restitution for "certain" Aleuts who had also been forced from their homes during World War II? We mention this because eventually there's an apology.

Early in the war, nearly nine hundred Aleutian residents of two of the Pribilof Islands—St. George and St. Paul—were jerked from their homes after the Japanese bombed Alaska's Dutch Harbor. Unlike the Nikkei, the Aleuts were not considered potentially treacherous. They *were* potentially in the line of battle. Their evacuation was brutally abrupt; they'd actually been preparing to evacuate, but the U.S. Fish and Wildlife Service suddenly ordered them to get on a boat with one suitcase. From the boat, the Aleuts saw their villages torched so no Japanese occupiers could use them.

Why was Fish and Wildlife involved? They managed the industry in the Pribilofs that killed northern fur seals—see? wildlife!—for their pelts. The Aleuts were forced to work in the sealing industry and were not allowed to leave. Before that, the Treasury Department had forced them to work in the sealing industry. Before that, the Russian-American Company (owned by the Russian government) had shipped them to the then-uninhabited Pribilofs and, yes, forced them to work in the sealing industry. Words that have been used to describe their situation include serfdom, peonage, and slavery.

Back to World War II: The Aleuts were sent to camps in abandoned cannery buildings so cold, ramshackle, and unsanitary that 10 percent died—they were literally decimated. Most were kept there until 1945, by which time the Japanese had been out of the Aleutians for two years. They were taken back to the Pribilofs, back to work in the sealing industry. In 1966 the Fur Seal Act was passed to protect fur seals and sea otters. Residents now catch halibut and snow crab, service fishing fleets, work for the government, and host zealous bird-watchers. (If you see Susan there, she'll be looking for the bristle-thighed curlew. *Teeoip!*) Not until the 1980s was the relocation investigated and folded into redress to the interned Japanese Americans.

Every year the Pribilof residents observe Evacuation Day. On St. Paul in 2017, Jim Kurth, acting director of Fish and Wildlife, made an Evacuation Day speech. Kurth extended "my and my agency's most sincere apology to the Aleut people interned . . . and their descendants who continue to carry this burden. For our actions during World War II in the Pribilofs and Funter Bay, I am sorry. For loved ones lost, and for internees who suffered from hunger, coldness, and illness, I am sorry."

That's good. He added, "[W]e cannot take back the course of history. But what we can do now is heal together. We can work together." SorryWatch suspects that when someone joins Fish and Wildlife, publicly apologizing for holding people in servitude is not something they expect to have to do. And in fact, Kurth *didn't* apologize for that, but only for the cruel, bungled evacuation and internment.

Did We Not Tell You About the Test?

Often a government apology doesn't come from the top but from a lower-level department or agency, as when the U.S. Fish and Wildlife Service apologized to the Pribilof Islanders. Another example was when the director general of the Health Service Executive (HSE), a division of Ireland's Department of Health, apologized to Vicky Phelan for bungling the handling of her test screening for cervical cancer.

In a letter to Phelan, HSE director general Tony O'Brien wrote, "While this apology will never undo the harm and distress suffered by you it is important that I emphasise the sincerity with which it is offered. I apologise to you for the failure to detect an abnormality in the original smear test that you underwent back in 2011. I also apologise to you for the failure to communicate in a timely and appropriate way the results of an audit that indicated a change in the interpretation of your original smear test." He explained how the HSE had altered its procedures to prevent a recurrence. "I hope you will accept my apology and I wish you the very best with your ongoing treatment."

That apology doesn't quite make clear what happened, does it? Here we go.

CervicalCheck is a free program from the HSE to do cervical smears (often called Pap tests in the United States). Its website described the test as "the most effective way to detect pre-cancerous changes in the cells of the cervix." It went on, "It's reassuring to know that Cervical-Check looks for early changes to cells that could one day become cancerous. If changes are found earlier they can be treated, making cervical cancer a truly preventable cancer."

The HSE had more tests than labs in Ireland could handle, so they farmed some out to a Texas lab, which used a different screening protocol. "Our scientists were screening 25 to 30 cases a day, whilst the American scientists were screening 80 to 100, so they were screening three to four times as many in a day," said Dr. David Gibbons, formerly chair of the quality assurance committee of the National Cervical Screening Programme.

Around 2008, Gibbons noticed that the American lab wasn't reporting as many positive (possibly precancerous) tests as the Irish ones. In fact, they were finding a third less. Worried, Gibbons reported this to Tony O'Brien, head of the National Cervical Screening Programme (who gave the above apology). "I expressed those concerns and I said that over a ten-year period, this will cause problems and the problems won't become apparent for ten years," Gibbons said. "And he dismissed my concerns." Gibbons quit, along with every other scientist on the committee. Politically, it seems that reducing the backlog of tests was more important to the HSE than heeding some doomsayers.

Of course, Gibbons and the other medical experts were right. Vicky Phelan was told in 2011 that her smear test was normal, but in fact it had detected precancerous cells. In 2014 she was diagnosed with invasive cervical cancer. She needed not just a hysterectomy but also radiation and chemo. In those three years her cancer had become terminal.

In 2014, HSE did an audit and discovered that there were more than two hundred women whose tests showed precancerous changes that the American lab had overlooked. It was almost as if the committee had been right. But HSE didn't feel like telling the women in question. After all, the audit had been done for "educational and training purposes." The year after that, they decided it was worth notifying those women's doctors. Then there was disagreement about who should tell these women— the program or the doctors? By the time they decided, it was 2016. Vicky Phelan wasn't told about her 2011 test results until 2017. She promptly sued the HSE and the American laboratory, getting a settlement of €2.5 million, some of which she is spending on last-chance cancer treatments. She is also fighting for an Irish right-to-die law, because she doesn't want her young children to see her die in pain.

In 2018 another audit found that 162 of the women had not been told about the revised results. Seventeen were dead. The Cervical-Check website said, "Failures in communicating with women about the CervicalCheck clinical audit have caused concerns. We are very sorry for any worries this has caused you." (Later, this was updated to extend "deepest apologies to women for any worry caused" and to provide more information.)

Sorry for Treading on You

On January 14, 1697, the legislature of the Province of Massachusetts Bay (now the state of Massachusetts) designated a day for fasting and atonement for the Salem witch trials. Samuel Sewall, one of the nine judges who had presided over those trials, had this personal statement read aloud in his church by his pastor:

> Samuel Sewall, sensible of the reiterated strokes of God upon himself and family; and being sensible, that as to the Guilt contracted upon the opening of the late Commission of Oyer and Terminer at Salem . . . he is, upon many accounts, more concerned than any that he knows of, Desires to take the Blame and Shame of it, Asking pardon of Men, And especially desiring prayers that God, who has an

Unlimited Authority, would pardon that Sin and all other his Sins;
personal and Relative: And according to his infinite Benignity, and
Sovereignty, Not Visit the Sin of him, or of any other, upon himself or
any of his, nor upon the Land: But that he would powerfully defend
him against all Temptations to Sin, for the future, and vouchsafe him
the Efficacious Saving Conduct of his Word and Spirit.

It's an interesting apology. It's addressed to his fellow citizens and mostly to God. It's way too much about him. Since the trials, two of his children had died and his wife had had a stillbirth. Sewall thought he was being divinely punished for his part in the trials of people who were hanged or pressed to death. In which, in his capacity as judge, he was acting for Massachusetts. States are no better at apologies than nations, it seems.

How Should a Government Apologize?

What makes a state's or nation's apology a good one? In many ways the elements are like those in an individual apology, though there are differences. Governments are so powerful, they can do worse things than most individuals. But because they are so powerful, they can also do much more to make up for what they've done. Theoretically.

A government apology should say "sorry" or "apologize." No, Queen Elizabeth II, it is not enough to "acknowledge" that the expulsion of the Acadians was "tragic." SorryWatch can do that too. It was indeed tragic that around ten thousand people from the Acadian region of the Canadian Maritimes were deported between 1755 and 1763 and shipped all over the world, in horrifying conditions, so that thousands died in transit of starvation and disease. But "acknowledgment" is an insufficient government response. Sure, you declared "A Day of Commemoration of the Great Upheaval," but that's feeble.

Governments tend to be formal and say "we apologize" more often than "we're sorry." That's fine. But it's crucial to say what the apology is *for*, to get it on record that it happened. The Armenians haven't gotten an apology for the genocide of 1915–1917, which was committed by the Ottoman Empire—now the Republic of Turkey—and, far more maddening, the government of Turkey continues to deny that it ever happened. Turkey pressures allies to do the same, which is why there was an outpouring of relief when President Biden deliberately used the term "Armenian genocide" in 2021.

Martha Minow writes that when people have been massacred, "disappeared," or raped in programs of "ethnic cleansing," there can be no adequate response. "Closure is not possible. Even if it were, any closure would insult those whose lives are forever ruptured," she wrote. ". . . Yet silence is also an unacceptable offense, a shocking implication that the perpetrators in fact succeeded. . . ." We agree with her sentiment. The word "closure" (like the words "Let's move on" and "It's time to heal") do not belong in an apology. Still, we have to apologize. No apology can change the past, but it is better than silence.

In addition to saying what the apology is for, governments must also speak for the record about the impact of the government's actions. Elizabeth II's proclamation did that part fairly well, saying the deportation of the Acadian people had "tragic consequences, including the deaths of many thousands of Acadians—from disease, in shipwrecks, in their places of refuge and in prison camps in Nova Scotia and England as well as in the British colonies in America." But a good apology should also speak to ongoing impacts. If the grandparents' generation was robbed, they were not able to help the generations coming after them.

Government apologies should not include excuses. They should say why their offenses won't happen again. They should clearly say what principles of justice were ignored. In that way, if a government comes for the Muslims, the Japanese Americans already have the principles to put in their legal brief.

A day of commemoration isn't much, unless it's an annual event, like Australia's Sorry Day, or the Pribilofs' Evacuation Day. That keeps history in living memory. And it's always good to have a new law to point to, one that bans whatever it was the government did.

And as far as making amends, it does not inspire hope when a proclamation includes boilerplate like this in the one to the Acadians: "Our present Proclamation does not, under any circumstances, constitute a recognition of legal or financial responsibility by the Crown in right of Canada and of the provinces and is not, under any circumstances, a recognition of, and does not have any effect upon, any right or obligation of any person or group of persons. . . ." Remember King Henry II atoning for Thomas à Becket's murder? Henry returned some confiscated lands. Just mentioning.

Reparations that cost a government money have real and symbolic value. If it didn't cost governments anything to make redress for injury, there'd surely be more apologies and more people doubting their sincerity and worth.

There will always be citizens beefing that *they* weren't the ones who did bad things and so *their* taxes shouldn't go for redress—because people need to be reminded that it's not about guilt; it's about national responsibility, national honor, and national justice.

ACTION ITEMS

❑ **A government apology requires fact-finding.** If it happened in living memory, survivor testimony is vital. Get it.

❑ **There should be an impartial investigation into the ongoing impact of what was done.**

❑ **Someone should write a really great responsibility-taking apology speech for the head of state, whoever they are.**

❑   **The United States still needs to apologize well to Native Americans and African Americans.** It is shameful that we have to say this.

5 Vile Political Apologies

1. Bill Clinton in 2018, interviewed by CNN's Craig Melvin:

Craig Melvin: *Have you apologized to Monica Lewinsky?*

Bill Clinton: I've apologized to everyone in the world!

CM: *But you haven't apologized to her?*

BC: I have never talked to her, no. I have never talked to her, but I did say publicly on more than one occasion that I was sorry. The apology was public.

CM: *You don't think a private apology is owed?*

BC: Do you think President Kennedy should have resigned? Do you believe President Johnson should have resigned? Someone should ask you these questions because of the way you've formulated the questions! I dealt with it 20 years ago plus, and the American people, two-thirds of them stayed with me, and I've tried to do a good job since then with my life and with my work. That's all I have to say.

2. U.S. attorney general Janet Reno, at a 1997 press conference about Richard Jewell's exoneration after false Atlanta Olympic bombing accusations destroyed his life: "Anytime a situation occurs where there is a leak and it subjects a person to such public focus, I'm sorry it happened."

3. Governor John Ashcroft, apologizing for his wife's use of the Missouri State Library on the Sunday night of Mother's Day in 1990 so that his wife and son could research the son's seventh-grade history project: "If anybody's been offended, I'm pleased to apologize to them. I don't want to offend people. That's not my intention nor is it the intention of my family." State Librarian Monteria Hightower noted that the state library should not have been opened after hours for a child and that the call had ended her and her family's Mother's Day. The governor responded: "I don't want to offend Mrs. Hightower."

4. Governor Andrew Cuomo in 2021, after New York's attorney general concluded that he'd sexually harassed eleven women: "There is a difference between alleged improper conduct and concluding sexual harassment. Now, don't get me wrong, this is not to say that there are not 11 women who I truly offended. There are. And for that I deeply, deeply apologize. . . . I thought a hug and putting my arm around the staff person while taking a picture was friendly, but she found it to be too forward. I kissed a woman on the cheek at a wedding and I thought I was being nice, but she felt that it was too aggressive. I have slipped and called people honey, sweetheart and darling. I meant it to be endearing, but women found it dated and offensive. My sense of humor can be insensitive and off-putting. I do hug and kiss people casually, women and men. I have done it all my life. . . . To my mind, I've never crossed the line with anyone, but I didn't realize the extent to which the line has been redrawn. There are generational and cultural shifts that I just didn't fully appreciate, and I should have. No excuses."

5. Hahns Copeland, a Republican House candidate in Virginia, in 2021, after he responded to a video in which Democratic Speaker of the House Eileen Filler-Corn, Virginia's first Jewish Speaker, discussed education policy: Copeland tweeted, "I was surprised to see a pair of eyes and a mouth with that NOSE." After an outcry, he tweeted, "My comment regarding Eileen Filler-Corn earlier today was immature and impulsive. It was never intended to be antisemitic or reference her ethnicity or religion. I apologize to anyone I may have offended. It is not an accurate reflection of my character, beliefs and values." He followed up with "Today there was a regrettable Tweet posted from my account. While the Tweet was ugly and regrettable it was never meant how the Democrats are portraying it. Many of my friends in the Jewish community know me and love me. They know me as a Christian and full of love."

BAD APOLOGY BINGO CARD #5
POLITICAL EDITION!

as a nation	dangerous precedent	lower the temperature	further divide	look toward the future
my adversaries	unity	rhetoric	none of this is binding	divisive
God bless America	on both sides	**FREE SQUARE**	we followed policy	that wasn't policy
not a black-and-white issue	my political enemies	my record	I love my country	the buck stops with me
I would never condone	it was wartime	with the help of my wife	not in power then	before we were born

CHAPTER 8

HOW TO ACCEPT AN APOLOGY AND HOW TO FORGIVE . . . AND WHEN TO DO NEITHER

Just as there are rules for apologizing, there are rules for accepting an apology. Must you accept an apology? And must you forgive? (Spoiler alert: no.) How can we discern when we should forgive and when we should allow for and even embrace our anger? If we do decide that we want to forgive, how do we get there? Finally, if someone else seeks our forgiveness, how can we tell whether they're sincere, whether it's to our advantage to forgive, how to open the door to further discussion about why we were upset in the first place, how to accept an apology that's decent, or how to get a better apology than the one they're offering?

How to Accept an Apology

Accepting apologies is part of the process of making things right again. It's what should usually happen. It's a good thing to do, and it's usually much easier than apologizing. Here's the short version of how to do it, which we'll expand on in a bit.

It's good to accept an apology explicitly. "Thanks. I accept your apology." Or "I accept your apology, and I appreciate it." Do not grunt enigmatically. (That's too enigmatic.) If the apology is for a minor thing, you can say, "It's all right," or "Thanks." But as we'll see, it's not kind to brush off a heartfelt apology with a casual "Don't sweat it." If someone made a serious effort to apologize, it's appropriate to acknowledge that. You already know how difficult it is. You might go with "Thank you. I'm sure that was hard for you to do."

If you choose to accept an apology, do it truthfully. You don't get to accept an apology *and* hold a grudge. It's one or the other. If you can't give up the grudge, do not accept the apology. But if you can't accept the apology, you should still respond to the person who offered it. You can say, "I don't accept your apology." We'll give some suggestions below on what to do if you need some time to think about it.

If the apology isn't good enough, you can ask them to try again. But that's only assuming you think it will be possible for you to accept a better apology. Writer and actress Franchesca Ramsey gives the example of the comeback for the bad apology, "Sorry if you're offended." That's not a good apology. Don't accept it. But Ramsey smartly suggests saying, "There's no need for 'if'—I *am* offended. So *are* you sorry?"

Susan once accepted a flawed apology—it was weak, it was evasive, it had an "if" in it—because it was from two classmates who had suddenly dumped her in high school, and it was such a vindication to get it. She said, "Thank you. I accept your apology." The long-ago friendships were revived, and later she got a really excellent and sincere apology, which truly put the matter to rest.

If the apology isn't good because they don't understand what they should be apologizing for, you can tell them. "I'm not upset that you let Jordan drink all my mulberry brandy. I'm upset that you let Jordan drive home afterward."

But if they don't understand what they should be apologizing for, *never* say, "You know what you did," or "You should know damned well why I'm upset." That's game playing, and it's not a nice game. If you've read this far, you're better than that. (What if you didn't read this far?

What if you just picked the book up and opened it at random and came upon this passage? Then it's *a sign*! Read the rest!)

Also, do not be a person who does not deserve stickers. A very charming 2015 study out of the University of Virginia created a scenario in which six- and seven-year-olds built a tower out of plastic cups, which a grown-up research assistant knocked over. (Christ, what an asshole.) Afterward, the kids got to decide whether to give the grown-up stickers—children appreciate the value of the sticker economy—or not. When the adult didn't apologize, the kids were stingy with the stickers. When the adult did apologize, the kids were still upset about the loss of their tower, but they gave more stickers to the grown-up than the non-apology-receiving kids did. "Even though an apology didn't make children feel better, it did help to facilitate forgiveness," study author Marissa Drell said. "They seem to have recognized it as a signal that the transgressor felt bad about what she had done and may have been implicitly promising not to do it again." And, hey, when the grown-up followed up the apology by helping kids *rebuild* their towers, the kids were even *more* generous with the stickers. "Restitution—some sort of active effort to make repairs after a transgression—can make the victim feel better because it may undo some of the harm, and it can repair the relationship by showing the transgressor's commitment to it," Drell noted.

If you are not six, and the person who is apologizing to you has not helped you rebuild your metaphorical tower, you are under no obligation to accept their apology. But you might want to think about why not. It may be that you want more time to think about whether you want to accept the apology or what recompense you might like from the person who hurt you. If so, you can simply say, "Thank you. I'd like some time to think about this." Easy. Then you can do the solo work of deciding whether you want to forgive (see below) or whether there is additional action the other person might take or further words they could offer that would help you forgive them.

In *Effective Apology: Mending Fences, Building Bridges, and Restoring Trust*, business consultant John Kador suggests using the phrasing "I appreciate the apology, but I'm not over it yet." The "it," he says, is deliberately ambiguous. If you're open to talking further later, he suggests several phrases:

> *I need some time. I hope you can be patient with me while I deal with this.*
>
> *I appreciate your coming to see me, but it's too soon for me. I want to talk to you but I need a few days.*
>
> *Give me some time to settle down, and we can talk. I'll let you know when I'm ready.*
>
> *I appreciate your coming to see me, but I'm just not ready to discuss what you did just yet. I need a couple of days to think clearly.*
>
> *It's good of you to take responsibility. I'm just not over it yet. Let me call you next week and we can pick it up when I'm thinking more clearly.*

"All these recommended phrasings have one factor in common," Kador says. "They locate the need for a cooling-off period not in the character of the apologizer or the quality of the apology, but in the recipient's need for time." He is not a fan of the negativity of "I'm not sure I can accept your apology. I need time to think about it." Skip the first part and just say the second part. (That is, if there is a chance that you'll accept the apology in the future, of course. If you don't want to hear the apologizer out, don't.)

The Minimalist Approach

If you want to keep the person at a distance, or don't want to get into a whole *thing* about what happened in the past, just say, "I accept your apology." This is often useful with people you haven't thought about in years who pop up suddenly telling you they want to be accountable. As we mentioned earlier, sometimes people who are newly in recovery reach out to everyone in their past as part of their 12-step or similar process. They may be flush with the excitement of beginning life anew, not really considering how their apologies are going to go over. Some treat apologies like fireworks, shooting them off gleefully in bright and sparkly bunches. If you don't have the time or inclination to share in this person's process, may we suggest the minimalist "I accept your apology." (If you do.) No need for further engagement.

Sometimes, though, someone apologizes long after the fact and you are delighted to hear from them. Marjorie once got a letter—a letter! with a stamp! in the mail!—from an ex, years after they'd broken up. He'd moved to another city and was getting married but wanted to write to say he was sorry for aspects of his behavior when he and Marjorie were dating. He wanted to tell her that because of some of the things she'd said to him when they were together, he was going to be a better husband. He told her that when it didn't seem like he was listening, he was.

The ex didn't include an email address or phone number, so there was no expectation of a response. It was just a card on nice heavy paper. The breakup was long enough in the past that Marjorie didn't feel fury or sadness when she thought of him. Yet the apology was welcome. It was just . . . nice.

Slow Down There, Pardner

Sometimes an apology comes quickly after the offense. Let's say your little brother has been ordered to apologize to you by your mom. Or someone you've just met wants to apologize for accidentally misgendering you. You are all "whatever" about their discomfiture. Again, this is a case for "I accept your apology." You're not saying what they did was okay. You're just saying some words to note that you want to end the interaction. But you don't say "whatever," because that would be brushing them off.

Now let's say the apology is super-duper welcome. A friend you haven't spoken to in months wants to apologize for the fight you had! Hooray! You're eager to accept the apology and you want to say that you feel responsible, too, and the thing that happened is both your faults, and there's enough blame to go around, and here's what you were thinking at the time and what you're thinking now . . . Great! *But wait.* Let them say their piece. This may be hard for them. (After all, they came to you. You didn't go to them.) Just listen. Pay attention. And when they've gotten all their words out, *then* you get to respond.

Be Gracious, You Rat Fink

Sometimes we accept apologies poorly, in a way that takes the wind out of the other person's sails and demoralizes them. Kador offers a great example: Janet and Ed are coworkers at a restaurant. They are kidders, yuksters. One night as they're closing up, Janet locks Ed in the walk-in freezer as a joke. But then she can't open it again and she doesn't have the key. Freaking out, knowing this will cause her to get fired, she calls the store manager and wakes him up. He gets there in an hour, fires Janet, opens the freezer . . . and there is no Ed. Ed has used a little-known service door to the parking lot! He's gone home without telling Janet. Janet calls Ed and says, "Ed, I am sincerely sorry for locking you in the freezer. I know that people have died from being locked into freezers. I can't believe I put you in that awful position and exposed you to that risk. I've learned my lesson. It was a terrible lapse in judgment and I feel terrible about it. I accept that I was fired. I just hope I don't permanently lose your respect. Again, I apologize."

Ed's response?

"Don't worry about it."

Pardon? How would you feel if you were Janet? "Don't worry about it"? That's it? Janet was *fired*. If someone has screwed up the courage to apologize to you, and apologizes well, as Janet has, you owe it to them to respond with the seriousness their apology is due. It's unsatisfying to hear "You have nothing to apologize for" or "Forget it" unless those words are an opening sally. If you respond to an apology with something like "Hey, it happens," please keep talking to make it clear that you aren't upset, that you admire the person for apologizing, and (if you're Ed) that you'd like to help balance the scales if possible.

Please Stop Talking

When accepting an apology, it's good practice to say, "Thank you." Unless you really, really do not want this apology and it horrifies you. In that case, you may reject the apology immediately. Don't even listen. Say, for instance, you are recovering from an eating disorder and have asked your mother not to talk about your weight to you under any circumstances, and you shut her down every time she persists, and then she perpetually calls you to say, "I'm sorry, but . . ." (feel free to fill that in: "you'd be so pretty if you lost weight"/"I'm only concerned for your health"/"I want to tell you about this amazing new plan I read about that's not a diet, it's a new way of looking at eating"/"you'll never get a man"/"you always get so nasty when I only care about what's best for you"/"I wasn't sure you were aware how many calories are in avocado toast"), it's not healthy for you to engage. This is a continuation of the original insult, betrayal, or abuse. Whatever interaction you have on the topic should be on your terms. Calmly say, "I've told you how I feel about this subject. I'm hanging up now."

Now Please Listen

If you feel that the person apologizing is genuinely sorry they upset you but not entirely clear on *why* you're upset, you might feel better—and do a good deed in the bargain—if you edified them. To wit: "Thank you for apologizing. I want you to understand why I was upset." And then tell them: "You called me 'Margie' and I've told you repeatedly I go by 'Marjorie' now"/"You persist in teasing me about my regional accent and I know you think it's funny but it's not funny to me"/"I realize that you thought you were expressing appreciation for my friend's culture, but what you said was unintentionally racist."

Sometimes, too-frequent apologies are a power play, a way to shut down further discussion: "I'm sorry! I'm sorry for living! I'm sorry you always get mad about the smallest thing! I'm sorry I'm human!" On the flip side, demanding too many apologies ("How dare you tell me it's my turn to do the dishes when you cheated on me five years ago!" "How dare you mention your hangnail when my gramma has CANCER!") can also be a power trip. If the person cheated on you and you've decided to stay with them, deal with the cheating in therapy, and fight fair about it. If you use it as a trump card to get your partner to apologize over and over, that's unfair. And if your friend constantly whines about their life without ever asking you how your grandma is doing, and you've talked about their tendency to do this, you're wasting your breath if you keep harping on it. They're self-absorbed. Accept it and keep them as a casual friend, or dump them. Do not dwell. (Then again, if you're using your grandma's health to win pity points or evade responsibilities, that's on you, pal.)

Extremely Logical and Self-Serving Reasons to Forgive

So you've probably heard a million reasons why you *should* forgive. Religious traditions tend to valorize forgiveness when not encouraging an eye for an eye and/or some nice recreational stoning. And there are tons of studies indicating that choosing to forgive lowers blood pressure, heart rate, and the amount of cortisol—stress hormone, essentially—your body releases. Holding on to anger and releasing excess cortisol (which happens when you silently rage at someone in your life instead of forgiving them) can cause headaches, indigestion, anxiety, depression, difficulties with concentration and memory, maybe even heart disease.

Practicing forgiveness is also linked to a better-functioning immune system and better overall health. A 2019 study published in the journal *Psychology & Health* found that forgiveness was even correlated with better sleep. Luther College psychology professor Loren Toussaint and other researchers surveyed 1,500 Americans and found that those who were more forgiving, of both themselves and others, tended to sleep better—and be healthier in general—than those who hung on to "anger, regret, and rumination." (Bonus fact: the study found that while forgiving yourself proved helpful for slumber, forgiving others worked better.)

Forgiving a wrong may also help you forget it, in a good way. A 2014 study by Saima Noreen (now at De Montfort University in Leicester, in the UK) and colleagues in the journal *Psychological Science* found that people who could overcome the desire for revenge against a person who did them dirty found themselves less able to recall the details of the wrongdoing. "It is well established that learning to forgive others can have positive benefits for an individual's physical and mental health," Noreen told the Association for Psychological Science (APS). "The ability to forget upsetting memories may provide an effective coping strategy that enables people to move on with their lives." Being able to handle your emotions and refrain from seeking vengeance demonstrates executive control. And executive control helps you manage and regulate cognitive processes, including the ability to forget.

Noreen had thirty volunteers read forty different scenarios involving (hypothetical) wrongdoings ranging from slander to infidelity to theft.

Using techniques from memory research, they tried to see whether feelings of forgiveness had any effect on the forgetting process. "Motivated forgiveness," as Noreen et al. put it, "is thought to be a function of an inhibitory control mechanism that can prevent unwanted memories from entering conscious awareness." When the subjects *hadn't* forgiven the sinner, they were far more likely to remember every aspect of the sin. When subjects did forgive, they were much less able to recall the exact details of what had happened. "We hope that, in time, new fields of enquiry may combine forgetting- and forgiveness-based interventions that might, in turn, give rise to powerful therapeutic tools that will enable people to 'forgive and forget' more effectively," Noreen told APS.

Love and Literacy

In *Achieving Emotional Literacy: A Personal Program to Increase Your Emotional Intelligence*, psychotherapist Claude Steiner tells of a good apology that came after many failed apologies. One of Steiner's emotional literacy workshops was attended by a couple, Edgar and Rose, who'd been married for forty years. After Steiner talked about apologies, Edgar spoke up. He said that the night their first child was born, he visited Rose in the hospital and then left in high spirits. He went to a bar, met a woman there, bought her drinks, went to her apartment, and had sex with her. The next morning he felt horribly guilty and confessed to Rose, saying he would never do anything like that again.

Rose was "inconsolable and unforgiving." Edgar had apologized many times over the years, but Rose never let it drop. Every time they had a fight she brought it up, still furious at the betrayal. Edgar asked Rose if he could try apologizing again, and she agreed. He knelt in front of her and said, "Rose, I know that I have apologized a hundred times . . . and I have complained that it doesn't seem to work. I realize from this discussion that even though I apologized, my apologies have been hollow, and I am not surprised that they haven't worked. I understand why. It is because I have not really acknowledged how much I hurt you. I really didn't want to accept that I had hurt you so much. So I made excuses and never stopped to experience your pain. Rose, after all these years, I realize how much what I did hurt you. I am so sorry that I did it and so sorry that it took me so long to realize the extent of your pain. Would you please forgive me?" She forgave him, right there in the emotional literacy workshop. A year later Steiner ran into Edgar, who happily said things were great and that Rose had never brought up his betrayal since that day.

Okay, but Do I Really Have to Forgive?

Again, no.

First of all, you own your own feelings. You get to feel what you feel. We don't believe that feelings are wrong. Actions, sure, but not feelings. Tamping down your emotions, as opposed to taking active steps to deal with them, is what's not good for you.

And make no mistake: not letting yourself feel your feelings is harmful to you and often to others. Why is it, do you think, that while women are far more likely than men to be diagnosed with depression, they're far less likely to kill themselves or others? American men are nearly four times more likely to die by suicide than American women; throughout the world, men are generally between three and four times more likely to kill themselves. Worldwide, 95 percent of those who commit homicide are men. Some experts attribute the disparity to the fact that women are encouraged to give voice to their emotions, while men aren't. For all that we talk about raising boys to become emotionally aware men, we still expect them to have tough skin. They're still not encouraged to seek help for feelings of depression and anger. When we allow ourselves to feel what we feel—fury and sadness included—we are less likely to turn those feelings into actions used to harm ourselves and others. Being pressured *not* to feel, or to forgive without receiving skills training for *how* and *why* to forgive, isn't helpful.

External pressure to forgive, without nuance and training and the allowance for exceptions, doesn't work. You'll only be resentful. Just as we say you shouldn't apologize if you're not sorry, we believe you can't simply forgive because you're told to forgive. The human brain and the human soul don't work that way.

There's a term called "spiritual bypassing," coined by psychotherapist John Welwood, which means calling on people to forgive without truly processing or talking about why they're distressed or angry in the first place. It means burying and repressing feelings. And it's no good—not for the person who's being told to forgive, and not for the person who wronged them. It does, however, tend to benefit the status quo and make other people more comfortable. People who urge you to forgive might just want the conflict or bad feelings to end, without really caring about the interaction with the person who hurt you or what it costs you. Being urged simply to forgive or move on—without engaging in the real work of intrapersonal, interpersonal, and societal change—sucks. So does tone policing: being told that your feelings are invalid because of the way you expressed them.

In *Practicing Forgiveness: A Path Toward Healing*, Richard S. Balkin, PhD, tells the story of a patient who nearly died during routine ankle surgery. The anesthesiologist accidentally screwed up the delivery of an injected painkiller, which caused the patient's heart to stop. To get it started again, doctors had to slice her open and crack her rib cage. The patient's husband said he "wanted to kill the anesthesiologist, flatten him," and the family visited a lawyer. But the anesthesiologist apologized, and apologized well, against the advice of the hospital's lawyers. (Sigh. See chapter 6.) He wrote the patient a personal letter telling her how sorry he was, then met her for coffee at a local diner and apologized in person. "I found out he was a real person," the patient said afterward.

"He made an effort to seek me out and say he was sorry I suffered." And the patient and her family decided not to sue after all. They weren't *pressured* not to sue, *pressured* to forgive, *pressured* to settle. Forgiveness needs to be a choice. As we like to say, apologies are mandatory, but forgiveness isn't.

The society we live in doesn't make forgiveness easy. (Again. Chapter 6.) The doctor in the example above is a powerful exception to the rule. Even when a crime victim would like the opportunity to forgive, the judicial system makes it difficult. Victims are often denied the right to meet face-to-face with criminals . . . even when they ask to. Arzoo Osanloo, associate professor of Law, Societies, and Justice at the University of Washington, asked in an essay for Princeton University Press, "What do victims' families want?"

> They want peace of mind. Forgiveness offers them that, but often, not before they have had a chance to expel anger and frustration. Often they seek, request even, meetings with perpetrators and their families. Beyond apology, they want to share their grievance with the only individuals who can begin to contemplate their pain—those over whom they hold the power to live or to let die. [. . .]
>
> A system of justice may rightly eschew the private right of retaliation as a form of vengeance, but the other end of the spectrum, cutting the victim off from the perpetrator completely, may also have its drawbacks for failing to allow for forgiveness to emerge as a presence of mind. [. . .] While forgiveness is not the end of injustice, it is a beginning that can forge the pathways to broader social and economic rapprochement.

And wouldn't that be satisfying?

The Insidious Pressure to Forgive

You do not have to forgive oppression. You do not have to forgive narcissists who have harmed you. You do not have to forgive simply to make things more comfortable for others. You do not have to forgive simply because you've received a half-assed apology. (You can, however, take steps to push a half-assed apology into a no-assed, full-throated, positive apology. Depending on the circumstances and the personalities involved, the attempt may work or it may not.)

In this book and on our SorryWatch website, we extensively discuss the role of power in forgiveness as well as in apology. The person apologizing has to voluntarily give up some of their power, put themselves in a one-down position, become a supplicant, take a position of acknowledging their own wrongdoing, and humbly ask for absolution. Forgiveness, on the other hand, involves being magnanimous with one's power.

In 1938, American sociologist Willard Waller coined a phrase (and concept) called "the Principle of Least Interest." It means that in any relationship—familial, romantic, business, societal—the party that has less investment in the relationship controls the relationship. This theory explains why police, corporations, and celebrities often apologize poorly: What incentive do they have to do better? They hold all the power cards! But when the person or party that has done wrong really craves forgiveness—when a politician is terrified that they'll be booted from office, an insurrectionist is facing the prospect of jail, a YouTuber is worried they'll have their channel stripped of ads, a TikTok star risks their partnerships, a cheating spouse really *wants* to preserve their marriage—it's the apology recipient who has "hand." (We don't even *like* that farshtunkiner show. But "hand" is such a useful concept.)

When the person who did wrong really wants to do better and maybe has suffered a little (or a lot) for their sins, it can be easier to forgive them. In *Practicing Forgiveness*, Richard S. Balkin discusses the "reward power" that a victim possesses when an offender truly wants to reconcile. "A victim may be more likely to express forgiveness when feeling empowered and when the victim feels that his sense of justice has taken place," he writes.

Forgiveness in Religious Traditions

A caveat: We're going to be sadly reductive here. Religious faiths, texts, tenets, and practices are complicated and often differ from community to community and even house to house. We're generalizing and offering an overview, and we encourage anyone interested in going deeper into a particular religious tradition's approach to apology and forgiveness to speak to a member of their clergy (or ask a librarian for book recommendations).

Many faiths stress the importance of forgiveness. In Christianity, Jesus died for humanity's sins. Christians are redeemed through Jesus's sacrifice; God has the power to grant absolution and grace regardless of a Christian's sins. Forgiveness is divine because it emulates Jesus and reflects a godly choice for reconciliation and healing. Attempting to "do the Christian thing" means forgiving and showing mercy as part of your identification with and desire to belong to a community of believers and the feeling of a personal relationship with God.

Hinduism has a diverse set of practices, and there isn't a single central holy book. (There are a bunch.) But a fair generalization might be that God's forgiveness can help purify humanity's inherently sinful karma. To be human is to cause harm to someone or something, to commit some offense or other, whether with or without intent. Human beings are inherently flawed, unlike God. The Bhagavad Gita calls forgiveness among human beings a divine virtue: Arjuna perpetually asks Lord Krishna for forgiveness for his ignorance. *Anavatva*, "vanity" or "egoism," can stand in the way of asking for forgiveness and granting forgiveness. When you successfully subsume your own ego to God, which is something every person should try to their utmost to do, you automatically forgive. There's a telling story about Bhagavān Buddha. In a past life he was a sweet and peaceful buffalo. A naughty monkey would tease him constantly, jumping on his back and pulling his horns. The devas said, "Why do you put up with this? Are you scared of a little monkey?" The Buddha said, "I could kill that monkey with one kick or one stab of my horns. He's far less powerful than I am, living at the mercy of everything in the world that's more powerful. A powerful being is noble when he forgives a weaker creature. That's why I choose to forgive."

Buddhists, too, believe in the potency of forgiveness. But Buddhism doesn't involve asking a deity for forgiveness as part of a quest to achieve eternal life or reach heaven, as Christianity urges. Forgiveness, according to Buddha, is an essential aspect to the way you live here on earth; you must practice *mettā*, loving-kindness, because reconciliation among all beings is vital, as all of us and all living creatures are interconnected. Meditation can help human beings do the work of forgiveness: *vipassanā* (insight) meditation involves recognizing your feelings of anger and blame as they pass through your mind, observing and processing them without attachment or judgment. The act of dispassionate observation clears space inside you for forgiveness. *Mettā* meditation involves using your breath to embrace feelings of interconnectedness. When you choose to remain attached to your anger, you cause suffering for yourself and others, but choosing to let go of negative feelings and embracing forgiveness gives you compassion for the entire world. These processes help you in your quest to attain nirvana, the only way to escape suffering completely. Buddhism's worldview, unlike many Western perspectives, doesn't emphasize eternal life in the world to come.

Both Islam and Judaism pay a lot of attention to the differences between sins committed against fellow humans and against a divine being. When you wrong a fellow person, praying to God or Allah for forgiveness isn't the way to deal with it. You have to earn forgiveness from the person you've wronged, and it takes work, not prayer. You have to show contrition to them, not to God.

In Islam, apologizing to others is essential, a sign of strength and good character, but forgiveness is perhaps even more important. The prophet Muhammad said, "My intercession shall not reach the person who does not accept the apology from another person—whether the apology is truthful or untruthful." Forgiveness is one of Allah's greatest attributes. Refusing to forgive, *even when you believe the apology is insincere*, is a disappointment to Allah. As the Qur'an says, "Those who control their anger and are forgiving towards people, Allah loves the good."

In Judaism, Yom Kippur is the big holiday of repentance, but Jewish texts are very clear that the Day of Atonement is about apologizing to both God and your fellow humans. When it comes to sins committed against other people, spending your day in synagogue praying and fasting does exactly bupkes. You have to apologize to those you've wronged before the Gates of Repentance slam shut that night.

The medieval scholar Maimonides wrote extensively about apologies and forgiveness. When you sin against someone else, you're obligated not only to apologize but also to do whatever you can to right the wrong: offer restitution and resolve not to commit the same sin again. ("Whoever merely verbalizes his confession without consciously deciding to give up his sins is like a person who immerses in a ritual bath to cleanse himself but is holding a dead reptile in his hand," Maimonides wrote. "His immersion will not cleanse him as long as the reptile remains in his hand." Friends, let go of that reptile.) Make sure your apology isn't just words: the test is when you're faced with a similar situation in the future. Will you behave differently this time? And Maimonides says that you must approach a person you've wronged three times to apologize and ask for forgiveness. If the person still doesn't forgive after the third time, the sin's on them. You're in the clear.

The upshot: In pretty much any faith tradition you might ascribe to, the pressure to forgive is generally a big honking deal. And while almost every religious text can be read with nuance, and can be interpreted to support the notion that there may be times that one needn't forgive, religious leaders often fail to convey this level of nuance to their congregants. Religion then becomes not a source of comfort but a source of guilt and stress for people who have been wronged and legitimately don't want to or aren't able to forgive.

In our view, choosing not to accept an apology can be the proper choice for one's emotional health. If it's possible to find support for this position in a religious text, in doctrine, in prayer, in an interpretive text, in the words of a given clergyperson, we hope you can find that support. If not, we'd argue that you need not allow religion to be a source of stress and guilt instead of an oasis of peace.

Our Societal Addiction to Forgiveness Stories

It's telling that our culture loves stories of Black forgiveness of white attackers, stories of Holocaust survivors forgiving Nazis, and stories of rape victims forgiving rapists. What they all have in common is that they're about people with less power forgiving people with more power. Our addiction to these stories is problematic, because these stories enforce the status quo, making us feel better about a world rife with inequality and injustice. We're not saying that no individual victim should ever forgive the person who harmed them or their loved ones. People have free will. If forgiveness is healing for them, it's not on us to tell them they're wrong. It is, however, on us to tell each other that celebrating these stories can be a feel-good choice that mutes our obligation to look hard at what needs to be fixed in the world we live in.

When Brandt Jean, the brother of Dallas police shooting victim Botham Jean, told his brother's killer, former police officer Amber Guyger, that he forgave her, and gave her a big hug in the courtroom, the press celebrated. But when a relative of a murdered Black person reacts with anger instead of hugs and sweet biblical sentiments, the public response is often furious. For example, after the New York City police officer who killed Eric Garner with an illegal choke hold apologized, a reporter asked Garner's widow, Esaw, whether she forgave him. She responded, "Hell no!" and was accused in a national news headline of "lashing out." But she was completely within her rights to say "Hell no." Anger in the face of injustice is warranted. (And why on earth did the reporter even ask that question?)

Yolonda Y. Wilson, a professor of philosophy at Saint Louis University who researches government obligations to rectify historic and continuing injustice, wrote in 2019:

> If anger can help us understand our place in the world and drive us to make the world that we occupy better, then good for anger. The most important feature of anger, properly directed, is the recognition that a wrong has occurred. To the extent that one's anger motivates one to right wrongs, anger can be a tool of achieving justice. [. . .] The pressure for black people to be especially forgiving in the face of wrongdoing cannot be disentangled from a racist history that has generally met black demands for justice with violence.

Eva Mozes Kor, a Holocaust survivor who in 2017 very publicly forgave a Nazi, was celebrated as a hero. She was among the many pairs of Jewish twins upon whom Dr. Josef Mengele did terrible medical experiments, and fifty years after World War II she connected with a Nazi doctor who'd worked at Auschwitz. At her urging, he wrote a letter of apology; she then wrote him a letter of forgiveness. A short BuzzFeed video about her has been viewed over 19 million times. How noble! How marvelous!

The fuller story: Kor, who'd long spoken to schools and synagogues about the Holocaust, decided that for the fiftieth anniversary of the liberation of Auschwitz she wanted to reach out to a former Nazi doctor she'd seen in a documentary she'd also appeared in. She said she wanted him to write that letter as proof to future generations that the Holocaust was no myth or exaggeration. The doctor did as she asked, writing, "I am so sorry that in some way I was part of it. Under the prevailing circumstances I did the best I could to save as many lives as possible. Joining the SS was a mistake. I was young. I was an opportunist. And once I joined, there was no way out."

Having read this far in this book, you recognize that this is a terrible apology. It doesn't take responsibility. It doesn't offer specifics ("in some way I was part of it"). It offers excuses ("I did the best I could" and "I was young"). The doctor *did* have a choice. Other "young" (and even old) people joined the Resistance, hid Jews in their basements and attics and barns, even elected to stand by passively without actively taking steps to join the SS, the top-tier political soldiers of the Nazi Party, as this doctor did.

Kor, however, was happy with the apology. And if *she* was happy, who are *we* to argue? Forgiveness is a choice.

A decade later, Kor also forgave Auschwitz's accountant. She publicly held his hand and graciously allowed him to kiss her cheek. She wrote a book, *The Power of Forgiveness*, which came out in 2021. (She died in 2019, but a colleague at her private museum in Terre Haute finished it in her name.) In the book she describes her healing process: she wrote down all the bad words she wanted to say to Dr. Mengele, and once she ran out of words, she realized she'd also run out of anger; then she was able to forgive. She decided to write a letter.

I, Eva Mozes Kor, a twin who as a child survived Josef Mengele's experiments at Auschwitz fifty years ago, hereby give amnesty to all

Nazis who participated directly or indirectly in the murder of my family and millions of others.

I extend this amnesty to all governments who protected Nazi criminals for fifty years, then covered up their acts, and covered up their cover up.

I, Eva Mozes Kor, in my name only, give this amnesty because it is time to go on; it is time to heal our souls; it is time to forgive, but never forget.

She asked the United States, German, and Israeli governments to stop investigating Nazis and to open up all their files to survivors so they could perhaps read about what had been done to them and learn useful information for their medical records. (Her twin, who had also survived, had terrible health problems; it would have been helpful to know what substances had been injected into her body.) Kor read a statement aloud on the ramp to the gas chambers at Auschwitz, saying she hoped "in some small way to send the world a message of forgiveness, a message of peace, a message of hope, a message of understanding."

Kor added that it gave her no joy to see any Nazi criminal in jail and didn't want to see any harm come to the Mengele family or their business. The press and public ate this up. But just as the footage of Brandt Jean hugging and forgiving his brother's killer dismayed plenty of Black people, Kor's actions horrified many other Holocaust survivors. As Holocaust scholar Deborah Lipstadt noted, "I watched them grimace as audiences gave her standing ovations and the media described her as someone 'who found it in her heart' to forgive, the implication being that survivors who did not follow her lead were unable to rise above their resentment. Survivors told me they felt they were being depicted as hardhearted, while Kor was being celebrated as the hero, someone bigger than they."

We Can Forgive Only on Our Own Behalf—Not on Behalf of Others

In her book, Kor says she did her forgiving in her own name only . . . but calling for amnesty for Nazis can't be considered acting merely for herself. "I know that most of the survivors denounced me, and they denounce me today also," she says in the video. "But what is my forgiveness? I like it. It is an act of self-healing, self-liberation, self-empowerment. All victims feel hopeless, feel helpless, feel powerless. I want everyone to remember that we cannot change what happened . . . but we can change how we relate to it."

This is absolutely true. In the book, Kor elaborates on how forgiveness made her "free to discover that I had power over my own today and tomorrow, again and again. It hurt no one, it doesn't hurt me. And it is free. Everyone can accomplish it." She then adds, "Also, there are no side effects. It works. But if you do not like feeling like a free person, it is possible to return to your pain and hatred anytime."

This statement was beautiful until that last sentence . . . which is a tad reductive, judgy, and dismissive. Make no mistake: choosing to forgive can absolutely be therapeutic. Kor's strategy of writing a letter to someone who harmed you, calling them all kinds of names, and then never sending the letter could work beautifully for some people. But her insistence that it *will* work is simplistic. To a woman who was raped and found it impossible to forgive her rapist, Kor suggested, "Write the letter again. And again. There's no limit. Maybe you need to write it 10 times, maybe 20. You might even need to write 100 letters." Couldn't this prove more hurtful than helpful for some survivors of trauma?

Kor's suggestions that gardening and spending time with animals can help people heal are also positive, also likely to be helpful to lots of readers. But again, the notion that these activities can lead *everyone* to forgiveness is facile.

People want to admire Kor and to find her generosity of spirit beautiful, because we want to live in a just world. We love cute, tough-talking old ladies with hearts of gold who remind us of our bubbes and bibis and nanas and nonnas. They charm us. They make us feel safe. They're familiar, like the cast of *The Golden Girls*. They convince us that the world has changed for the better since the Holocaust. (Feel free to substitute "since slavery." Or "since that rapist realized the error of his ways and cried on camera.") The danger lies in wanting Kor's story of forgiveness to be every victim's story—and blaming the victim who refuses to conform to her narrative.

So You Think You Want to Forgive?

The key here is choice. If you feel the need to forgive, as Kor did—because you'd like to feel better about the world, because you'd love to have all the health benefits of forgiveness mentioned at the beginning of this chapter, because you're exhausted from feeling as though you're toting a heavy load all the time—go, you! But many of us who'd like to forgive need some help in figuring out how to do it.

Fortunately, the work is doable. One 2014 review of fifty-four studies of "forgiveness interventions" found that such interventions help people increase their feelings of hopefulness and decrease their feelings of anxiety, depression, and anger. Fred Luskin, PhD, director of the Stanford University Forgiveness Projects, is one such expert who offers "skills-based forgiveness training." He's explored "forgiveness therapy" with survivors of violence in Northern Ireland, Sierra Leone, and the World Trade Center attacks on 9/11. And he believes that forgiveness is a learnable skill, like riding a bike or training for a marathon or doing higher math or developing better sleep practices. There are different kinds of forgiveness, he says: interpersonal (forgiving someone else, which doesn't necessarily mean having a relationship with them again), intrapersonal (forgiving yourself), and existential (forgiving God, nature, or fate for what's been done to you). Forgiving, he says, does not mean that you believe what happened to you was okay.

Luskin, the author of *Forgive for Good: A Proven Prescription for Health and Happiness*, says that true forgiveness begins with recognizing that your hurt and anger are causing you emotional or even physical harm. When you have the skills to forgive a big wrong that's been done to you, the benefits reach forward as well as backward: you'll find that you can let go of future hurts in your life more easily and even learn not to take offense in the first place. Luskin believes you can eventually change your worldview so that you can decide whether to tackle a problem or let it go. You may discover that you're missing much of the wonder and beauty in the world if you spend a ton of time ruminating over wrongs in the past. Learning to recognize that everyone (even you) acts out of self-interest means understanding that different people's goals will invariably conflict.

Luskin outlines nine steps toward forgiveness. To (drastically) summarize, they are:

1. *Be able to articulate why what happened to you is not okay and talk to a few trusted people about your feelings.*

2. *Commit to doing the work to feel better and remind yourself that you deserve to feel better. You don't have to confront or reconcile with anyone. This process is for you.*

3. *Understand that the goal is for you to feel the peace that comes from "lessening the blame of that which has hurt you, taking your life experience less personally, and seeing the cost of holding a grudge."*

4. *Understand that you're addressing how you feel now, not what happened then.*

5. *Learn deep breathing and stress management techniques (outlined in Luskin's book) to use when you start feeling distressed.*

6. *Don't expect other people to change or start giving you what you need if they never have. Celebrate the power that you have, but don't look to others for affirmation or apology if they don't have a history of delivering for you.*

7. *Set new goals. Luskin calls this "finding your positive intention." Find better ways to meet your needs and move on emotionally from a situation that's not working for you.*

8. *"Remember that a life well lived is your best revenge." Find things to rejoice in and appreciate. Observe moments of kindness happening all around you. Remind yourself of what's good in your life. "You will start to see that the sun still shines, people still fall in love, and beauty still exists everywhere."*

9. *"Amend the grievance story you are telling." When you consciously change the story about yourself, you tell yourself, "That feeling of peace is the experience of forgiveness."*

Even if you never get an apology from the person who harmed you most, accepting the fact that the apology is not forthcoming can be a powerful, fulfilling act. You can be a happy, successful person without that apology. You may never learn why a horrid experience befell you; accepting that there is no answer can be hugely freeing.

Still More Forgiveness Paradigm Options!

In *The Forgiving Life: A Pathway to Overcoming Resentment and Creating a Legacy of Love*, psychologist Robert D. Enright offers a forgiveness model consisting of four phases: *uncovering* (thinking about how you've been harmed, trying to be as objective as possible); *decision* (choosing, of your own free will, to begin the process of forgiveness); *work* (trying to understand the motives and contexts of the person who harmed you, and choosing to view them with compassion); and *deepening* (finding meaning in your suffering, and pondering whether you, too, might need to seek forgiveness). Enright's model is imbued with his religious Christian perspective, so it might not work for everyone or might require some adaptation.

Enright notes that while lots of people say things like "I'll never forgive! I'll keep fighting!," they need to understand that these two concepts aren't mutually exclusive. You can "seek this goodness in the face of injustice and seek justice" simultaneously. Like most forgiveness researchers, he distinguishes between *forgiveness* and *reconciliation*. "Forgiveness is a moral virtue like justice," he says. "Reconciliation is not a moral virtue. It takes two people or more to come together again in mutual trust. One can forgive without reconciling; one does forgive without ever excusing; when one forgives it is never from a position of weakness."

Perhaps the most influential forgiveness researcher out there is Everett L. Worthington Jr., now professor emeritus of psychology at Virginia Commonwealth University. His interest in forgiveness began after his mother was murdered in 1996. He and his brother and sister all forgave the murderer, but living with what had happened to them was nonetheless agonizing. His brother committed suicide in 2005.

Worthington's research—again, from a Christ-centered perspective, so it may not resonate with all readers—is imbued with self-awareness about his own feelings of guilt; his work is particularly strong on the subject of self-forgiveness. He developed a forgiveness model he calls REACH. (You can read more about implementing this model in his many books; the most recent one is 2013's *Moving Forward: Six Steps to Forgiving Yourself and Breaking Free from the Past.*)

R = Recall the hurt. *Decide not to pursue payback even so.*

E = Empathize with your partner. *Try to imagine the other person's perspective.*

A = Altruistic gift. *Remember a time you wronged someone—a parent, a friend, Mr. Slinger—and were forgiven, and how that felt. You can give that same gift to someone who hurt you.*

C = Commit. *When you've forgiven, write a note to yourself saying so to help your feelings stick.*

H = Hold on to forgiveness. *You may be tempted to un-forgive. Reread your note.*

There is a huge difference between forgiveness and pseudo-forgiveness. The latter can involve continuing to tolerate abuse, which is not okay. But abusing yourself isn't healthy either. We at SorryWatch find that if we think of forgiveness as a gift we give ourselves, not inherently one we give to someone else, we find it easier to feel at peace and not be ruled by anger.

How to Practice Self-Forgiveness

Lots of us carry around a heavy load of shame and self-blame. As we saw in chapter 6, family members of people harmed by doctors often feel tremendous guilt. So do the doctors who do the harm. People who are raped often blame themselves, and it doesn't help that they're often blamed by others. Domestic violence victims are disparaged because they didn't "just leave." (They may have tried. They may have few resources. They may fear losing their kids or having the abusers kill their kids. They may be debilitated by shame and guilt and self-blame.) Poor people are often accused of laziness despite living in a culture that has few safety nets, little affordable childcare, and multiple barriers to economic advancement. Sadly, society is full of roadblocks, biases, and hatreds—based on race, religion, size, gender identity, sexual orientation, and many more isms—making it all too easy to internalize self-hate.

We also live in a world where the least powerful people are the least permitted to screw up. Despite all the jibber-jabber on social media about cancellation, the people who are most harmed by their mistakes tend to be the ones at the bottom of the org chart, not the top. Bear in mind when you yourself are in a cycle of self-blame that your acts and failures to act don't occur in a vacuum. External forces have an impact on all of us. Life is not fair. Don't hate the player; hate the game.

In addition to the forgiveness and reconciliation strategies discussed earlier, you can try some other techniques for forgiving yourself. Therapy can help. So can reevaluating a terrible thing that happened to you by imagining it from a different perspective. Try to see it from an outsider's point of view. Would you blame the person you're seeing in your mind's eye if they weren't you? We're often kinder to our friends than we are to ourselves.

You might also consider all the good things you've done in your life. You weren't crushed by your mistakes or the bad things that have happened to you. You're strong. And your story isn't finished; you're on a journey and can continue to make changes, both to see yourself as and to actually become a better human being.

Forgiving a Public Apology

Most of this chapter has been about personal apologies. But let's take a moment to talk about public apologies.

People are very, very quick to point out when someone on the internet is wrong. Sometimes this is a good thing. Being accountable isn't the same thing as being canceled. It can be super-fun to pillory someone, to turn into Mean Girls with a virtual burn book. When social media censure blitzes occur, people really want SorryWatch to join in. When a famous person apologizes badly, we're flooded with emails and direct messages: *Roast them! Flay them alive!* The posts on our website that get the most traffic are the ones that excoriate terrible celebrity and political apologies. We know this, and yet we do not want to spend all our time mocking crappy apologies. We want to point out good apologies. We want people to do better. We want everyone to know that it's *hard* to apologize well, despite the fact that we're all positive that if we were in that other person's position, *we* could do it. (We might be able to and we might not. See chapter 4.) Constantly being snarky isn't fun or productive. It's essential to leaven our outrage and sarcasm with moments of delight. (Kids' sincere yet misspelled apologies are good for that.) We're not just talking about ourselves here: being angry on the internet isn't healthy for you, either.

Yes, an online pile-on is fabulous barn-burning fun when a famous person deserves it. When a homophobic politician gets caught in a compromising position with a lithe and slinky young man; when a person who bellows for violence and sedition winds up sobbing a snot-filled apology as his brick-throwing image is identified and he realizes jail time is an actual possibility; when a misogynistic actor rolls his eyes while apologizing dickishly for the genuinely lousy thing he said about his female costar. *Stone him! Whee!*

When a non-famous person does something dumb and apologizes, but people continue to excoriate them all over the internet, mock their looks, write to their employers, dox (reveal their address and phone number for direct abuse) and swat (send cops to their house under a malicious pretense), spew hate, or make threats against them and their children? Not helpful. (Often criminal.) Comedians talk about punching up versus punching down. Mocking the bad apologies of people whose careers certainly are going to bounce back from them is sporting; it's punching up at someone powerful. Mocking the bad apologies of people whose lives could be destroyed is ill-humored; it's punching down at someone without tons of power. Some rando who said they're sorry, even badly, shouldn't be subject to abuse. (We're not talking about people who keep doubling down on, say, spewing Nazi ideology, then apologizing with "Sorry those slurpers of Christian baby blood are so sensitive." It is okay to virtually punch them.)

We also may not know the full story. We once retweeted a Black politician's lousy apology for an anti-Asian thing she'd once said and were immediately contacted by two Asian Americans in the same community asking us to undo our retweets. They DM'd us that people were quietly working in good faith behind the scenes to build bridges between Black and Asian American folks in the community, and raising the temperature online wasn't helping. People with nefarious motives were trying to get the politician fired so they could replace her with someone of their choosing. We had no idea. We shouldn't have joined a rampage that we were clueless about.

Let's say an author is being eviscerated on Twitter for attacking Goodreads users who gave her book only four (out of five) stars. Is her behavior terrible? Yes! (Should authors ever look at Goodreads? No!) But Twitter users emailing the author's agent insisting they fire her, demanding that her publisher drop her, giving her book one star on Goodreads despite not having read it? Not cool. Especially if, say, the book is *about* the author's lifelong struggles with mental illness and abuse. Not that this excuses calling people who give her books four stars "nerds," but maybe instead of attacking the author . . . just do something else? Go for a walk, read a book by a different author, give five stars to a book you adore that hasn't received enough attention?

One time we did a SorryWatch post about a random sports fan's sloshed shenanigans and crappy apology. He reached out to us a few years later to ask that we take the post down. Half a decade after his

offense, stories about his drunken antics that day are the first thing anyone sees when they do a web search for his name. Now he's job hunting
and there it is on the first page of search results, stopping potential hiring
managers cold. We opted to keep the story up (we are journalists!), but
we gave him a pseudonym. Our bad-apology-parsing lesson still works if
you don't know the guy's name. Could people do their own detective
work and figure out his identity if they wanted to? Sure! But we won't do
it for them. Even if he's a schmuck, he doesn't deserve to have his life and
livelihood ruined. Celebrities and politicians can afford to have image-
improving companies manipulate their search results so that negative
stories about them don't show up for pages and pages. Regular people
can't. The playing field is not level.

When we at SorryWatch think a performer—even a very famous
one—is truly mentally ill, we don't cover them. It doesn't seem right or
helpful for anyone. Marjorie is reminded of the sign in her child's kinder-
garten classroom: "Before you speak, think: Is it true? Is it kind? Is it necessary?" (This quote is attributed to both Socrates and mid-century
radio host Bernard Meltzer.)

And finally: Always remember that someone is getting rich off your
outrage. Your fury isn't organic or isolated. Social media is TRYING to
piss you off. More pissed-off people means more engagement means
more clicks means more money. Let's get that fury trending! Let's get
those algorithms messing with your feed so you'll be more angry more
often! As Tressie McMillan Cottom, the sociologist and cultural critic,
told *New York Times* columnist Ezra Klein, "One of the problems right
now is that social shame, which I think in and of itself is enough usually
to discipline most people, is now tied to economic and political and cultural capital." Why opt in to raising your blood pressure, getting some
dimwit fired, and enriching Mark Zuckerberg and Jack Dorsey?

Before leaping into the digital fray, maybe ask yourself if you're piling
on, being your best self, offering up more light than heat. When Hank

Azaria apologized in 2021 for voicing the character of Apu on *The Simpsons*, lots of white people responded by retweeting a 2020 tweet by comedian Hari Kondabolu, who'd made a documentary about how hurtful the character was to South Asians:

> *POC: Yo, that shit is racist!*
> *WHITE: It's just a movie/ TV show/ book/ song/ any piece of media!*
>
> *10 YEARS LATER . . .*
> *WHITE: You were right. My bad.*

True that. But consider Kondabolu's 2021 response to Azaria's apology: "Hank Azaria is a kind & thoughtful person that proves that people are not simply 'products of their time' but have the ability to learn & grow. Nothing. But. Respect." Why were people so eager to "gotcha" Azaria's sincere, decent apology, one that was backed up by action, since he also quit voicing Apu? What benefit did it serve except to showboat? Neither Azaria nor the rest of us are time travelers (as far as we know), and we can only change our behavior moving forward.

Public shaming is best deployed when someone says something truly and undeniably hateful. A private, personal attempt to educate, aimed at encouraging reflection rather than eliciting a reaction, may offer less of a dopamine hit but can put forth more good in the world.

In 2021, during the trial of Derek Chauvin for the murder of George Floyd, Cher (always a wild ride on Twitter) tweeted "Whites Can No Longer Stand On The Side-lines . . . We 'MUST STOP GOP BIGOTS!' " Some people called her out for centering white people in a Black narrative and assuming that white people needed to step in to rescue Black people.

But others called her in. The next day she tweeted:

I Just got off phone With Friend Karen.Told her what Happened,& Realized,You Can Piss Ppl Off,& Hurt Them By Not Knowing Everything That's"NOT Appropriate"To Say.I know Ppl Apologize When They're In a Jam,BUT 🤚 TO GOD,🙏 IM TRULY SORRY If I Upset AnyOne In Blk Community.

It wasn't a perfect apology, but Friend Karen (finally, a positive media depiction of a Karen!) clearly helped Cher understand that she'd hurt people and how. And Friend Karen did so in a way that didn't cause Cher to feel so defensive and persecuted that she shut down (or, worse, blamed the victim).

Is It a Social Media Kerfuffle? Could You Maybe Just . . . Not Wade In?

We were taken with a 2019 *New York Times* essay by Smith College professor and activist Loretta J. Ross, who asked whether "today's call-out culture unifies or splinters social justice work, because it's not advancing us, either with allies or opponents . . . call-outs are justified to challenge provocateurs who deliberately hurt others, or for powerful people beyond our reach. Effectively criticizing such people is an important tactic for achieving justice. But most public shaming is horizontal and done by those who believe they have greater integrity or more sophisticated analyses."

As thoughtful, grown-up people, we need to be able to engage in discussion and handle debate. We don't have to do it all the time. But standing on the sidelines and yelling at the cloud and acting self-righteous isn't terribly useful to anyone. People on the internet who have been directly harmed are not on the hook to educate everyone else about what harmed them. But if you, a person who is not directly involved in whatever the current mess is, have the emotional space to take a friend or relative aside and do a little non-shame-y teaching about the topic at hand? Do that! It may feel empowering or exhilarating to leap into someone's mentions and start throwing virtual brickbats, but is that the most effective way to create real change?

Indeed, sometimes people just need a little leg up in understanding rather than a hectoring lecture by someone more interested in scoring virtue points than actually being helpful. To quote Ted Danson's character on *The Good Place*, "People improve when they get external love and support. How can we hold it against them when they don't?"

ACTION ITEMS

❑ **Be gracious in accepting apologies.** Don't tell the other person "No biggie" or "It's cool" if it clearly *is* an uncool biggie to them.

❑ **If the other person is capable of apologizing better, tell them.** (Perhaps by giving them this book.) Don't settle.

❑ **If someone is making a sincere effort to apologize, let them have the floor before you jump in and talk.** That's important whether you want to say you're sorry, too, or whether you want to tell them that you're considering forgiveness but aren't quite ready.

❑ **You needn't accept any apology right away.** You can tell the person apologizing that you need to think about it and get back to them.

❑ **Only you can decide if you're willing to forgive.** External pressure be damned! Talk to a friend or therapist if you're pondering forgiveness and want help clarifying your thoughts.

How to Get a Better Apology

Ask them to be specific about what they're apologizing for. "I can't tell if you're apologizing for TPing the neighbors or just for getting me arrested."

Tell them what you're displeased about. "It's not that you were late, it's that you didn't call. I don't care so much about the food getting overcooked, but I hate feeling that you don't care enough to respect our plans."

Call out creepy language. "Please don't say you're sorry *if* you hurt my feelings. You know you hurt my feelings. That's why you're apologizing, right?"

CHAPTER 9

"WHAT I SAID ON MY PRIVATE ISLAND WAS TAKEN OUT OF CONTEXT": AN EVISCERATION OF CELEBRITY APOLOGIES

Among the most teeth-gnashing parts of SorryWatching, for better and for worse, is being bombarded with godawful celebrity apologies.

Here's the chicken-or-egg question: Are celebrities worse at apologizing than normal people or are we just more aware of their bad apologies by virtue of their fame? Perhaps the issue is that their fans refuse to call them on their bullpucky? If Susan apologizes badly, her friends and family are likely to roll their eyes. When a famous person apologizes badly, people tell them (a) they did not have to apologize at all, and (b) they are brave and heroic for apologizing and they are totally forgiven! (Cue the Greek chorus of celebrity stans chanting, "You were young! You've changed! King! Kween!")

A 2006 study—conducted by media personality Dr. Drew Pinsky, who years later had to apologize for calling Covid-19 "a press-induced panic" and "way less serious than influenza," so maybe take this with a grain of salt—found that celebrities *are* more narcissistic than the general population. In collaboration with his colleague S. Mark Young, a professor of accounting, management, and communications (but not psychology) at USC, Pinsky found that reality TV personalities had the highest celebrity narcissism scores, followed by comedians, actors, and finally musicians. Length of time in the public eye wasn't correlated with narcissism, an indication, Pinsky says, that celebrities may have had narcissistic tendencies prior to becoming famous.

Pinsky's research method was to ask famous guests on his radio show *Loveline* to complete the Narcissism Personality Inventory, a long-established clinical tool. (In other words, he paired a useful self-assessment quiz with a methodologically suspect application.) Pinsky found that female celebrities were notably more narcissistic than male celebrities . . . but couldn't that be because they answered honestly the NPI's questions about their relative attractiveness? Female celebrities, particularly those who might be guests on *Loveline*, probably are more attractive than average! Acknowledging that isn't narcissism; it's truth.

Still, it makes sense that celebrities might be more self-absorbed than average. They're people who are drawn to the public eye; they're confident; they persevere in competitive environments that involve a lot of rejection. And since the folks who took Pinsky's survey were successful—judging from the fact that they were booked on his show—they've also experienced some of the perks of celebrity: adulation, money, free stuff. All this may make them more likely to believe in the Just World hypothesis. As we saw in chapter 4, a belief that life is fair is correlated with both privilege and faith in God's goodness. Celebrities may be confident that they deserve and have earned all that they've gotten, when in fact they've been lucky and/or benefited from privilege.

An illustration: When Black film executive Franklin Leonard wryly tweeted, "Hollywood's a meritocracy, right?" after an announcement about Steven Spielberg's daughter casting Sean Penn's son in a film written by Stephen King's offspring, Ben Stiller (son of Anne Meara and Jerry Stiller) replied, "Too easy . . . everyone has their path." When Leonard replied that the spawn of the famous perhaps take a different path than most, Stiller replied, "I would bet they all have faced challenges. Different than those with no access to the industry. Show biz as we all know is pretty rough, and ultimately is a meritocracy." Leonard followed up: "How do you explain the utter lack of diversity behind the camera? Lack of merit?" Stiller replied that diversity is "a much bigger issue." In actual fact, of course, it is the same issue: certain people are way more likely than others to get a shot because the playing field isn't level. Meritocracy, schmeritocracy.

Sorry You Don't Think I'm Marvelous, as I Do

Whether it's because of their innate attributes or the consequences of being famous, celebrities tend to be not great at taking responsibility for their bad behavior. Their first reaction to a call-out is usually to blame the press for reporting on whatever they did, a strategy that is not available to The Non-Famous. But when the evidence of their poorly considered conduct is incontrovertible, they may pivot to "I never claimed to be perfect" or "No one's perfect." (Funny how an inordinate number of terrible apologies contain the word "perfect." But apparently it can still be very hard to admit any *particular* instance of not being perfect.)

It's *true* that no one's perfect! It's a great point! One that does not belong in a great apology! On the one hand, yes, if we hold ourselves to a standard of utter crystalline perfection, we'll always fail, even if we're actually kind of superb. (Which we are! And we bet you are too!) We should all expect to make mistakes, no matter how hard we try. And if we know how to apologize for these mistakes, we're ahead of the game. However, when you yourself are called on the carpet for something, it is neither helpful nor non-weaselly to protest that no one's perfect. Acknowledging imperfection doesn't give us carte blanche to be a jerk; it also doesn't excuse us from having to examine our own behavior and make amends for it.

Bad Celebrity Apologies Are Enraging yet Often Fun

On SorryWatch, our most trafficked post is an apology from Reese Witherspoon in the aftermath of a DUI situation, which rapidly became a "Don't you know who I am" situation. When her husband was pulled over for driving drunk, Reese responded poorly and was ultimately charged with disorderly conduct. She later apologized: "I am deeply embarrassed about the things I said. It was definitely a scary situation and I was frightened for my husband, but that is no excuse. I was disrespectful to the officer who was just doing his job. The words I used that night definitely do not reflect who I am." *This is not who I am! It was scary, y'all!*

We're not sure why people keep clicking on that particular bad apology. (Do people really dislike Reese Witherspoon?) Regardless, she's hardly alone in generating SorryWatch site traffic. In general, our posts about bad apologies by celebrities, athletes, and politicians tend to get way more eyeballs than, say, our deep dives into literary or historical apologies or analyses of academic apology research. It's understandable: as a culture, we have a love-hate relationship with famous people, and there's something viscerally schadenfreude-y and delicious about the mighty being brought low. Still, mocking celebrities feels a bit like hitting low-hanging fruit with a mallet. The spatter is fun and cathartic, but can we really *learn* from it?

Then again, must everything be educational and nutritious? Can't it just be tasty, tasty intellectual junk food? Consider, for instance, a classic from the annals of celebrity history: Sharon Stone, in 2008, on the red carpet at Cannes. She was asked for her thoughts about an earthquake in China a few days earlier, which had claimed over seventy thousand lives. She responded that the Chinese "aren't being nice to the Dalai Lama, who is a good friend of mine." She continued, "And then all this earthquake and all this stuff happened, and I thought, 'Is that karma? When you're not nice, that the bad things happen to you?' "

When the "Sharon Stone said *what*?" karma hit the fan, Stone responded: "I misspoke. I could not be more regretful of that mistake. It was unintentional. I apologize. Those words were never meant to be hurtful to anyone. They were an accident of my distraction and a product of news sensationalism."

This is practically a complete Bad Apology Bingo card in only thirty-nine words. Please pick up your daubers and mark "misspoke," "regretful," "unintentional," "never meant," "anyone," "accident," "distraction," and "news sensationalism." Stone then compounded the badness with a statement to the *New York Times*: "I am deeply saddened that a 10-second poorly edited film clip has besmirched my reputation of over 20 years of charitable services on behalf of international charities." Again, blaming the media, but now with a bonus gloss of: I have been a saint for over twenty years and was *entrapped*.

See? Delicious in its terribleness.

To reiterate: a good apology is not All About You. Giving your narcissism free rein by blaming others, saying how you've suffered, touting your long record of being awesome, accusing people of not understanding your intentions—these behaviors cheapen any apology you manage to make and say more about your arrogance than your humility. Celeb or not, you need to keep the *recipient* of the apology foremost in your mind. What matters is the real victim's perception, not your heroic intentions.

Famously out of Touch with Reality

Let's say, for instance, that you are a celebrity wife from Massachusetts and sometimes imply that you are from Mallorca and sometimes speak in a Spanish accent and sometimes pretend to forget the English word for cucumber. When you semi-apologize poorly on Instagram for people being "confused," despite your seeking of "clarity," you trigger a second wave of mockery, and when your husband proceeds to defend you on his Twitter by making fun of a *different* celebrity's accent—one that, it turns out, is not fake at all—this triggers a third wave of mockery, and when your husband responds to *that* wave of mockery by deleting his Twitter account and calling the platform "where all the assholes in the United States and beyond go to get their advanced degrees in assholiness"—which is true—it triggers a fourth wave. Some people claim this cycle constitutes "cancel culture," despite the fact that your husband still makes a bazillion dollars a minute and your only personal consequence seems to be that your endorsement deal with a diaper company was terminated. Fortunately, you can afford to buy your own diapers.

This particular kind of celebrity apology is more of an explanation than a remorseful act. In this way it's like Plato's *Apology*. In Plato's recounting of Socrates's trial, Socrates says that he's been entrapped by malicious enemies, that he answers to divine authority rather than to flawed human jurisdiction, and that he's accused of corrupting students yet no student has testified against him. The Greek word ἀπολογία, "apologia," from which we get the word "apology," actually means a formal defense. When celebrities launch into prolonged explanations of why they said or did the apparently awful thing they said or did, and it seems as though they're really justifying their behavior rather than apologizing for it, one might say they're apologizing Platonically. Forthwith, you can also raise your eyebrow, on the inside of your brain if not visibly, when someone fancily uses the word "apologia" when they mean "apology." The words aren't synonymous.

We're now familiar with the genre of celebrity social media apology videos, which are so often wince inducing, and so often wince inducing in the same ways, that parodying them has become an entire comedy genre inevitably starting with "Heeeey, guys!" We're partial to the one by British comedian Harry Trevaldwyn, in which an influencer attempts to monetize an apology: "Hey, guys, I'm sure you've seen the news and what's happened. Thank you so much for giving me the time and space to tell my side of the story. . . . This jumper is from Zara and you can get 15 percent off if you use the code 'Apology15.' Now back to the murder. The *alleged* murder."

Then there's writer Lauren Bridges in the *New Yorker*'s "Shouts & Murmurs" humor column, parodying a real-life celebrity spin instructor (we live in times in which this is not an oxymoron) who jumped the line to get her Covid vaccine. "Hey, guys. There's been a lot of backlash about why I, an esteemed twenty-eight-year-old life-style Insta influencer, was able to get the covid-19 vaccine by calling myself a teacher. I'd like to sincerely apologize if I offended anyone. But I'd also like to say that I did nothing wrong. First of all, there should be no question that I am, in fact, a teacher. Have I not taught you, my one million followers, how to improve your style by posing in new outfits every day?"

Playwright Jeremy O. Harris offered up apologetic YouTuber mockery on Instagram: "Time to get to the half-assed apologies!" he sings out. "I literally can't even believe that you guys would interpret what I said as *that*. If you knew me, you would know there was a Black person in one of my classes one time!" Harris's character knows how the liturgical ritual works, explaining, "And then I turn off my comments and wait about two weeks for people to forget about what I did! It usually works because I'm white and pretty!"

Saturday Night Live excels at mocking very bad celebrity apologies. In 2020, Senator Ted Cruz, played by Aidy Bryant, told the public he was very sorry for abandoning frozen-solid Texas during a statewide crisis to go to Cancún with his family during the Covid pandemic. "I deeply regret my actions over the last couple of days—mostly flying United," he said. "I'm sorry, I'm pretty bad at human stuff." He blamed his daughters (as he did in reality), noting that they were really looking forward to "swimming with sick dolphins."

Our favorite *SNL* celeb apology parody involved Kyle Mooney playing a TikTok star and *Prank Posse* host who repeatedly goes viral for douchey activities that are "problematic and/or crimes." He apologizes, then does a new bad thing, like filming a video in which he drops a flat-screen TV on his friend (played by Daniel Kaaluya). To the accompaniment (again) of somber music, he says, "Hey, guys, I would like to take this opportunity to apologize for dropping a TV on JP's head." He goes on, sincerely, "I know a lot of you thought my last apology was insincere. You were right. I was lying. But this time I mean it. It was cool and it was funny, but it was wrong. That's why, out of respect, we are gonna delay the release of the 'tricking JP into kissing my penis' video until next Thursday." Jump-cut to another apology video for the penis-kissing-trick video.

Celeb apologies are easy to parody because of their same-sameness. A Twitter user who goes by Madame Novelette illustrated this with a composition called "Every Single Public Male Apology" (she graciously gave us permission to reproduce it here):

> *Hey everybody. Humble statement of confession to alleged wrongdoing. Immediate reiteration that from my perspective I was not doing anything wrong in that moment, but it's come to my attention that in fact my actions may have caused harm.*
>
> *It's crazy that I, in particular, would have made such an error in judgment, given what a good person I know myself to be. These actions which I took, usually repeatedly, do not represent the utterly blameless man I try so hard to embody.*
>
> *Uncomfortably personal, mostly unrelated anecdote about my own childhood trauma. I'm doing ok, even though this true accusation about my knowingly chosen behavior has triggered those painful memories.*
>
> *Statement about how this has been an experience of profound growth for me, and I'm so thankful for your support. Gentle insinuation that those who do not forgive me aren't yet as*

enlightened as I am, but I'm such a humblegood that I respect their decision, though I dream of a world where forgiveness is constant and evergreen.

Please congratulate me on this press release or humanity itself will suffer, because good men like me won't be inspired to apologize when they do something wrong. After all, what incentive will they have, if we don't teach them that apologies don't magically remove consequences?

Sincerely,
A Man

Where's the lie?

I'm Sorry You're Threatening My Endorsement Deals with Samurai Vapes and Cinnabon

Celebs rarely apologize in a vacuum. Sometimes they apologize so they can keep their endorsement deals, athletic eligibility, acting gigs. Sometimes they consciously choose not to apologize because not apologizing is their brand: politicians and talk show hosts who want to be perceived as tough and/or anti-woke will talk endlessly about their noble refusal to bow to pressure to apologize . . . which is less heroic when your fandom would be furious at you if you *did* apologize.

Whatever conceptual efforts we regular folks make to avoid apologizing, celebrities are even more likely to engage in. Because being famous is a mind-altering drug. Years ago, Marjorie gave her name to a maître d' at a fancy restaurant and was greeted with a gasp. "The writer?!" Marjorie was flattered. "Well, yes," she said modestly. She was immediately shown to a superb table and seated with great ceremony, even though she was a woman dining alone, a condition that often leads to sneering and being seated next to the bathroom. Marjorie saw the maître d' whispering to a server and pointing excitedly to her. The server came over to offer Marjorie still or sparkling water, and burst out, "I have to tell you we are such huge fans! We all love *Little House on the Prairie!*"

Marjorie had been mistaken for Laura Ingalls Wilder, who has been dead since 1957. But she is sorry that this mistake has not been made since, because being famous was intoxicating! The best table! Admiring glances! Probably free food if she'd had the forethought to say, "Thank you for so warmly welcoming me here from my pig-bladder-tossing time-travel adventures!"

And she would no longer have to write her own apologies. High on entitlement, famous people even have people who craft their apologies for being entitled. We will never *not* be obsessed with Ariana Grande's apology claiming that her public donut licking was designed to call attention to America's obesity epidemic. Normal human people would not come up with that. A raft of publicists and damage-control managers? Sure!

Grande's crisis management team was actually being serious. We can't say that about former baseball star Pete Rose, who was banned from the sport for betting on it when he was manager of the Cincinnati Reds and now makes his living autographing baseballs. A signed Pete Rose ball usually goes for $99.99, but for $299.99, Rose will write "I'm sorry I bet on baseball." Or "I'm sorry I broke up the Beatles" or "I'm sorry I shot JFK." At least the sarcasm is more honest than Grande's wide-eyed innocence. And people who buy those baseballs know exactly what they're getting, unlike whoever might have purchased Grande's spittle-flecked pastry.

Another Vile Apology from the Dust Heap of History

A truly gag-worthy apology belongs to the late Jerry Lewis. During a 2000 Q and A session, he was asked which female comics he admired.

He replied, "I don't like any female comedians." Martin Short, whom we believe to be a mensch—if he's not, don't tell us—tried to hand Lewis a paddle as the elderly gentleman ventured up Defecation Creek. Surely Lewis must have admired Lucille Ball, with whom he'd worked? "No," Lewis replied. "A woman doing comedy doesn't offend me but sets me back a bit. I, as a viewer, have trouble with it. I think of her as a producing machine that brings babies into the world."

This did not play in Peoria or anywhere else. *People* magazine wrote that the audience got up and left. Reporting on the story for Knight Ridder, Tom Sine noted, "Lewis ought to have realized long ago that a woman can produce a baby and a big joke at the same time. After all, his mother did it."

Lewis later issued a non-apology. "There are times when half statements get misinterpreted, and that's what happened at the Aspen U.S. Comedy Festival last week," he said. He explained that he believed that women are "incredibly strong people who deserve our undying respect" but that this didn't "sit right with the media," who have to "trash someone to make a deadline." In reality, he said, he admired Whoopi Goldberg, Elayne Boosler, and Phyllis Diller. "But when women, doing comedy, do routines written for them by drill sergeants, I take objection. Their filth makes me and many ashamed to be in our business." He was apologizing, he said, not because he'd done anything wrong—he hadn't—but because people might take it out on his beloved muscular dystrophy telethon. "My kids are innocent, and they deserve your care and goodwill. Please accept my humble apology, and let's get back to where we were." Think of the children!

Lewis was truly gifted at monstrous apologies. The next year, when people who used wheelchairs objected to Lewis's invoking viewers' pity to get donations for his telethon, Lewis snapped, "You don't want to be pitied because you're a cripple in a wheelchair? Stay in your house!" Wow, we can't imagine how that failed to placate anyone. He later clarified, "The statement I made on the May 20 CBS Morning Show was made in error. It is certainly not how I feel. I admire people with disabilities. That's why I've worked so hard for all these years." Why did he say it if it's not how he felt? Who knows? It probably went over really well in France.

Even Famous People Get It Right Now and Then

Terrible celebrity apologies can serve as a bonding opportunity: you and I may not be famous, but at least we're not clueless assholes. Mocking celebrities on social media can also be a potent performance opportunity. Leap into the fray and watch the "likes" roll in. Social media approval is addicting.

Good celebrity apologies are less fun than bad ones. They're the same as good normal-people apologies (albeit rarer): they use the word "apology" or "sorry" instead of "regret" or "error"; they're specific about what they did wrong; they acknowledge and own their wrongness instead of blaming the press or "haters"; they make clear that they know they've caused hurt; they explain the steps they're taking to ensure they won't make the same mistake again; they make amends if they can.

One example of a good apology is actress Florence Pugh's response on Instagram after being called out for culturally appropriative fashion choices in her past. She rambled and was sometimes cringey, but it was clear that she'd actually written the words; they didn't feel filtered by an army of handlers. She seemed to really want to do better; the apology felt authentic. She used the term "white fragility" about her past self, an indication that she was tuning in to the wider discourse. She told a story about showing off her "Corn Rows" to a friend who criticized them; she realized that by co-opting an aspect of Black culture as a fashion trend, she was participating in a process by which "Black culture was being so obviously exploited." She'd had her hands decorated with henna, think-

251 Getting to Sorry

ing, "I was an exception," because she had an Indian friend, but she wasn't an exception. She braided her hair and wore a Rasta cap and referenced Shaggy's "Boombastic." ("I am ashamed of so many things in those few sentences," she noted, and who can blame her? We're embarrassed just reading them. But she *did* note them, rather than eliding them in "an incident years ago when I was young.") "Stupid doesn't even cut it," she wrote of herself. "I was uneducated. I was unread." She concluded, "Black, Indian, Native American and Asian cultures and religions are constantly used and abused every new shopping season. It's not wrong to appreciate the beauty of a culture but rebranding them for the sake of a fashion trend and a $ most certainly is."

Is it a perfect apology? No. She says "sorry to all of you that were offended" (apologize to everyone, not just those offended) and doesn't quite seem to understand that her story of having "befriended" an Indian shop owner when she was eight doesn't mean that she and the shop owner were truly friends. (Hi, capitalism. Hi, white saviorism.) But she's legitimately trying here. She's clearly done some reading and listening. We at SorryWatch believe in education and redemption; being eager to point fingers without allowing someone—even someone famous—the chance to do better isn't helpful.

The People on Our Screens Are Not Our Friends!

Why do we care so much about celebrities and their apologies, anyway?

Thanks to social media, we can interact with famous folks in a more intimate way than previous generations did. Authors almost always respond to "I loved your book!" tweets; movie stars sometimes retweet a fan's song or joke; Instagram lets us join beloved singers in their kitchens. There aren't a ton of degrees of fame anymore. Reality stars are on the covers of magazines; people who create dances on TikTok or play *Magic: The Gathering* can get sponsorships. There's no studio system now, no

Hedda Hopper or Walter Winchell carefully crafting palatable, vetted narratives about starlets and himbos that kept fans of yore at arm's length but made them *feel* as though they were getting access. Now we really *do* have access. (And during an endless-seeming quarantine—resulting in massive amounts of TV watching and an explosion in popularity of Cameo, the app that lets us pay for personal messages from famous people—we sometimes felt we spent more time with famous people than with our actual friends.)

So when today's celebrities make us feel angry or hurt, we demand explanations. Then we pick their apologies apart like meat from a drumstick. But what's the utility? Why should we look to someone for moral leadership just because they're good at throwing balls? Why do we care when Kardashians and Jenners fight?

One-sided relationships with celebrities, known as parasocial relationships, aren't inherently a bad thing. They make us feel happy, engaged, connected. In a 2007 study, researchers found that the more media people consumed, the more they tended to form parasocial relationships with characters. The viewers didn't actually know the celebrities or the characters they played, but their feelings of connection were real. Is it so hard to believe, especially in a time period that kept us isolated far more than usual, that the consistency and regularity and appointment television-ness of our relationships inside an electronic box were meaningful to us? When we're adrift, shows can provide a sense of community and belonging. And research has shown that we actually gain the psychological benefits of friendship: comfort, ease, self-esteem. For those of us with some degree of social anxiety—again, the pandemic ramped up those feelings of discomfort and self-consciousness about being out in a group—our TV/video friends let us feel invested in relationships without the awkwardness, uncomfortable small talk, stress, and fears of rejection we can feel out in the "real world."

Finding our sense of connection through social media, though, may be less healthy. In 2017, University of Pittsburgh professor Brian Primack and his colleagues studied 1,787 subjects between the ages of nineteen and thirty-two. One group spent more than two hours a day on social media, the other a half hour or less. The heavy social media users felt twice as lonely as the light social media users. Another study, published in January 2020—a couple of months before the pandemic ramped up—found that 61 percent of American adults self-report that they sometimes or always feel lonely. Again, heavy social media use correlated with loneliness: 71 percent of heavy users, compared to 51 percent of light users, reported feeling lonely. Still another study offered a more nuanced picture of what kinds of social media use are harmful to our sense of well-being. It found that "positive interactions, social support, and social connectedness" on social media lessened depression and anxiety, but negative interactions and "social comparisons"— comparing yourself to others (their looks, their perceived happiness levels, their success)—on social media were related to higher levels of depression and anxiety.

And remember, Facebook is eager to provide content you'll interact negatively with; bad feelings mean greater engagement and more time spent on the site. It's no accident that Instagram makes us feel crappy about our bodies and social lives even though we know that everyone else is curating their feed to look happier and hotter, and that even famous people are using filters, trickery, and facial fillers to look better. As a Facebook whistleblower noted in 2021, Instagram consistently exacerbates young people's mental health issues and eating disorders, but its powerful algorithms are designed to keep you scrolling on through.

Time for the Dive into Cancellation!

When we tip too far into celebrity culture, we're not only overly committed to famous folks being our buddies but also overly committed to believing that those we stan have no faults. When they do screw up, as humans all do, we tend to excuse their failings: "He had no idea what that antisemitic slur meant! Those syllables just popped out of his face!" "He only implied that his costar is a whore because he was exhausted from doing the press tour!" "Those girls are all false accusers out to make a buck!"

First and most important: when a celebrity does something that causes people—particularly marginalized people—to feel disrespected or harmed, fans do not have the authority to dismiss those concerns on the grounds of "he would never do that" and/or "people are too sensitive."

Let's remember that people all over the political spectrum can be jerks, and social media exacerbates it. Sometimes the person under fire is racist, homophobic, transphobic, misogynistic, antisemitic. Sometimes the person *doing* the attacking is racist, homophobic, transphobic, misogynistic, antisemitic. (One member of Team SorryWatch has been told more than once on Twitter to "get in the oven.") People on the left and on the right can both be execrable on social media. The question for all of us playing along at home is whether we're doing anything of value when we wade into a social media fray. Are we merely showing off how highly evolved we are? Might our attention be better spent in meaningful service to the causes we care about?

It must be said, however, that although people of all political persuasions go on social media rampages, the right has been far better at *actual* cancellation. For example, in 2020, the last year for which American Library Association stats were available, the list of the most frequently banned and challenged books consisted of seven books objected to by people with a right-wing perspective and two objected to by those with a left-wing perspective. The right attempted to ban or challenge three young adult books (*Stamped: Racism, Antiracism, and You* by Jason Reynolds, adapted from *Stamped from the Beginning* by Ibram X. Kendi; *All*

American Boys by Jason Reynolds and Brendan Kiely; and *The Hate U Give* by Angie Thomas) and a picture book (*Something Happened in Our Town: A Child's Story of Racial Injustice* by Marianne Celano, Marietta Collins, and Ann Hazzard, illustrated by Jennifer Zivoin) that depict police brutality; a young adult book (*Speak* by Laurie Halse Anderson) about a rape that was deemed "biased against male students"; a book about a trans kid (*George*—now retitled *Melissa*—by Alex Gino) accused of "not reflecting the values of our community"; and a book for adults (*The Bluest Eye* by Toni Morrison) deemed "sexually explicit" and objectionable for depicting child sexual abuse. The left attempted to ban or challenge two books for racial slurs and racist depictions: *Of Mice and Men* by John Steinbeck and *To Kill a Mockingbird* by Harper Lee. One book has the great honor of being banned and challenged from both the left *and* the right (great work, everyone!): *The Absolutely True Diary of a Part-Time Indian* by Sherman Alexie. Conservatives objected to its references to masturbation, "profanity and sexual references"; liberals objected to dozens of accusations of sexual misconduct against the author.

Look, we could talk all day about the intricacies of book bans and challenges, but for our apology-related purposes, let's merely note that despite the right's fondness for words like "cancellation," "wokeness," "heresy," "Orwellian," "tyranny," "mobs," silencing," "orthodoxy," "shamed," and "McCarthyism," the stats tell a different story. We've just seen that by a score of 7 to 2, the right is far more prone to "cancellation" than the left. And of course, the right is also far more likely to cancel people in a far more literal way: driving cars into protesters; storming the Capitol; plotting to kidnap a governor; and shooting up mosques, Black churches, synagogues, and massage parlors employing Asian women.

What are the consequences of "cancellation," anyway? Can a good apology forestall it? Does it matter? (We are speaking here of the "Don't buy this book" and "Don't see this guy's movies" kinds of cancellation, not the murder kind of cancellation.) It's worth noting that the vast majority of people who go viral for lousy apologies—and who spark calls for cancellation—are famous and powerful. In general, no one outside our immediate circle of fellow nobodies really cares when we mere mortals apologize poorly. The exception is when a nobody has been caught on video saying or doing something horrifying, then uses the apology to muck things up even further. If, say, you are a light-skinned woman who screamingly accuses and attacks a brown teenager in the lobby of a hotel where he is a guest (and you are not), shrieking that he stole the iPhone that you actually left in an Uber, and then you apologize by saying, "I don't feel that that is who I am as a person. I don't feel like this one mistake does define me. But I do sincerely from the bottom of my heart apologize that if I made [the kid] feel as if I assaulted him or if I hurt his feelings or the father's feelings," and then you say, "Okay, I apologize, can we move on?"—well, you deserve all the snark that is aimed at you.

For most celebs, vast depths of bad behavior and vast quantities of bad apologies still have minimal long-term effects. Mel Gibson was not canceled for his drunken, antisemitic tirades and physical abuse of his partner, followed by his "Hey, sorry my drunk mouth said things sober me totally doesn't believe" apology. He's still making movies. Dolce & Gabbana's clothes are all over red carpets around the world, despite the company's history of anti-Asian racism and tepid apologies. J. K. Rowling, despite online claims that she's transphobic, still rakes in big movie, merch, and amusement park bucks. Louis C.K. is touring, doing stand-up about the perils of "political correctness." True cancellation of a famous person is rare indeed.

Here's some overarching advice: Just forget celebrities as behavioral touchstones. Celebrities are not good to emulate.

The Five Worst Celebrity Apologies, Which Are So Bad, They Are Way Too Long for a Sidebar, but Oh Well

1. In 2017, disgraced movie mogul Harvey Weinstein (who will now always be known as Disgraced Movie Mogul Harvey Weinstein), accused of sexual assault, harassment, or rape by more than eighty women, responded, "I came of age in the '60s and '70s, when all the rules about behavior and workplaces were different. That was the culture then." Yet somehow many men of this era managed not to rape anyone! "I have since learned it's not an excuse, in the office—or out of it. I realized some time ago that I needed to be a better person, and my interactions with the people I work with have changed. I appreciate the way I've behaved with colleagues in the past has caused a lot of pain, and I sincerely apologize for it." He appreciates it now! Also note the term "colleagues" as opposed to "young women with far less power who depended on him for income"! "My journey now will be to learn about myself and conquer my demons." A champion! "I so respect all women and regret what happened." Ah, the ever-ambiguous "what happened." "I cannot be more remorseful about the people I hurt and I plan to do right by all of them." Doubtful. "I am going to need a place to channel that anger, so I've decided that I'm going to give the NRA my full attention. I hope Wayne LaPierre will enjoy his retirement party. I'm going to do it at the same place I had my Bar Mitzvah." Ha, jokes! Japery!

"I'm making a movie about our President, perhaps we can make it a joint retirement party." Nice rhetorical strategy, mentioning two men he wants to remind people might be worse than he is. "One year ago, I began organizing a $5 million foundation to give scholarships to women directors at USC. While this might seem coincidental, it has been in the works for a year. It will be named after my mom, and I won't disappoint her." See, he loves women! And respects them! Especially his mother!

2. Then there's Lena Dunham. The apology that lands her on this list—though she's had to apologize for a bunch of things—occurred after a friend and cowriter on her show *Girls* faced allegations of sexually assaulting a seventeen-year-old. Dunham issued a statement with her show's cocreator saying that the accuser was lying. "While our first instinct is to listen to every woman's story, our insider knowledge of Murray's situation makes us confident that sadly this accusation is one of the 3 percent of assault cases that are misreported every year," she wrote. "Misreported" is a nice touch, arguably blaming the media rather than the young woman making the accusation. Dunham's statement did not go over well, and she decided to walk it back. She tweeted, "I naively believed it was important to share my perspective on my friend's situation. . . . I now understand that it was absolutely the wrong time to come forward with such a statement and I am so sorry." Did she really think the problem was the *timing*? "Every woman who comes forward deserves to be heard fully and completely, and our relationship with the accused should not be part of the calculation anyone makes when examining her case." In other words, we should listen to women's

accusations as a matter of politeness and policy, even when we *know* our friend didn't do it. She concluded, "We apologize to any women who have been disappointed." Any women! What about the one specific woman she maligned? Not so much.

3. And how can we ignore Mario Batali, who, after four women who worked for him accused him of groping them, initially seemed to blame the notion of *merriment*. "We built these restaurants so that our guests could have fun and indulge, but I took that too far in my own behavior," he said. He was just having fun, you guys! When an additional five women accused him of sexual assault, he issued another statement: "As many of you know, this week there has been some news coverage about some of my past behavior. I have made many mistakes and I am so very sorry that I have disappointed my friends, my family, my fans, and my team. . . . I will work every day to regain your respect and trust." No apologies to the women in question, of course. "PS. In case you're searching for a holiday-inspired breakfast, these Pizza Dough Cinnamon Rolls are a fan favorite." Nothing like a recipe to spice up one's response to sex crime accusations! Adding insult to injury, the Pizza Dough Cinnamon Rolls are apparently terrible.

4. It's typical for an abuser to play the card of being abused. After being arrested in 2009 for beating up Rihanna, Chris Brown offered an apology statement: "Words cannot begin to express how sorry and saddened I am over what transpired." "What transpired"? That could be anything. Spilling cereal. The Packers losing the Super Bowl. "I am seeking the counseling of my pastor, my mother and other loved ones and I am committed, with

God's help, to emerging a better person. . . . Much of what has been speculated or reported on blogs and/or reported in the media is wrong." He has religion and a mom, so he's going to be okay! And whatever you think he did, he didn't, because media. In a successive apology video, Brown said he was sorry about "those few moments," about "what I've done," about "the situation," about "what happened," and about "my mistake." Only once does he actually use the term "domestic violence," and it's when he is mentioning the domestic violence that *he* witnessed growing up. "I have let a lot of people down, and I realize that," he said. "Nobody is more disappointed in me than I am." Rihanna might be.

But even that tepid apology was apparently too much apology for Brown. In 2011 he told *Page Six*, "At the end of the day, if I walk around apologizing to everybody, I'm gonna look like a damn fool." He also tweeted, "I'm so over people bringing this past shit up!!! Yet we praise Charlie Sheen and other celebs for there bullshit." (We really do not praise Charlie Sheen, who was fired from *Two and a Half Men* that year, but okay.) When asked about the incident in 2011 on *GMA*, Brown picked up a chair and smashed a window; shards of glass fell onto Forty-Third Street and Broadway. He later apologized with "I want to apologize to anybody who was startled in the office or anybody who was offended or really looked disappointed at my actions, because I was disappointed in the way I acted. I kept my composure and did my performance, and when I got back, I just let off like steam. I didn't try to hurt anyone, I just wanted to release, just the anger that I had inside me." There were more abuse allegations from more women over the years, and more apologies, but, honestly, we're done here.

5. One of the five worst apologies hasn't happened yet. Sadly, we wait.

ACTION ITEMS

❑ **Teach kids not to indiscriminately idolize celebrities.** Instead, offer them examples of real heroes in the community, in activism, and in the wider world. For a performer or athlete to be a hero, they should do something that benefits the world apart from being good at their job.

❑ **Try to spend less time on social media.** Send emails, write post-cards, pick up the phone. Start a mailing list for your former high school class rather than idly sharing data about yourself hither and yon.

❑ **Think before you type.** Before joining in on a celebrity social media pile-on, consider whether there are less performative, more concrete actions you can take to help whatever communities are affected by the celebrity's dumb or toxic actions.

❑ **There are no guilty pleasures.** All this said, please don't feel bad for enjoying bad celebrity apologies or gossiping about famous people's private lives. Such things are a nice distraction in a scary world. Just consider when you're getting too invested, you know?

Influencer Apology Mad Libs

Hey, guys! It's me. So I just wanted to _____ (verb) about the _____ (noun) that's been going around. I need to be real with you guys because you're my _____ (plural noun). You guys, I am emotionally _____ (adjective). The incident that happened was _____ (adjective) and I really wish I could go back in time but _____ (self-exculpatory phrase). If I didn't have _____ (product) right now, I don't know what I'd do. Swipe up to learn more! Aw, I _____ (verb) my puppers. Anyhoo, I now realize _____ (vague cliché) and want to apologize to anyone who has been touched by _____(noun). My own history of _____ (negative noun) should have made me more _____ (adjective). The world we live in is _____ (adjective) and my goal is always to _____ (verb). I really appreciate your _____ (noun) and_____ (body part). I am _____ (adverb) _____ (adjective) of myself and I will be better. I love you guys; thank you so much for manifesting _____ (noun). _____ (adjective) vibes!

BAD APOLOGY BINGO CARD #6
CELEBRITY EDITION!

the Hollywood machine	my art	boundary pushing	edgy	my heart goes out to
old tweet resurfaced	the role of comedy	use my platform	as an artist	in a private moment
I got into this business	born in an era	**FREE SQUARE**	my younger self	my entire career has been about
push the envelope	satire	my [Black/ gay/lady] friend wasn't upset	meant in jest	lynch
fighting my demons	gift	positivity	The First Amendment	the media

GIRL, STOP APOLOGIZING, OR MAYBE DON'T, UGH, IT'S COMPLICATED: GENDER, RACE, AND POWER

You know the stereotype. You've heard it a million times. Women apologize too much. Women simply cannot stop apologizing. If you look at a woman sideways, she apologizes. If you drop an anvil on her, she says she's sorry to the anvil. Don't forget to lock your door at night, because otherwise an apologizing woman will tiptoe abjectly in. Female apologies are an epidemic! They're a disease! They're a sign of weakness; they're a girlie vocal tic! They're like *uptaaaalk?* And *vocal fryyyyyy?* They harm women in the workplace, turn women into doormats, sap women's authority, make women shrink into tiny sad shriveled things like wool sweaters accidentally washed in hot water.

Yikes.

As with most sweeping generalizations and proscriptions, the situation's a lot more nuanced than that.

Let's get this out of the way first: women do apologize more than men. There's a ton of social science research backing this statement up. In isolation, though, all those studies don't tell you much. The knottier questions: *Why* do women apologize more than men? And what would happen if they didn't?

To begin, let's look at two small, creatively designed studies by

Karina Schumann and Michael Ross, psychologists at the University of Waterloo. They published "Why Women Apologize More Than Men: Gender Differences in Thresholds for Perceiving Offensive Behavior" in the journal *Psychological Science* in 2010.

Two Studies, One Result

Both studies found that men apologize less than women because men simply don't feel their conduct is so bad. They have a much higher threshold for what constitutes an apology-worthy offense. And lest we roll our eyes at men doing their annoying men things, it's worth noting that men also don't feel they're as *deserving* of apologies compared to women. They tend to view not only their own transgressions but also transgressions committed *against* them way less severely than women view these transgressions. *However,* when men *do* feel they've done something wrong, they're just as likely to apologize as women. Men and women both apologized for 81 percent of the offenses they felt warranted an apology, and men and women both apologized with equal intensity. The difference, again, is that men were way, way more likely to think they'd done nothing wrong.

In other words, the commonly held view (by women) of men as stubborn jackasses who simply refuse to apologize despite knowing that they've screwed up is incorrect. Perhaps men aren't deliberately rationalizing away their bad behavior like recalcitrant toddlers; men really, truly don't think they need to apologize. Bless their hearts.

Knowing that men sail through life not understanding that they've hurt people but also genuinely not feeling hurt themselves means they're not deliberately being obtuse. Which is a relief? But what the study *doesn't* look at is *why* men are less offended than women and *why* they're less likely to believe their behavior is offensive.

Why Do Men Take Less Offense Than Women?

SorryWatch's supposition: Men live in a way comfier place in the world than women do. They're challenged less often on their conduct than women are. Strictures about what constitutes politeness and what behaviors are acceptable are less . . . well, *strict* for men than for women. Men live in a world that's built for them: many pharmaceuticals are tested only on them, lest women's girlie hormones and pregnancies cloud the data. Crash test dummies come in manly sizes, leading to more women being killed in car crashes because their seat belts don't fit right. Smartphones fit big ol' man hands better, leading women to text things like "{Gwt DORTOS I', Starvimg~" (actual text received by Marjorie from a non-drunk human woman).

Men, particularly men of a certain race and class, can be blithe about fairness and justice more easily than women can, because as far as they're concerned, the world is mostly fair and just. And unfortunately, a culture that gives preference to male experience and male ways of being hurts men as well as women. As the feminist critic Jude Ellison (formerly Sady) Doyle put it, "This is just how sexism works: When we privilege men's voices and perspectives over women's, men naturally develop an inflated idea of their own intelligence or skill. They're biking with training wheels and they think they're winning the Tour de France." As the world becomes fairer, the guys who most believe things were just fine as they were are the ones who are going to have the worst time. (We choose to believe the world is changing for the better because we are optimists who see change happening in the justice system, workforce, and Disney World where they got rid of the rapey pirates in the Caribbean.)

Let's get more granular about how women and men apologize. In *Sorry About That: The Language of Public Apology*, Edwin L. Battistella discusses the research of linguist Janet Holmes. In one paper she examined

183 apologies and found that women apologized three times as much as men and tended to apologize more to other women—particularly their female friends—than they did to men. Men, on the other hand, apologized much more often to women than they did to other men. (Fully two-thirds of the men's apologies were to women.) Holmes concluded that men see apologies as "face-threatening acts . . . to be avoided where possible," while women see them as "other-oriented" acts "aimed at facilitating social harmony." Men seem to be less threatened by apologizing to women than they are to other men; they apparently view apologies to women as less of a loss of face. Hmph.

Much of the research on gender and apology dovetails with research on gender and teasing. Women find teasing in romantic relationships much more distressing than men do. Even when men think they're being affectionate or funny with their teasing, women are much more likely than men to feel hurt or angry. And when studies were designed in which women were supposed to *be* the teasers, they rated their own behavior as far more offensive than men did.

The default in this society is male, a fact that men sometimes forget or may not understand. When women are told to forgive, to forget about it, to lighten up, to *jeez, stop taking this so seriously* . . . they're just taking the thing more seriously than men do. Why does that make it *too* seriously? Why do men get to establish the default? Rather than saying, "Women are overly sensitive to the emotional states of other people," what if we presented study findings as "Men aren't sensitive *enough* to the emotional states of other people"?

Women don't want to be taunted, and they don't want others to be taunted. It's odd that this is considered weak or aberrant when what it is is kind. It's also a reflection of how women are socialized in our society: they're expected to monitor others' feelings, to be aware of nuances and tiny aggressions, to do the emotional labor of being in society with others. (And then they're criticized for doing precisely what they've been socialized to do. Joy.) This all jibes with research showing that women consistently report more guilt after committing transgressions than men do. They also feel greater empathy for victims of violence and crime and are more willing to forgive wrongdoing aimed at them. Are women inherently nicer, or are women more socialized to forgive? Does it matter, since there's no way to tease those two things apart while we marinate in the culture we all marinate in?

We've discussed the fact that powerful people are more likely to have Just World bias. They're doing well, and they're good people, so they clearly *deserve* to do well, and people who do less well surely must be at fault for not achieving as much. We're not saying that this applies to many straight white Christian men, but, y'know, if the popped collar fits . . .

We also think that some women who grew up with difficult parents learned to be placating as a survival strategy. When you're perpetually worried that a parent will fly off the handle or launch into narcissistic wailing, you grow up on tenterhooks. You may respond to the fear of violence or manipulation with knee-jerk and/or incessant apologies and continue to do so well into adulthood, even when the threat is no longer present. Men who grew up with difficult parents seem less likely to choose reflexive apology; they're more apt to withdraw or lash out in response.

Women who grew up in chaos may also tend to apologize for things that aren't their fault and for the behavior of others in the past or present. Same goes for women who are or were partnered with difficult people: they apologize *for* the partner or *instead of* the partner, whether or not the partner is present. While we don't think this phenomenon applies to *most* women, we do think it's real. We think we've been apologized to by some of those women. For no reason! We love you, we value you, and you don't have to apologize for anyone else or for who you are.

Manly-Man and Girlie-Girl Offenses and Their Corresponding Apologies

There's plenty of evidence that the rules of apology and forgiveness are different for women than for men. A 2016 study by researchers at York University in Toronto, published in the *Journal of Management Development*, looked at how difficult it was for men and women to earn back trust after a misdeed. When women commit an offense that defies gender stereotypes, they experience a "double backlash," in the words of the study authors, Shayna Frawley and Jennifer A. Harrison. Because women are supposed to put others first, in both the workplace and in politics, while men are supposed to be competitive and independent, women are punished more for not hewing to the way women are "supposed" to act. They get a double whammy for not conforming to societal expectations.

"With the Hillary Clinton email scandal, her critics were claiming she put national security at risk for her own convenience, putting her own needs ahead of her responsibility as a public official," Frawley explained. "This is a clear example of breaking trust and gender expectations." The office parallel: if a woman violates her colleagues' trust by doing something ethically shady or acting in a way that makes others perceive her as "not a team player," it's far harder for her to regain trust than if she'd done something that indicated she was merely underperforming at her job. But men aren't *expected* to put others first. If they aren't helpful to a coworker or if they make a coworker look bad, they don't experience the same sort of trust consequences.

It's not all roses and office birthday cake for men, either, though: men are judged more harshly for underperformance, since they're supposed to dominate on the metrics of pure achievement. It's fine if they're not collaborative—no penalties there. It's *not* fine if they actually screw up. Unlike women, who are more likely to get second chances, because women are *expected* to screw up—silly things that they are, always thinking about Louboutins and whatnot.

This dichotomy, incidentally, is why Donald Trump was repeatedly furious about measurements in which he was found wanting, such as indications that his inaugural crowd size was smaller than Barack Obama's or the particulars of his declarations of bankruptcy. "What these claims are trying to get at is that despite Trump's reputation and his connections, he's not performing so well at things that men traditionally are viewed at being good at," Frawley stated. "They were saying he can't be trusted to perform well . . . which plays into gender stereotypes."

This Is Why We Say "Toxic Masculinity Hurts Everyone"

Apologizing is viewed as weak and feminine by men who are focused on hypermasculinity. (The actor Jim Belushi's memoir-meets-self-help-book is called *Real Men Don't Apologize*; the title is depicted as a tattoo on Belushi's flexed biceps, because of course it is.) And indeed, apologizing can be harmful to men. It's especially bad for men when they're dealing with other men who value gender stereotypes. If a man breaks the public trust in a way that squares with gender stereotypes—say, if he cheats on his wife or leers at or grabs other women—the male offender is unlikely to irk the kind of folks who view his behavior as "Boys will be boys." In fact, being seen as "weak" would be riskier for him in terms of helping him regain lost trust.

Apologizing, some researchers say, can prove helpful to men when they're perceived as taking responsibility. But as you know by now, we at SorryWatch feel that a preponderance of apologies out there fail to do that. It's arguably the hardest part of apologizing, and the reason for all the use of passive voice, victim blaming, lack of specificity, and excuses in so many apologies. And as we discussed earlier, crappy apologies almost invariably do more harm than good.

Finally, Frawley and Harrison note that much gender stereotyping around issues of trust is unconscious. *Of course* women shouldn't be penalized more than men for hogging credit, and *of course* men shouldn't be penalized more than women for making a mistake. But that's not how the world works. At least, not right now. In short, apologies are inherently gendered, and studies that fail to examine the role of gender in apologies are flawed studies.

Our takeaway: when women apologize, it's often a necessary strategy in the way it isn't for men. When women *don't* come off as tentative and self-effacing, they're called bitches. Apologizing—like uptalk, like vocal fry—are attempts, sometimes unconscious ones, to seem approachable and humble. Which, again, are often important tools for women in a world that posits maleness as the default. When experts opine about how apologizing undermines women's gravitas, they're not being fair, because women are judged on entirely different metrics from men.

Alexandra Petri, the *Washington Post*'s brilliant humor columnist, parodied the apologetic quality of female speech by showing how famous orations by men would sound if delivered by women. Patrick Henry's "Give me liberty or give me death!" would become "Dave, if I could, I could just—I just really feel like if we had liberty it would be terrific, and the alternative would just be awful, you know? That's just how it strikes me. I don't know." The biblical Moses's "Let my people go!" would come out, "Pharaoh, listen, I totally hear where you're coming from on this. I totally do. And I don't want to butt in if you've come to a decision here, but, just, I have to say, would you consider that an argument for maybe releasing these people could conceivably have merit? Or is that already off the table?"

It's funny because it's true.

Sort of.

More evidence that the apology-related playing field is different for women: women are much more frequently interrupted than men. Men perceive women as dominating a conversation when they speak 30 percent of the time. A 2017 study found that men in academia gave 69 percent of colloquium studies, while women gave 31 percent. Perhaps this is why so many female comics joke about systemic inequities: it's a good way to keep from crying. It's also a good way for women to bond and acknowledge shared experience. Exaggeration is funny and a good way to cope with the fact that the rules of communication are different for women than for men, and this is frustrating. Ah, life, she is a rich pageant!

It would be fabulous if women could always simply be direct, if they could always simply speak their minds and be heard and listened to. But we do not live in that idyllic world. Whatever coping strategies help folks of any gender make it through the day without throwing hands are legit coping strategies. Blaming women and gender-nonconforming folks for trying various work-arounds in a sexist culture is blaming the victim.

We're reminded of the knee-jerk editorializing that women are underpaid because they fail to compare salaries with colleagues and with others in their industry and because they don't ask for raises. Oh, these foolish women, undervaluing themselves! As it turns out, NOPE! BIG LIE! Actual science has found that women *do* ask for raises; they just don't *get* them. A 2017 study of more than 4,600 people conducted by researchers in the United States and the UK found that women are just as likely to negotiate promotions and raises as men are. But the study—called "Do Women Ask?"—found that women were simply more likely to be turned down.

Look, we are not saying that we know that a particular man at one of our previous workplaces was getting paid more than twice what one of us was getting paid for doing less work, but we're not NOT saying that.

I'm Sorry I'm Rejecting You; Please Don't Be Scary About It

Another way in which apologies function differently for women than for men has to do with rejection. Women spend a lot of time worrying about men's hurt feelings, because the consequences of men feeling hurt can range from sulking to retaliation. We're obliged to remind you of that Margaret Atwood quote: "Men are afraid women will laugh at them. Women are afraid men will kill them."

And it seems that, yep, again, women are damned if they do and damned if they don't. A 2017 study by researchers at Dartmouth and UT Austin, "When Saying Sorry May Not Help: The Impact of Apologies on Social Rejections," published in the journal *Frontiers in Psychology*, found that when social rejections—like "I don't want to go on a date with you"—are accompanied by apologies, the rejected party doesn't admit to feeling hurt but feels angrier than if the rejection *hadn't* been accompanied by an apology. The rejected person who *receives* an apology—"I'm sorry, I don't want to date you"—feels more compelled to express forgiveness than the person who didn't get an apology, even if they don't feel forgiving. Women's concerns about the impact of rejections are clearly well-founded.

The conclusions here are dismaying, especially because the study was so clever and well done. It was constructed with a gender-neutral person as the target. Participants got to choose how much hot sauce to force Taylor to ingest—knowing that Taylor did not like hot sauce—each time Taylor rejected them. When participants received an apology, they dosed Tayor harder with hot sauce than when they didn't get an apology. "As predicted, rejections that contained the words 'I'm sorry' led to worse outcomes than rejections without apologies," the researchers said. The theory is that people are angrier when you apologize because they know they're *supposed* to forgive you, and they don't want to, so—consciously or not—they feel even more punitive.

To embroider on this finding: women are supposed to be nice and let men down gently, but when they do, unbeknownst to them, men are actually angrier than if they hadn't said "I'm sorry" at all. The authors noted, "The devastating consequences of social rejection highlight the value in understanding ways in which to soften the blow. Together, the findings provide a first step in evidence-based advice for how to socially reject someone in a less damaging way."

But SorryWatch's reaction, again: Why is it on the shoulders of the party who says "No" to make the rejected party feel less vindictive and hot-sauce-squirty? Why are the no-sayers responsible for the other person's feelings when they simply express their own preference? In a real-world situation, is it coincidence that feeling spurned by women is a thing that makes men shoot people? *Why is that responsibility on women??*

Women should not have to focus their attention on whether apologizing or not apologizing for not wanting to go on a date will make men angry. Why aren't we focusing our academic, interpersonal, and political attention on fixing the angry people rather than the women who reject them? (Don't answer that. We all know the answer already.) Here at Team SorryWatch, our central focus is crafting better apologies, not suggesting ways to lessen the impact of toxic masculinity on our culture, because we don't want to write a book that's one million pages long. There are many other fine books that address how-tos for creating a more just, feminist, and ethical world (get yourself a copy of *Man Up: Reimagining Modern Manhood* by Carlos Andrés Gómez; *Asking for It: The Alarming Rise of Rape Culture—and What We Can Do About It* by Kate Harding; *Rage Becomes Her: The Power of Women's Anger* by Soraya Chemaly; *The Will to Change: Men, Masculinity, and Love* by bell hooks; *The Descent of Man* by Grayson Perry . . . We could go on, but as the saying goes, the lightbulb has to *want* to change). From a pure apology perspective, if we all focus on tuning in to our gender biases about apologies and observing how the rules differ depending on who's apologizing, we'd all be better off. A journey of a thousand miles begins with a single step, and cluefulness is the first step in this particular journey.

Sorry, Sorry, Sorry: The Case for Good Apologies is about addressing the real world we live in right now as well as about instilling hope for the future. So let's look at whether women should apologize for their offenses, and how. Apologizing, for all genders, can be an attempt to forestall the consequences of a mistake. But for women, the consequences of making a mistake are often far worse than they are for men. The aftermath of a major social error, for instance, often leads to harsher and more lasting consequences for the ladyfolk.

What a Shock: Women Are Far Less Likely to Be Forgiven for Their Offenses

Many of us have read Jon Ronson's witty *So You've Been Publicly Shamed*, about the cruelty of social media. It was published back in the Pleistocene era, meaning early 2015, before we even knew the term "cancel culture." Today, the list of people Ronson profiled is instructive. Many of the purportedly shamed men in the book have bounced back, like the two developers who told a sexist joke at a public conference. They experienced temporary career setbacks but wound up getting rehired for more money elsewhere. The woman who took *offense* at the joke, on the other hand, wound up losing her career. She made the unforgivable error of calling attention to toxic bro culture.

In *So You've Been Publicly Shamed*, the man who gets the most ink is journalist and author Jonah Lehrer, who fabricated quotes in a book about Bob Dylan and initially lied about it and repeatedly self-plagiarized in his work for the *New Yorker*, *Wired*, and other publications. He was also accused of inventing anecdotes. Lots. As he said years later on the *Moth*, what he'd done was "breaking the most basic rule of journalism: Don't make shit up."

Sure, dude got mocked on the internet, and his publisher withdrew two of his books from circulation. But wasn't a bit of mockery, you know, reasonable? And did it even matter, when Lehrer ultimately got another hefty book deal? The consequences to him were not exactly dire.

The *woman* Ronson devotes the most time to, on the other hand, is publicist Justine Sacco. You remember her. In 2014 she tweeted a joke as she sat down on a plane: "Going to Africa. Hope I don't get AIDS. Just kidding. I'm white!" Undeniably this joke was in bad taste. It also wasn't funny. (Jokes that are designed to shock but that are clear in their sympathies for the powerless *can* be funny. Do a search for Wanda Sykes's routine about wishing she had a detachable vagina.)

Sacco was, we think, attempting to point out a disparity. She was trying to mock the kind of comfortable white women who say racist things blithely, who don't understand the depth of the privilege they have. But her attempt at social commentary failed abysmally. By the time her plane landed, her career had self-destructed and she was getting death threats. The fact that she apologized quite well didn't matter. Here's the apology:

> *Words cannot express how sorry I am, and how necessary it is for me to apologize to the people of South Africa, who I have offended due to a needless and careless tweet. There is an AIDS crisis taking place in this country, that we read about in America, but do not live with or face on a continuous basis. Unfortunately, it is terribly easy to be cavalier about an epidemic that one has never witnessed firsthand.*
>
> *For being insensitive to this crisis—which does not discriminate by race, gender or sexual orientation, but which terrifies us all uniformly—and to the millions of people living with the virus, I am ashamed.*

This hits almost all our elements of a good apology: Sacco says "I'm sorry" instead of "I regret." She takes responsibility. She doesn't make excuses. She shows she understands the impact of her words. She doesn't make amends . . . but how on earth would she do that authentically in a public statement? If she'd said, "I've made a donation to the AIDS Foundation of South Africa," people would've seen it as a play for sympathy from a craven, manipulative little bitch. Sacco also failed to repeat precisely what it was she said, but in her case it probably wasn't necessary: *everyone knew.* It was all anyone on social media could talk about. There were hashtags—#HasJustineLandedYet—as people salivated over her inevitable comeuppance.

Sacco told Ronson later, "I had no business commenting on the epidemic in such a politically incorrect manner on a public platform. . . . Living in America puts us in a bit of a bubble when it comes to what is going on in the third world. I was making fun of that bubble." Again: She did not do this well. (And we hate the term "politically correct.") Again: It was not a good joke.

But let's compare the sins of Sacco and Lehrer. She had her entire life torpedoed and received death threats. He did something much worse: stole other people's work, extensively and repeatedly, for years, dissembled about multiple studies and fabricated quotations, defrauded his publisher and employer. Yet he was redeemed in the public eye a hell of a lot faster than Sacco and had a hell of a lot less venom aimed at him. (In fact, an article in the *Harvard Business Review* actually made the argument that Lehrer wasn't nearly as bad as Enron or Lehman Brothers. Sure, and he was also not as bad as Hitler, but does that make his conduct okay?)

The woman in the book who gets the second-most coverage after Sacco is Lindsey Stone, a young woman who worked with people with special needs. She and her friend had a running joke in which they took pictures of themselves acting like jerks. They documented themselves smoking in front of nonsmoking signs and mocking the poses of somber statues. Undeniably stupid. In the incident that caused her shaming, she Facebooked a selfie at Arlington National Cemetery in front of a sign saying "Silence and Respect." In the photo, she was pretending to yell and give the finger. Oh ho ho ho, what a card.

It turned out that Stone didn't really understand the difference be-

tween public and private Facebook settings. (It was 2012, a more innocent time.) If only her friends had seen the picture, they might have said,
"Oh, that Lindsey." But the world saw her picture. And then she compounded her error by apologizing badly: "Whoa, whoa, whoa . . .
OBVIOUSLY we meant NO disrespect to people that serve or have
served our country." As we've noted elsewhere, the word "obviously"
never belongs in an apology, let alone in ALL CAPS. And why would
her lack of disrespect be obvious? That photo was worth a thousand
"obviouslys."

Stone lost her job and, worse, could barely leave her house for a year.
She got rape threats and death threats and went into a crushing depression. (So did Sacco.) It took her two years—and the donated services of
the website Reputation.com, which specializes in making negative mentions of you on the web drop lower in search results for your name—to
get another job. (After four years, Sacco was rehired at her old job.)

Again: Stone messed up. She was shamed. But the consequences
were far outside the realm of reason compared to, oh, we don't know,
someone whose name rhymes with Blonah Shmerer.

When Lehrer apologized, long after his initial sin, after laying low for
a year, it was in a speech for which he was paid $20,000 and in which he
said that his extremely high IQ caused his tendency to lie, and that journalism requires a set of rules and processes to ensure that mistakes like
his don't happen again (it's journalism's fault, not his! funny that so many
journalists have managed to resist the urge to invent quotes and plagia-
rize press releases despite a lack of formal rules and processes!) and that
he should be compared to Charles Darwin and Niels Bohr. Imagine if we
at SorryWatch tried that: *My name is Susan McCarthy. I was traveling for
three weeks and never found time to pick up presents for my loved ones back
home. It's the kind of error Chekhov might have made, distracted by pondering his next scene in* The Cherry Orchard, *widely regarded as a classic in
twentieth-century theater.*

Lehrer's tepid apology—like that of other privileged white men like swimmer Ryan Lochte and actor Jeremy Renner, whom we have dispatched, figuratively, on our website—was sufficient for his redemption. It's ironic—we're not sure that's the word we're looking for, but we'll go with "ironic"—that women's apologies seem to help them get out of jams less than men's apologies do, despite the fact that women are starting from a place of less power. You'd think, given women's perceived weakness, they'd be more easily forgiven. You would be wrong.

Apologies and Power—but Wait: We Gotta Look at Gender, Too, Surprise, Surprise, Again

A recent study in the *Journal of Experimental Psychology* found that apologies from people with high status are judged less believable and sincere than apologies from people with low status. But as we've seen with many male celebrities, believability doesn't seem to translate into *gaining power*, and lack of believability doesn't seem to cause *loss of power*.

Let's take a closer look. Professor Arik Cheshin at the University of Haifa led an international team of researchers in studies involving hundreds of participants. The subjects were shown a variety of scenarios in which someone committed wrongdoing in a business setting. Sometimes the study participants were told the person who did the bad thing was the CEO, and sometimes they were told it was a junior-level employee. The subjects also watched the real video clip of the CEO of Toyota weeping and apologizing for failing to act on the knowledge that there were potentially fatal brake problems in his company's cars. Sometimes the study participants were told that this guy was Toyota's CEO; other times they were told he was a low-level employee.

In every case, when the participants were told a CEO was apologizing, they found the apology less sincere than when they thought he was a regular schlub apologizing. Overwhelmingly, they felt that CEOs were better than less powerful people at strategically manipulating people's emotions. "The assumption is that the CEO has much more to lose and accordingly has a stronger motivation to try to use emotions to create empathy," Cheshin said in a statement. People were far more willing to forgive junior employees' transgressions, offering detailed and elaborate explanations about why the less senior people should be forgiven.

We offer a caveat about Cheshin's findings, though. It doesn't necessarily *matter* that powerful men's apologies are viewed as suspect. Because (unlike Justine Sacco) they often manage to keep their power anyway.

Cheshin felt that the study's findings were transferable to other fields, such as politics. "The more senior the politician, the more we are inclined to assume that they are better at controlling their emotions and are using emotions strategically," Cheshin said. Again, we find his reasoning suspect. The problem is that male apologies are often viewed as a sign of weakness. So, SorryWatch would argue, it actually might not matter—and might even *help* a male politician—if his apology is viewed as insincere. And women politicians, alas, might be better off not apologizing at all, whether they're viewed as ball-busting (Hillary Clinton) or weak (Kirsten Gillibrand, blamed by voters for the implosion of Al Franken's career).

We'd like to think that ossified gender views around apology are changing. And, indeed, it seems that they might be. These days certain men know full well that if the truth about their pasts come to light, they're going to have to apologize. Many sexist behaviors that flew in the past are less likely to fly now.

This doesn't mean men apologize *well*. But we're getting there, and we hope this book will help. For now, all any of us can do is hope to find good, fair, and justice-minded bosses of any gender—as we all know, not all women are terrific at supporting other women—and use our instincts to figure out when it's wise to apologize and when it isn't. And when you *are* the boss, lead by example. Make sure you let women speak, and be aware of the distinctly not-level playing field.

Working Twice as Hard to Be Seen as Half as Good: Black Women and Apologizing

Black women are held to even more exacting standards than white women. Where white women have to steer between the Scylla of being perceived as likably nonauthoritative sweeties and the Charybdis of being seen as competent but ball-busting bitches, Black women have it tougher still. Because if they're not perpetually agreeable, tentative, and apologetic for taking up space, they risk being caricatured and dismissed as the Angry Black Woman. Professor Wendy Ashley at California State University, Northridge, sums up this "pervasive and parasitic" stereotype: "The mythology presumes all Black women to be irate, irrational, hostile, and negative despite the circumstances. . . . Angry Black women are typically described as aggressive, unfeminine, undesirable, overbearing, attitudinal, bitter, mean, and hell-raising . . . tart tongued, neck rolling, and loud mouthed."

The consequences of NOT being perceived as docile, scraping, and apologetic can be dire for Black women, even in childhood. A 2017 study by Georgetown Law's Center on Poverty and Equality indicated that Black girls are universally seen as more mature and more aggressive than white girls and receive harsher penalties for perceived misconduct. A few years ago we saw agonizing footage of a six-year-old Florida girl arrested for throwing a tantrum—though she was calm and listening to a story by the time the police arrived. As she was loaded, sobbing, into a police car, her hands zip-tied behind her—they were too small for the cuffs—she pleaded, "Please give me a second chance!" Black girls are not allowed to make mistakes.

When Black and brown women speak up about concerns or micro-aggressions, they risk their jobs. Witness the story of Timnit Gebru, PhD, blowing the whistle on problems with hiring practices and bias issues embedded in artificial intelligence at Google. Despite doing what she was hired to do, she was fired.

The psychologically safe environments we discussed earlier in this book—those that allow employees to ask questions, be open about mistakes, apologize, and move on—are even harder for Black women to find. One study found that while more than 80 percent of white women and men say they see themselves as allies to people of color at work, less than half of Black women feel they have strong allies.

When Black women are perceived as too assertive, white people get anxious. And that is frequently dangerous. "Being sorry is literally a lesson in our DNA," writes activist and poet Sonya Renee Taylor in *The Body Is Not an Apology: The Power of Radical Self-Love*. "In the Jim Crow South, an apology could at times be exacted by death sentence." Celeste Walley-Jean, a professor of psychology and dean at Clayton State University in Morrow, Georgia, who has studied Black women and anger, found, "contrary to popular belief, that rather than exploding when minimally provoked (or even unprovoked) as the image of the 'angry black woman' stereotype summons, African American women in the current sample are actually *less* likely to experience angry feelings even when faced with situations in which they are criticized, disrespected, or evaluated negatively." It doesn't matter: the stereotype remains pernicious.

When a Black woman doesn't conform to the role she's supposed to play, the majority culture is horrified. Witness what happened in 2019 when a U.S. Open line judge accused Serena Williams of being illicitly coached by someone in the stands. She exclaimed, "I didn't get coaching! I didn't get coaching! You need to make an announcement that I didn't get coaching! I don't cheat, and I didn't get coaching! You owe me an apology. You owe me an apology. I have never cheated in my life. I have a daughter, and I stand for what's right for her. And I've never cheated, and you owe me an apology." She smashed her racket—something men have done without penalty since time immemorial; if John McEnroe had been held to this standard, he would have left the sport owing the USTA money—and was fined $17,000. She got no apology.

The report *The State of Black Women in Corporate America, 2020* found that for every one hundred men promoted to manager, only eighty-six women—and only fifty-eight Black women—are promoted, despite the fact that Black women ask for promotions at the same rate as men do. "Compared to white women, Black women are less likely to have managers showcase their work, advocate for new opportunities for them, or give them opportunities to manage people and projects," the report said. "Black women are also less likely to report that their manager helps them navigate organizational politics or balance work and personal life." The 2019 study "Race and Reactions to Negative Feedback: Examining the Effects of the 'Angry Black Woman' Stereotype," published by the Academy of Management, found that Black women who were perceived as angry tended to receive lower performance evaluations and lower recommended raises.

Nope

There's an increasingly popular slogan out in the world: "Unapologetically Black." The website for Massachusetts's first Black congresswoman, Ayanna Pressley, sells "Unapologetic" bumper stickers. Their genesis: In 2020, Pressley stopped wearing a wig and announced that she had alopecia. Jeered by white men for not conforming to their beauty stereotypes, she tweeted a photo of her bald self in tight close-up, with, "Dear Trolls, You really think I look like 'Mr. Clean'? Please. He never looked THIS clean. Sorry not sorry my unapologetically rockin' my crown triggers you. Proud #alopecian." Her colleague Alexandria Ocasio-Cortez backed her up, tweeting, "They're just mad because you pull off any & every look thrown at you, meanwhile they can't even put on a hat on their head without looking like a baby peanut."

Sonya Renee Taylor writes:

> *For decades, I spread out before the world a buffet of apologies. I apologized for laughing too loudly, being too big, too dark, flamboyant, outspoken, analytical. I watched countless others roll out similar scrolls of contrition. . . . We apologized for our weight, race, sexual orientation. We were told there is a right way to have a body, and our apologies reflected our indoctrination into that belief. Not only have we been trying to change our "wrong bodies," but we have also continued to apologize for the presumed discomfort our bodies rouse in others.*

Women who are Black, brown, old, fat, trans, disabled, or otherwise seen as outside the norm "awaken daily to a planet that expects a certain set of apologies to already live on our tongues," Taylor writes. "There is a level of 'not enough' or 'too much' sewn into these strands of difference." The pressure to be perfect, unassuming, and unthreatening is powerful, yet more women from different marginalized communities are being increasingly vocal about pushing back. Australian Paralympic medalist and disability activist Elizabeth Wright wrote in *Conscious Being*, a magazine by and for women with disabilities, "I'm done apologising to wider society for making them feel uncomfortable with my missing limbs, curvy spine, and demands for accessibility and inclusion."

The Menfolk, Granting Themselves Absolution Hither and Yon

Women, as we've discussed, are more likely than men to apologize to the person they've mistreated. Men, when circumstances dictate (as in, say, a #MeToo apology), may simply choose to fling their apology into the public sphere like a Frisbee. They may fail to address the apology to the person who most needs to hear it. Bill Clinton, for instance, acknowledges that he's never apologized to Monica Lewinsky, though he's apologized *about* Monica Lewinsky. It doesn't seem to trouble him one iota that he's never actually said the words "I'm sorry" to the person whose life he destroyed.

Bill Clinton's belief that because he's reflected and prayed on his offenses and lies and has addressed them in the public sphere he's off the hook is . . . not uncommon among the male populace. The essayist Lili Loofbourow has written about men's use of the phrase "I've reckoned with this," which was uttered by, among others, actor Jeffrey Tambor. In Tambor's case, the phrase took the place of an actual apology to the person he'd repeatedly screamed at and denigrated, his *Arrested Development* castmate Jessica Walter.

Tambor's male costars, who were sitting in the same room as Tambor and Walter when Tambor's "reckoning" occurred, "eagerly accepted this and considered the matter settled," Loofbourow writes. "It didn't much matter to them (or to Tambor) that Jessica Walter, the injured party, did not." Loofbourow went on, "*I've reckoned with this* is a handy phrase. It lets a man's monologue (often phrased as a journey of self-improvement) stand in for making amends to the people he's wronged. This is in some ways traceable to our theological heritage: The Reformation turned confession into a more internal, private 'reckoning,' and that spiritual model still has power. America has a tender spot for men who admit their flaws. The story of a man who's done terrible things and sincerely repented is enormously romantic." (Hello, Maxim de Winter.)

But "self-pardoning" should not be a thing. It's not like self-checkout at the grocery store. You cannot cut out the middleman—the person you actually need to apologize to.

"If you want to know why women are so angry, it's because this ritual tends to exclude the injured party," Loofbourow points out. "This 'talk about how you're going to do and be better' stuff isn't actually a great formula for reconciliation. It offers neither retributive nor restorative justice. It privileges public acceptance over making things right with the actual victims, who barely seem to register at all. But it's pretty effective: In an age of never-ending public relations wars, we're so starved for any sign of sincere spiritual struggle that we rush to reward self-proclaimed sinners who say they're trying to make good."

The Power of Imagination

Women seem way less likely to award themselves a self-absolution medal. It's not unheard-of, though. In *Eat, Pray, Love: One Woman's Search for Everything Across Italy, India and Indonesia*, Elizabeth Gilbert has a huge "I forgive myself" scene on an ashram roof in India. Many people found the scene moving and beautiful and felt it answered their own inchoate yearnings.

"I thought of how many people go to their graves unforgiven and unforgiving," Gilbert writes. "I thought of how many people have had siblings or friends or children or lovers disappear from their lives before precious words of clemency or absolution could be passed along. How do the survivors of terminated relationships ever endure the pain of unfinished business? From that place of meditation, I found the answer— you can finish the business yourself, from within yourself. It's not only possible, it's essential."

Gilbert decides to invite her ex-husband, metaphysically, to join her on that roof. The two have split, bitterly; he's still furious at her. But she feels him arrive on the roof, at her request. "His presence was suddenly absolute and tangible," she writes. And suddenly, they forgive each other. Wait, no, it's even easier than that! She and her husband "were just two cool blue souls who already understood everything. . . . They didn't need to forgive each other; they were born forgiving each other."

SorryWatch does not approve. We believe you have to sit with discomfort, to use another hippie phrase. If someone is upset at you and you know you are on any level responsible, you have to apologize to their face, and if they don't forgive you, welp, you have to live with that. You don't get to decide how other people feel. Marjorie and Susan both really want people to like us, and both of us find it distressing that there are apparently people out there in the world who do not like us. (Well, they don't like MARJORIE. Everyone likes Susan. Sucks for Marjorie.) We suspect Elizabeth Gilbert has similar desires to be liked. It seems unsporting that she gives herself the absolution the rest of us want, too, even for things we don't deserve.

Gilbert's imagined forgiveness is materially different from the imagined apology created by V (formerly Eve Ensler). In her book, fittingly called *The Apology*, the feminist critic and *Vagina Monologues* author writes the words she'd love to hear from her late father, who was physically, emotionally, and sexually abusive. (The book is dedicated to "every woman still waiting for an apology.")

"Dear Evie," V writes, using her father's nickname for her. "I have asked myself, What is an apology? It is a humbling. It is an admission of wrongdoings and a surrender. It is an act of intimacy and connection which requires great self-knowledge and insight." In real life, V's father was incapable of such self-knowledge and insight. But imagining that he *is* capable, long after his death, and that he would choose to interrogate his own behavior and make things right with his daughter is a powerful act of healing for her. And this is a story V is entitled to tell, because— unlike Gilbert's ex-husband—her father can't tell it himself.

And craving an apology isn't the same thing as craving forgiveness. Gilbert could have kept seeking forgiveness from her ex or accepted that it wouldn't be forthcoming; what she *doesn't* get to do is to unilaterally decide that forgiveness has been granted to her. V, on the other hand, while revisiting her nightmarish childhood in graphic detail (all the trigger warnings for this book), is futzing with a finished narrative. Her father's story is over. She's telling only her own. How can an adult make sense of her childhood sexual abuse when the abuser is dead and there isn't the slightest hope for an apology? Storytelling has this re- demptive power. We hope V's book, and way of processing horror, helps other victims heal. We do wonder if maybe it helps V that she imagines her father's dreadful afterlife torment.

Ultimately, what becomes clear is that apologies can be a minefield for women in a way they simply aren't for men. Perhaps that's why there's currently a movement to encourage women to say "Thank you" instead of "I'm sorry."

Maybe Reframing Everything Will Fix Our Broken Language and Broken Gender Essentialism?

Maybe!

Queens-based cartoonist Yao Xiao got the ball rolling a few years ago with a comic suggesting alternatives to apology. SorryWatch approves of several of them. Instead of "Sorry I'm rambling," she suggests "Thank you for listening." Instead of "Sorry I'm kind of a drag," say, "Thank you for spending time with me." These phrases are nice because they're not self-negating. But saying "Thank you for your patience" instead of "Sorry I'm late"? No! You *should* apologize for being late! When you've inconvenienced someone else, you owe them that "Sorry!" It's inherently different from thanking someone for spending time with you.

An appropriately deployed "Sorry" is about making sure the person you're apologizing to feels seen and heard, while the misguided "I regret . . ." is about the narcissistic need for the apologizer to say how they feel. SorryWatch feels that "Sorry" and "Thank you" each have a place in our discourse. Let a thousand linguistic flowers bloom. Regret doesn't have a place here, though. Go away, regret. Regret is self-absorbed, ungenerous, a feeling that belongs on the *inside*. We do not need to wave regret at other people. They will invariably be annoyed at it.

In general, though, it is irksome that women are expected to police their own language so desperately and constantly. It's anti-feminist to be told that you, as a woman-person, should obsess about every word coming out of your mouth. Men are not told this. And look, honestly, women's apologies are going to be judged more harshly than men's, because in this culture women's words and actions are judged more harshly than men's. (Sorry. It's true.) Here's a contrary opinion: If you tend to reflexively say "Sorry" all the time, maybe don't stress about it? Because someone's going to find something wrong with your speech anyway as long as you exist as a female human in the universe. Unless saying "Sorry" a lot super-bothers you, in which case, sure, work on it! But please don't be too hard on yourself.

We know nuance is difficult. So, with some reservations, we'll share a bit of advice, in addition to select bits of Yao Xiao's cartoon, on how to say "Sorry" less often.

How to Say Sorry Less Often . . . if You Want To

In 2018, *Forbes* magazine offered a roundup of career coaches suggesting "sorry" alternatives; as with the "thank you" cartoon, we like some of the suggestions and not others. We liked career coach Heather Murphy's suggestion to avoid "Sorry" when it's accompanied by an excuse for a missed deadline. Instead, try "Thank you for your patience as we navigate this project. You'll have it by Friday of next week." This is good because it acknowledges the inconvenience the other person has experienced, implies that the complexity of the work is at fault, and offers a solution to the problem.

Career coach Loren Margolis abhors "Sorry to bother you." In a meeting, Margolis suggests, simply speak up politely, with no preamble, when there's a pause. And if you knock on your boss's door needing a moment of their time, say, "Is now a good time for a quick question?" Margolis clarifies: "Don't apologize for having an opinion or a question that will enable you to get your job done." And if you're on the receiving end of criticism, Jay Steven Levin suggests avoiding a reflexive apology and instead saying, "Thank you for pointing that out; what else is worth knowing here?" He explains, "Focus on what's needed to bring about the desired outcome." We like this advice!

Sometimes, though, female apologies are about solidarity and empathy. Those are beautiful, fine things. Monica Lewinsky once said that after years of trauma, the seven words that undid her were "I'm so sorry you were so alone." She'd always had family and friends supporting her, but everyone involved in that White House intern scandal, including people she thought were her pals and confidants, pretty much abandoned her. "Swimming in that sea of Aloneness was terrifying," she said. "Isolation is such a powerful tool to the subjugator."

The social apology—"I'm sorry you're hurting," "I'm sorry for your loss," "I'm sorry that happened to you"—is nothing to apologize for, especially when it's accompanied by listening to the other person's story. This apology is a beautiful kindness. And women tend to be good at it. That's something to celebrate, not slough off like an ill-fitting shoe.

Finally: the title of this chapter, obviously, is a nod to Rachel Hollis's bestselling books *Girl, Wash Your Face* and *Girl, Stop Apologizing*. We find them reductive. Pulling yourself up by your bootstraps, as these books recommend, may work for blond, straight, cisgender, thin, able-bodied, Christian, financially secure women like Hollis. But they're the literary equivalent of Cher smacking someone across the face in *Moonstruck* and exclaiming, "Snap out of it!" Simplistic. Easier said than done. Any meaningful look at apologizing has to examine the structural inequities that make apologies—or the lack thereof—meaningful.

ACTION ITEMS

❑ **Understand that apologies are burdened with gendered and race-based stereotypes and expectations, like pretty much everything else in society.** Consider your own biases and the cultural milieu when you feel you're being pressured to apologize or owe an apology.

❑ **If you're a woman, don't feel pressured to say "Thank you" instead of "Sorry" . . . unless you want to.** You have enough on your plate already. If, however, you'd like to give it a shot because you think it would increase your authority, start with some easy ones:

  ❑ "Thanks for helping me" instead of "Sorry I couldn't do this myself."

  ❑ "Thanks for listening" instead of "Sorry I'm so whiny."

  ❑ "Thanks for catching that!" instead of "Sorry I made that typo."

❑ **If you're a man, use your privilege.** Have you noticed that men, say, do most of the talking in your meetings, causing women to hesitantly say, "Sorry, can I add something?"? You can help! Say in your loud man voice, "I'd like to hear what [female colleague name] thinks." When women think their contributions are welcome, they're less likely to apologize for them.

❑ **Empathetic apologies** ("I'm sorry about your dog," "I'm sorry you stubbed your toe on that boulder," "I'm sorry you lost the TV remote and couldn't turn off *Dirty Grandpa* starring Robert De Niro and Zac Efron last night") **never go amiss, no matter what gender you are.**

Times to say "Thank you" instead of "I'm sorry"

"Thank you for holding the elevator." (Not "I'm sorry for making you hold the elevator.") "Thanks for being a stand-up guy about the oil change." (Not "I'm sorry you had to deal with the oil change.") "Thanks for drinking that white chocolate raspberry Irish Crème–flavored swill when you specifically told me you wanted it black." Wait, no. You *should* apologize for that one.

BAD APOLOGY BINGO CARD #7
SEXUAL HARASSER EDITION!

twisting my words	affectionate	just being friendly	father of daughters	isolated incident
the accusations	all the facts	determine the validity	their motivation	get the help I need
indiscretion	so sensitive	**FREE SQUARE**	not my intent	if I crossed the line
respect	taking responsibility	some things were said	baseless	any offense
God knows my heart	characterized as	horrified to think that	as a young man	misinterpreted

CHAPTER 11

LET THE MOMENT LAST;
LET THE RIPPLES WIDEN

Certain words associated with certain attributes seem to have certain political leanings. Here's what we mean: The word "honor" is beloved by conservatives. The word "justice" is beloved by liberals and progressives. It's not completely clear to us why this is, since we don't think conservatives would say they're *against* justice, or that liberals and progressives have anything *against* honor. The word "respect" doesn't appear to slant right or left; everyone values respect. (To be fair, people on one side of the spectrum talk a lot about respecting *institutions*, and people on the other side of the spectrum talk a lot about respecting *individuals*.)

Words are often coded. But "apology" is a word that should cross all political lines. As Michael in that great philosophical text called *The Good Place* noted, "What matters isn't if people are good or bad. What matters is if they're trying to be better today than they were yesterday."

No one on this planet is perfect. Everyone makes mistakes. Everyone needs to be allowed to fail, to get things wrong, to learn without being slammed and shamed for what they don't know. These are ugly times, in which many politicians and religious leaders of many nations are trying very hard to set people against each other. People say foul things about lovely people like ourselves, and we're outraged and goaded to respond in kind. Ugly feelings get ugly responses. Ugly responses increase contempt and fear and rage. Examples in public life encourage us to show those feelings. We have to make a conscious choice to resist. The world's in rough shape, and we need to work together to save it.

Harvard Business School professor Amy C. Edmondson has found that in workplaces where people are encouraged to own and report their mistakes, without fear of shaming or reprisal, workers feel more confident discussing what went wrong, how to correct it, and how to prevent similar issues from recurring. The most cohesive and effective teams, she says, are the ones that report the most mistakes, because they don't feel the need to bury evidence, point fingers, or avoid ownership of problems.

Apology Adjacencies

Again, we are not telling you to be profligate with your apologies and forgiveness. We stand by our belief that if you're not sorry—and if after seeking a reality check, and talking with trusted friends and/or a therapist about whatever happened, you're *still* not sorry—do not apologize. And we stand by our belief that you don't have to accept an apology, either. Being fake and chirpy about forgiveness isn't healthy.

There are, however, ways to feel more connected and more like the world isn't an entirely transactional and self-serving place. Let's call them apology-adjacent strategies. Like apology itself, they're undervalued and underappreciated acts that have the power to make human beings feel better about the planet we share.

Psychologist Sonja Lyubomirsky at UC Riverside did a study asking participants to keep a gratitude journal, writing down a few things for which they were grateful or thankful. Half the participants did it once a week and half did it three times a week. They expressed gratitude for all kinds of things: their mom, not getting sideswiped by a surprise test in class, getting a valentine. But only the group that expressed gratitude one night a week saw a benefit to their happiness. Lyubomirsky hypothesized that the ones who wrote only once a week felt the activity remained relatively fresh and meaningful, whereas the ones who wrote three times a week felt pretty quickly as though they were doing homework. Similarly, apologies and forgiveness should not be homework.

But seeing the good in your life and maintaining an appreciation for it? That's valuable. "When you become truly aware of the value of your friends and family," Lyubomirsky writes, "you are likely to treat them better, perhaps producing an upward spiral, a sort of 'positive feedback loop' in which strong relationships give you something to be grateful for, and in return fortify those very same relationships."

Kindness is a self-fulfilling prophecy. Treating someone else with kindness and charity can have a positive impact on your own self-perception: you see yourself as an altruistic and compassionate person. This is a rubber-and-glue situation that means you feel more confident, optimistic, and helpful, which makes you behave in more confident, optimistic, and helpful ways.

A line in Jennifer Weiner's very funny novel *Little Earthquakes* sticks with us. The main character, Becky, is pondering her monstrous mother-in-law, a shrew who perpetually insults Becky's weight, finds fault, even tries to sabotage Becky's wedding to her son. In a moment of soul-deep irritation, Becky forces herself to breathe deeply and imagine this horrible woman as a baby. There she is, "in the crib, wailing away, crying for parents who wouldn't come. [Becky] thought of what it would be like to grow up without the one certainty that every baby deserved—*when I'm hurt or cold or scared, someone will come and care for me*—and how that absence would warp you so that you'd lash out at the people you loved, driving them away when all you wanted to do was pull them closer." Picturing her mother-in-law as an ignored, unloved, terrified infant, her little fists wrapped around the bars of the crib—something that might even have been true, once upon a time—Becky is able to be the bigger woman (figuratively as well as literally). We're not trying to tell you to forgive monsters. We're trying to tell you how to give them less power in your psyche, which can in turn fuel what you say and do in ways that are more productive and less stressful for you.

You're More Appreciated Than You Think

Another example of a small, apology-adjacent act that makes the world better: sending a thank-you note. We tend to think that shooting off a note or email is not a big deal. It turns out we're wrong.

A study published in the journal *Psychological Science* in 2018, "Undervaluing Gratitude: Expressers Misunderstand the Consequences of Showing Appreciation," by social psychologists Amit Kumar and Nicholas Epley, provides valuable insight. Kumar and Epley asked participants in several different experiments to write a letter of gratitude to someone who did something nice for them and to predict how the letter recipients would respond. The letter writers figured the recipients would be a little surprised and pleased—but also maybe a little weirded out by receiving a lot of compliments?

Nope on both counts!

People *loved* getting the thank-yous. Loved it! While the people who sent the thank-yous worried that the recipients might view them as insincere, that their writing might be criticized, that the letters might make the recipients feel uncomfortable (ugh, awkward), no! The recipients often said they were "ecstatic" to get the thank-yous! It wasn't awkward; they didn't scrutinize the writing; they were just delighted. Thrilled. Who knew it was that easy to make people ecstatic?

The mismatch between expectation and reality was huge. Apparently we humans suck at predicting other people's responses to our kindness. Kumar and Epley wrote, "We found that expressers may worry inordinately about *how* they are expressing gratitude—their ability to articulate the words 'just right'—whereas recipients are focused more on warmth and positive intent."

In other words, don't freak out about the perfect wording or crumble with performance anxiety. There's no need, because people will be happier to accept your gratitude than you think. Just reach out.

Thinking about this research, Marjorie did an experiment of her own. When she was a kid, her hometown repertory theater had a program that took middle school students to special daytime performances of Shakespeare plays. Marjorie has never forgotten the production of *The Tempest* in which Caliban was played by an actor in street clothes with tall kitchen stools strapped to his feet and Ariel was played by a dude with a hairy chest in a pink tutu, flying in and out on an obvious wire. It was a revelation to a kid who'd had no idea that Shakespeare could be funny or surprising or moving. She wound up studying Shakespeare in college in large part because of this experience as a child. Feeling stupid but also sentimental, adult Marjorie sent an email to the theater's education department about how much it had meant to her. She got an email back from the current director of the theater's education program—who probably wasn't yet born when Marjorie saw that show—saying how thrilled he was to get her email and how he'd shared it with his current team to remind them of why they did what they did. Good energy all around.

Kumar and Epley noted that their study participants often chose people they were pretty sure would be receptive. "So people's willingness to express gratitude is guided by the expected value of a recipient's response," Kumar says.

We've been thinking about how this finding might dovetail with the world of apologies. And here goes: People wrote expressions of gratitude to those people who they thought might be open to receiving them. So what if we went through life as the kind of people who seem willing to listen in general? What if we conveyed a vibe of openness to a good apology, rather than vibrating with the kind of performative energy of people on Twitter who seem eager not to accept *any* apology or who clearly want to jump down the throat of anyone who apologizes imperfectly?

The Importance of Reaching Out

In a study correlated with gratitude letter writing, Kumar and Epley asked people to send a card to someone else "just because." Checking in, sharing a joke, saying hi. The duo wrote, "Here, too, participants underestimated the positive consequences of this warm, prosocial engagement with another person."

One small good thing to come out of the Covid-19 pandemic has been an increase in letter writing. One USPS survey found that one in six consumers had sent more mail to family and friends during the pandemic. (Susan wasn't able to visit her mother, so she sent a daily postcard, and her mother claimed to appreciate them. Marjorie exchanged cat postcards with a cat-obsessed pal in another city.) Social isolation, which so many of us have experienced, is associated with depression. Symptoms of anxiety in the general population also skyrocketed during the pandemic. But finding moments of connection helps us feel a little better. A classic study conducted at Stanford from 1969 to 1974 looked at 843 people who'd been discharged from the hospital after being treated for depression or suicidal ideation. Half the subjects received four or five hand-typed letters a year from someone they'd met in the hospital; the letters were short and said some variant of "Hey, thinking of you, hope you're doing okay, write back if you'd like." The other group didn't get these letters. In the five years following their discharge, the group that got letters were far less likely to commit suicide than the other group. This was especially true in the first two years after discharge; it seems that this is when we're the most in need of contact and support.

And that kind of "I'm thinking of you" buttressing is perhaps unknow-ingly what many of us have tried to provide for others and gain for our-selves during the pandemic.

Again, it takes so little to send a note. You don't have to write a novel or be particularly witty. Just a couple lines can tell someone you care. If we fail to reach out to others because (as Kumar and Epley's study sug-gests) we think the recipient will judge the way we express ourselves or we think they already know how we feel about them, we miss an oppor-tunity for connection. To put that in academic-ese: "Expressers may as-sume that recipients are already aware of their gratitude, a 'curse of knowledge' that makes expression seem unnecessary."

What is this "curse of knowledge"? The term was coined in a 1989 *Journal of Political Economy* article and refers to a cognitive bias in which we wrongly assume that someone else has the same information or knowledge that we do. For instance, less skilled teachers may be unable to put themselves in the shoes of a student because they can't quite un-derstand how it feels not to have the background they themselves do. A naive do-gooder may assume that others care about the same things they do rather than considering what others' worldviews might be and how and why they differ from the would-be reformer's. An example of the curse of knowledge from the cartoon world: Marjorie recently saw a one-panel comic of a dude saying, "Making espresso is easy. Start with the brew ratio. A brew ratio of 1:1 (18 grams in/18 grams out) to 1:2 (18 grams in/36 grams out) as a 'ristretto' . . ." while another dude is smiling politely and thinking, *wut*.

We think that the "curse of knowledge" might put a damper on our apologizing and our accepting of apologies because the person who *should* apologize might think, *Oh, Jordan knows I'm sorry*, and the person who is *owed* the apology might think, *Eh, Other Jordan knows I'm not mad*. What if we actually said the words *Hey, Jordan, I wanted you to know I'm sorry for X*, and *Hey, Other Jordan, I wanted you to know I forgive you for Y*? Unburdening ourselves of the curse of knowledge might help everyone.

Similarly, we may not seek out someone we happen to know is griev-ing (beyond a quick "Sorry for your loss"), because it feels awkward. What if they don't want to hear from you? They already *know* everyone is sorry, right? What if they want privacy? What if they don't want you to remind them of their loss?

But they are never *not* reminded of their loss. Keeping silent about it only makes them feel more alone. When Marjorie's father died, all she wanted was stories about him. She was grateful for every card, every "Re-member that time when . . . ?" And years later, whenever someone found a photo of him she hadn't seen before and shared it, she felt a little stab of pain but a far greater burst of joy.

Self-doubt hinders positive social connections in daily life. We have this wonderful source of well-being right there, and we don't tap into it. Indeed, Kumar and Epley's studies showed that expressing gratitude made the note writer, not just the recipient, happier.

But we so rarely avail ourselves of this hit of happiness. Claude Steiner, working in the field of transactional analysis in 1971, developed the concept of the "stroke economy," which confronts most of us with an *artificial shortage* of kindness and compliments. Our lives are full of peo-ple we respect, like, or admire—but we seldom tell them so. Those un-voiced compliments create an artificial shortage. The flip side of that is that your life may be full of people who have good thoughts about you that they don't share. Unspoken compliments, hidden praise. People who love the way you laugh, who think you're the best cook ever, who wish they had a tenth of your social savvy, who would elect you captain of the expedition every time—and they never mention it. It just doesn't come up. It might be awkward.

But wouldn't it be nice to find out about that secret praise?

Go Ahead, Invite Them

On a similar note, we may stress about inviting others—especially folks we don't know well—to a party. What if we come off as desperate or needy? What if our party sucks and we look uncool? They'll probably be busy anyway, so why even bother?

But, really, people are almost always happy to get invitations, even if they can't make it. It's a compliment to be asked. People may get offended if they're *not* invited. If Sleeping Beauty's parents had just *invited* the wicked fairy to her christening, they would've saved So Much Trouble. Yeah, she might have eaten all the blackbird tarts, tried to shatter mead glasses with her high C, maybe insulted Prince Charming's breeches—but that's better than having your kid in a coma for a hundred years.

We all love true stories of people having something surprising and wonderful done for them. The story of a teenager who helps a little kid learn to skateboard instead of telling her she doesn't belong in the skate park. A customer who overhears a server talking about her money woes and leaves a huge tip and a note wishing her success. When Susan's friend Bill used to drive across the Bay Bridge into San Francisco, he'd look for out-of-state cars full of luggage/stuff. He'd get in line ahead of them and pay for their car, asking the toll collector to tell them, "Welcome to San Francisco!" He did that as often as he could and enlisted others to do it too. (Since the bridge phased out toll collectors in favor of electronic passes, he has lost this pleasure.)

People love these stories because we desperately want the world to work this way. We want it to be a caring community. And it's delightful to find unexpected instances when it is.

It's also nice to see ordinary examples. Even when we haven't been mistreated ourselves, we enjoy seeing others receive good apologies. Suppose we're waiting in a long line. Behind us, maybe where the line bends around a corner, we see someone cut in. Because we're ahead of that spot, this doesn't do us any harm. But we don't like seeing it. Then suppose someone says, "Hey, the end of the line is over there," and the person who cut says, "Oh, sorry! Didn't mean to cut—I thought *this* was the end of the line!" and moves to the actual end of the line. That's reassuring. People are trying to act right. Things are working as they should.

On Generosity

We may tell ourselves there's no reason to send those thank-yous, to voice those compliments, to apologize for little things. The other person might think we're manipulative, or insincere, or simply *too much*. It's easier to think that these small things are not really important, but it's just not true. Those excuses also save us from making an effort.

A 2008 study in the journal *Science* titled "Spending Money on Others Promotes Happiness" shows that it's not just emotional generosity but financial generosity that conveys rewards to the giver. Study participants were given a small sum of money. They predicted that they'd be happier if they spent the money on themselves than on someone else. But randomly selected participants who were told they had to spend the money on someone else wound up much happier than those who had the option to spend it on themselves and did.

Apologies are just one way in many to build communities and keep them intact. Recently we read an article about the genesis of "Buy Nothing" groups. People in a given neighborhood who want to get rid of things or need things post in their local Facebook group, and other people say they want the thing or they have the thing the poster wants. "I think that our participation in these groups is allowing people to tap into that deeper truth about who they are and how they want to live and what it really means to be in a community," said one of the founders. The groups encourage neighbors to get to know and trust each other, to be of service to one another, and to ask for help when they need it. Within a few years, there were 5,500 Buy Nothing groups in forty-four countries. During the Covid-19 pandemic, healthy people assisted sick ones. (When Marjorie's whole family got Covid, early in the pandemic, her six-floor New York City tenement sprang into action. They picked up medicine, went grocery shopping, dropped off meals. When Marjorie and her family felt better, her husband found a stash of N95 masks, which were then nearly impossible to get. A neighborhood volunteer picked them up and brought them to one of the nightly celebrations for essential workers at a nearby hospital, where they were gratefully accepted by a group of firefighters. Help begets help begets help.)

Buy Nothing groups aren't a utopia. The same racism and classism that pervades real life still rears its head online. Yet group administrators don't deny that biases exist. They just work on ways to fight them. "Potential admins now undergo additional training on redlining—or excluding people from certain neighborhoods—and diversity," a piece in the *Washington Post* said. "The equity team also has created an evolving community agreement that serves as both a mission statement and a commitment to keeping Buy Nothing equitable."

Marjorie and Susan are reminded of how they've felt at Burning Man, which also has a gift economy. There are only two things you can buy at Burning Man: ice and coffee. Self-sufficiency is integral to Burning Man's ethos, but so is sharing. Camps offer drinks and snacks; people surprise strangers with little presents. It's fun to give gifts of art, noshes, attention. It's clear to us that much of life on the desert playa is about how badly people want to feel seen. As middle-aged women, we often feel invisible in the real world. At Burning Man, though, everyone looks into everyone else's eyes. People want to feel known and appreciated.

Sending spontaneous letters, sharing memories, volunteering apologies, making the effort to see people as they are, giving gifts and trading in a way that's divorced from our capitalist economy—all these help create a better world. (Of course, use your judgment. Don't apologize to someone you know never wants to hear from you again. Don't throw a surprise party for someone who hates surprise parties. Never gift anyone an impulse puppy.)

Practice Makes Perfect

Apology is a muscle. When Susan first realized that pointless pride was keeping her from admitting fault, thus making her less nice to be around, she practiced saying, "You were right and I was wrong."

She started with trivial things. "The scissors were in the kitchen drawer, after all. You were right and I was wrong." She worked up to harder things—things that were harder to admit. She found that people like hearing that sentence. Occasionally they remark, "I don't think anyone ever said that to me before," or even "I'm not sure I've ever heard anyone say that." This rare sighting pleases them.

Kids adore it. We think it's great for them to hear adults say those words. They might be able to imagine saying it themselves.

Susan claims she gets a sinister thrill from her own graciousness. She recommends the exercise. She also recommends caution with postscripts. Like "You were right and I was wrong. Wow! How often does *that* happen?" As in: Don't say that.

Remember to start small. "Huh, the salt's over here. You were right and I was wrong." It could be too hard to start with bigger stuff. "Looking back, it was silly to do that gender reveal explosion in the national forest. You were right and I was wrong. Since they're only giving me one phone call, would you be a sweetie and get me a lawyer?"

I Speak Out About Your Bad Behavior

An illustrative anecdote: It was a baking North Carolina day when Rebecca Landis Hayes pulled into a "Reserved for Veterans" parking spot and raced into the grocery store. She wasn't gone long, but it was long enough for this note to be left on the vehicle: "This parking is for Veterans, lady. Learn to read & have some respect."

On Facebook, Hayes posted a photo of the note with a withering reply:

> To the person who left this note on my windshield today . . . It was the first time, and I won't do it again. I'm sorry . . .
>
> I'm sorry that you can't see my eight years of service in the United States Navy. I'm sorry that your narrow misogynistic world view can't conceive of the fact that there are female Veterans. I'm sorry that I have to explain myself to people like you. Mostly, I'm sorry that we didn't get a chance to have this conversation face to face, and that you didn't have the integrity and intestinal fortitude to identify yourself, qualities the military emphasizes.
>
> Which leads to one question, I served, did you?

To her surprise she soon got an anonymous letter from someone who said a friend had shown them the Facebook post. It said:

> I would like to apologize to you. I know it's no excuse, but I've seen so many young people park in retired vets' spaces, along with handicap lately, and I lost my cool. I'm sorry you were the one who got the result of that angry moment. I know it was a mistake and I'm glad I saw your post. I immediately felt horrible about a situation—where I assumed I was standing up for someone. . . . You didn't deserve that, and I hope you can accept this apology. I appreciate your service to

this country and I highly respect military men and women. It was an
error in judgment, and again, I'm sorry for that. Thank you for all
that you've done.

Now Hayes was happy and posted an image of the letter, calling it "a much appreciated, sincere apology." She and the anonymous note writer weren't so far apart after all. The note writer wanted to live in a caring community where people save parking spaces for veterans to show respect. Hayes wanted to live in a caring community where strangers assume she's worthy of respect and don't make unwarranted hostile judgments about her and express them in anonymous nastygrams. They each had their vision of a caring community damaged, and then restored, by more complete information followed by an apology. They both felt better. As the note writer said, "I'm glad I saw your post." The apology reduced the amount of fury in the world.

Incidentally, to Anonymous? And everyone else? Just as you can't always tell whether someone is a veteran—and veterans can be young!—you can't always tell if someone is disabled just by looking at them. You gave a nice apology there. Now work on keeping your cool in the future.

In *Effective Apology*, John Kador tells of being at a highway rest stop bathroom when a man who used a wheelchair entered. There was only one wheelchair-accessible stall, and it was taken. The man using the chair was audibly, loudly peeved. Kador writes, "When, after a few minutes, a seemingly able-bodied man emerged from the stall, the man in the wheelchair lit into him for using the one handicapped stall when there were other stalls he could have used. The other man looked stricken and without a word raised his shirt. He had a colostomy bag taped to the right side of his abdomen. The man in the wheelchair turned red and said, 'I apologize. I didn't know.' The other man said, 'I'm sorry, too.'"

In general, Kador has observed, "In many ways the escalation of apology is a good outcome. It signals the final gasps of a world that has systematically maintained its power and privilege at the expense of women, people of color, sexual minorities, and other oppressed groups. Simply stated: the demand for so many apologies today is compensation for not nearly enough apology in the past."

Oh, Grow Up, Social Media

We've talked about how social media catches people saying poorly considered things, immature things, things that were *supposed* to be funny but really aren't, and how that can lead to an enormous uproar and outrage. It can be dismaying, but we like to think it's symptomatic of a culture's growing pains. People are learning that words/conduct/assumptions that seemed acceptable before really don't play well when more people—and more kinds of people—see the words/conduct/assumptions in action today. Apology plays an important part in turning call-out culture into call-in culture. If people who say stupid stuff get called on it, and apologize thoughtfully, and are welcomed into the circle of humanity for what they've learned, we'll have more thoughtful, smart people with a better grasp on inclusive community.

Two creators of social media sites that called out bad behavior have recently spoken out about changes of direction they are making and would like to see. Dion Beary created the influential Tumblr blog *This Is White Privilege* in 2013. Beary told *Slate*, "It took a very complex topic, which was privilege, and it simplified it into these small bite-sized chunks that were easier to understand. The basis of the blog was: If you're someone who doesn't believe in privilege and you say, 'Oh, show me an example,' well, here are a million bajillion examples." For instance, he offered: "White privilege is textbooks being written by people who speak the same dialect that you speak," and "White privilege is every hiring manager that you meet looks like you."

Although he thinks people learned important things from the blog, Beary also worries about unintended effects. "It was . . . so digestible and easy to understand that it taught people a lot, and also dumbed the conversation down so much that it was difficult to come back from." It was too surface-y, too easy. "We weren't teaching any critical thinking. We were discouraging critical thinking. There was a time where we said that it was problematic to ask a question, and that is wild to me."

In 2016, Beary stopped running the blog. He wanted to make things more transactional. Less one-way. "When I was 20 or 22, I felt like I knew everything. I felt like it was so simple and it was so black-and-white and so easy to understand, and that if you disagree with me, that means you hate Black people. If you don't like the way I run the blog, it means that you're just a racist, period. I was so full of vinegar and anger. And I don't think that reflects the way I feel now."

To be clear, Beary doesn't think we live in a changed world. He just thinks that a reductive response to white privilege wasn't doing the work of educating he really wanted to do.

Similarly, Liat Kaplan created another influential Tumblr blog, *Your Fave Is Problematic*; she, too, has had some second thoughts. Kaplan spent hours researching celebrities. "The posts contained long lists of celebrities' regrettable (racist, sexist, homophobic, transphobic, ethnophobic, ableist and so on) statements and actions—the stuff that gets people canceled these days," she said recently. She'd originally started a blog when she was in high school about classmates' bad behavior, taking down posts only after they apologized. The school ordered her to stop, so she switched to addressing the flaws of the rich and famous.

Kaplan encountered a lot of anger about her blog. She began posting less and eventually stopped altogether. "In the years since, I've looked back with shame and regret—about my pettiness, my motivating rage, my hard-and-fast assumptions that people were either good or bad. Who was I to lump together known misogynists with people who got tattoos in languages they didn't speak? I just wanted to see someone face conse-quences; no one who'd hurt me ever had." But over time she, too, gained an appreciation for nuance and wanted to go deeper and have more im-pact. "I was angered by hypocrisy and cruelty; what I did about it was apply a level of scrutiny that left no room for error," she says. "I just know what we all should know by now: that no one who has lived publicly, on-line or off, has a spotless record."

We at SorryWatch also understand that it's depressing to live in a way that's all gotcha, little joy. We know from doing the site that people crave the quick hit of an eviscerating, rage-filled analysis of a terrible apology. We sometimes feel the irresistible urge to metaphorically disembowel a horrid political apology, to hurl monkey poop at a pathetic celebrity apology. As we've said, our angriest posts tend to be the ones that get the most traffic. And yet we find ourselves yearning more and more for ex-amples of good apologies. They feel better to write about. They don't make us hate ourselves afterward. They don't make us feel as though we're grappling in the mud with a pig but rather frolicking in a gentle, cleansing summer rain with pigs and many other kinds of mammals, all of whom yearn for a more thoughtful, mindful farm.

What if We Lived as Though Human Redemption Were Possible?

When Marjorie was in her twenties, she read a book by another woman in her twenties about how the phenomenon of college date rape was exaggerated. Marjorie and the writer had been college classmates. The writer, after cherry-picking data and blaming feminists for a supposed wave of unwarranted panic and infantilization of women on campuses, asked something like (and we paraphrase) "If one in four of my friends were date raped, wouldn't I know it?" And Marjorie's visceral response was "No, you wouldn't! Because your whole *vibe* means that anyone who *was* date raped wouldn't tell you!" Maybe a valid parallel here is: If you've shown yourself to be a person without mercy, why would someone come to you when they seek mercy?

There's a chance for bridge building here if we choose to take it. Kumar and Epley felt, as we do, that their findings had broader implications. "We believe the asymmetry in attention to competence versus warmth could create mistaken expectations across a wide range of prosocial actions," they wrote. In other words, people's fears of sounding dumb or naive or calculating or insincere could stand in the way of connection making across many different chasms. Maybe don't act as though educable people are perpetually bad or dumb? Are you verbally slapping them to be performative, or really trying to change the world for the better?

So again we ask: What if we conveyed that it's okay to make a mistake as long as you're willing to apologize, learn from it, and make amends? We're not talking about accepting deliberately obtuse, gaslighting apologies. We're not saying anyone has to forgive the unforgivable. We're talking about allowing folks who are capable of learning to have the opportunity. What if we didn't hover like vultures ready to pounce?

Culture Change in Action

The cultural shift in thinking described by Kaplan and Beary leaves room for people to acknowledge errors, try again, and be accepted. Given that no one's perfect, we must leave room for people to be imperfect *when they're doing their best.*

There are always doomsayers who say change can't happen. (Sometimes they say, "Get over it." No.) Which brings us to a related cultural shift in . . . macaques. This comes from a fascinating experiment done by the great primatologist Frans B. M. de Waal and Denise L. Johanowicz. They were familiar with the behavioral differences between two different species of macaque, rhesus macaques and stump-tailed macaques. They wanted to know what would happen in a mixed colony.

Rhesus macaques are edgy and somewhat combative monkeys, extremely interested in who is dominant to whom, and don't you forget it. They have nice, long tails. Stump-tails are calmer, gentler, and quite interested in everyone getting along. They have a big set of reassuring gestures they use when reconciling after fights. They reconciled three times more often than the rhesus did. Aww. But don't forget, their tails are little stubby things.

The researchers introduced groups of the two macaques into a large new enclosure. All were juveniles but, stacking the deck a little bit in favor of pacifism, the rhesus were two-year-olds and the stump-tails were two-and-a-half-year-olds. First the stump-tails mooched around, exploring the new digs, and the rhesus monkeys clung to the ceiling in a fearful group. Then the fiercest rhesus made threatening grunts down at the stump-tails. That's the sort of thing that would have gotten a reaction from another rhesus, but the stump-tails paid no attention. Finally, the rhesus came down from the ceiling and everyone made chitchat. They played. They squabbled. And then the stump-tails insisted on reconciling and wouldn't take "I'm still mad!" for an answer. Also, the stump-tails were charmed by the rhesus's tails and insisted on grooming them, and how can you stay mad at someone who so clearly thinks you're gorgeous? At first the monkeys slept at night in separate heaps, a rhesus heap and a stump-tail heap, but soon they got along so well, they all slept in one big monkey heap. Fuzzy.

Five months into the experiment, when the researcher took the stump-tails out, the rhesus had adopted their peacemaking ways. After fights or disagreements, they were now just as likely to reconcile as the stump-tails were. Without their stump-tailed buddies to show them how? They went right on being nice. Although they still used rhesus calls and gestures, they had adopted the kind, community-mindedness of the stump-tails, and they liked it too much to change back.

One Way We Do It

Apologizing is part of a network of things we do to make the world feel kinder, more connected. And if we do these things, then it *is* kinder and more connected. To apologize well is to learn something. Because the person apologizing needs to show they understand what they themselves did, they are forced to examine their behavior and/or their previously unthinking assumptions. They—we—become wiser.

We may never know the impact of our apologies: forestalling a lawsuit, changing a worldview, showing someone who was convinced evil was everywhere that maybe people are capable of being better.

In a world that desperately needs more kindness and respect, apologizing is a concrete way to provide those things. It's what strong, good people do to build a strong, good world. This is one of the ways to make the world what we want it to be. You have this power. *We* have this power.

ACKNOWLEDGMENTS

This book! We're extravagantly grateful to those who helped bring it into being.

At Gallery/Simon & Schuster, we are lucky to have found our helpful and supportive editor, Hannah Braaten. Tons of thanks, too, to the delightful Andrew Nguyễn and to the savvy legal and production teams who made our idea into reality. Jen Bergstrom provided astounding moral support exactly when needed. And can we just mention our amaahhzing agent, Sarah "Fierce Shepherdess" Burnes, and her able aide-de-camp, Sophie Pugh-Sellers, at the Gernert Agency? We're grateful for practical help on the SorryWatch.com website from David Gallagher. We've been fortunate to have many readers who call our attention to interesting apologies—among them Elizabeth Crane, Wendy M. Grossman (who doubles as our Senior Tennis Correspondent), Barry Hayes, Kali Israel, Jonelle Patrick (Our Woman in Japan), and sagacious frequent commenter Tanita S. Davis. Thank you to anyone who's ever brought our attention to an apology, good or bad.

Radical gratitude goes to PlayApology Camp at Burning Man, particularly David Wollock, Liz Bronstein, Sue Fernandez, Catherine Melina, D-Stracted, Fruity Felix, Liz, MadKap, and Other Matt. Also xtrasilky and Dr. Cheezie, who tipped us off that PlayApology exists. We are also grateful for the considerable assistance of Binky and The Horse Doc. And to The WELL, where we first met, and which has provided to

SorryWatch more assistance of divers kinds than we can mention. Special plates o' shrimp to David Gans, Jon Carroll, Paul Belserene, Katherine Catmull, Mike Godwin, G. Jack King, David B. Doty, Ernie in Berkeley, Frako Loden, Felicity O'Meara, and Randall Swimm. We've also been helped by Sumana Harihareswara, Teresa Moore, Michele H., and William Benjamin Abbott IV.

We're indebted to Harriet Lerner, who writes eloquently about using apology concepts in her psychotherapy practice. Thanks, too, to Helen Zaltzman, Laura Beaudin Lakhian, and Maggie Balistreri. Anyone who writes about apology without thanking Aaron Lazare for his groundbreaking work needs to apologize.

Going way back, Susan thanks some of the lovely people at *Salon*, which ran her first writing on the cravenness that is "Sorry if," especially Laura Miller, Andrew Leonard, Karen Croft, Scott Rosenberg, Gary Kamiya, and David Talbott. Marjorie adds thanks to Wayne Hoffman (first at the *Forward*, then at *Tablet*), Paula Derrow (first at *Glamour*, then at *Self*), and Danielle Claro (first at *Sassy*, then, well, everywhere) for teaching her tons.

We super-mega-thank our brilliant early readers, Carol Ingall, Ed.D., and Gayle Forman. Having a professor mom whose field is moral education is helpful when writing about doing things that are correct but difficult. And as for Gayle, as some pig once said, "It is not often that someone comes along who is both a true friend and a good writer." Gayle is a true friend, a good writer, *and* a great editor, and therefore better than a spider.

We've had so much help and kindness in our quest to understand apology. We know it and we appreciate it. Thank you. If we missed mentioning you, it's probably because you're the most essential person of all, and that means, ironically, we're going to have to apologize to you. Damn, it's *so* hard not to screw up.

NOTES

Chapter 1: The Importance of Apologies, Good and Bad

9 *he was asked by Jimmy Fallon:* "Donald Trump on 'Tonight Show': Will Apologize 'If I'm Ever Wrong,'" Associated Press, September 12, 2015, https://www.jacksonville.comstory/news/nation-world/2015/09/12/donald-trump-tonight-show-will-apologize-if-im-everwrong/15679585007/.

11 *"Gadsden had the quixotic notion":* William Oliver Stevens, *Pistols at Ten Paces: The Story of the Code of Honor in America* (Boston: Houghton Mifflin, 1940), 20.

12 *"Modern progress has brought":* Vivek H. Murthy, MD, *Together: The Healing Power of Human Connection in a Sometimes Lonely World* (New York: Harper Wave, 2020), 98.

12 *"indignant disagreement":* Pew Research Center, "Critical Posts Get More Likes, Comments, and Shares Than Other Posts," February 21, 2017, https://www.pewresearch.org/politics/2017/02/23/partisan-conflict-and-congressional-outreach/pdl-02-23-17_antipathy-new-00-02/.

12 *It's akin to getting high:* Dar Meshi, Anastasia Elizarova, Andrew Bender, Antonio Verdejo-Garcia, "Excessive Social Media Users Demonstrate Impaired Decision Making in the Iowa Gambling Task," *Journal of Behavioral Addiction* 8, no. 1 (March 1, 2019): 169–73, https://doi.org/10.1556/2006.7.2018.138.

13 *ChadMichael Morrisette was minding his business:* Rachel Bertsche,

"Bully's Powerful Apology to Student He Tormented—20 Years Later," Yahoo! News, May 14, 2015, https://www.yahoo.com/news/bullys -powerful-apology-to-student-he-tormented-118953377332.html.

17 *took his granddaughter:* Angela Sterritt, "Indigenous Grandfather and 12-Year-Old Handcuffed in Front of Vancouver Bank After Trying to Open an Account," CBC News, January 9, 2020, https://www.cbc.ca /news/canada/british-columbia/indigenous-girl-grandfather-hand cuffed-bank-1.5419519.

17 *There was a branch manager:* IN THE MATTER OF THE *HUMAN RIGHTS CODE* R.S.B.C. 1996, c. 210 (AS AMENDED) AND IN THE MATTER OF A COMPLAINT BEFORE THE BRITISH COLUMBIA HUMAN RIGHTS TRIBUNAL BETWEEN: MAXWELL JOHNSON SR. AND TORIANNE, COMPLAINANTS, AND: VANCOUVER POLICE BOARD, RESPONDENT: APPENDIX IN RESPONSE TO COMPLAINT, https://www.strongascedar.ca/wp-content/uploads /2021/05/2021-02-17-VPD-Appendix-to-Response-to-Complaint _Redacted.pdf.

19 *The bank let it be known:* Simon Little and Sean Boynton, "BMO Apologizes for Handcuffing of Indigenous 12-Year-Old, Denies Racism a Factor," Global News, January 16, 2020, https://globalnews.ca/news /6422079/indigenous-handcuffing-bmo-apology/Li.

21 *"Better Late Than Early":* Cynthia McPherson Frantz and Courtney Bennigson, "Better Late Than Early: The Influence of Timing on Apology Effectiveness," *Journal of Experimental Social Psychology* 41, no. 2 (March 2005): 201–7, https://doi.org/10.1016/j.jesp.2004.07.007.

22 *Loretta J. Ross:* https://lorettajross.com.

Chapter 2: Six Simple Steps to Getting It Right

29   *two most powerful words in the English language:* Harriet Lerner, *Why Won't You Apologize?: Healing Big Betrayals and Everyday Hurts* (New York: Gallery Books, 2017), 175.

29   *"If you can't stomach an apology":* Guy Browning, *Never Hit a Jellyfish with a Spade: How to Survive Life's Smaller Challenges* (New York: Gotham Books/Penguin Group, 2005).

31   *comedian Franchesca Ramsey:* Franchesca Ramsey, *Well, That Escalated Quickly: Memoirs and Mistakes of an Accidental Activist* (New York: Grand Central Publishing, 2018), 67.

31   *vague sentiments delivered somberly in Italian:* Yuhan Xu, "Dolce & Gabbana Ad (with Chopsticks) Provokes Public Outrage in China," NPR, December 1, 2018, https://www.npr.org/sections/goatsandsoda/2018/12/01/671891818/dolce-gabbana-ad-with-chopsticks-provokes-public-outrage-in-china.

31   *"by zombies":* Dr. Rebecca Johnson (@johnsonr), October 18, 2012, Twitter, https://twitter.com/johnsonr/status/259012668298506240.

33   *grown-up sports announcer:* Kay Jones, Laura James, and Alaa Elassar, "Announcer Who Hurled Racist Insults at a High School Basketball Team Has Issued an Apology," CNN, updated March 14, 2021, https://www.cnn.com/2021/03/13/us/oklahoma-high-school-basketball-announcer-trnd/index.html.

34   *When a woman attending a wedding:* Maressa Brown, "This Woman Had the Perfect Response When Told She Couldn't Breastfeed at a Museum," *Cosmopolitan*, March 23, 2016, https://www.cosmopolitan.com/lifestyle/news/a55663/woman-shamed-breastfeeding-western-reserve-cleveland/.

34   *If last night I said I would clear the dishes:* Shawna Potter, *Making Spaces Safer: A Guide to Giving Harassment the Boot Wherever You Work, Play, and Gather* (Chico, CA: AK Press, 2019).

38 *you might want to line up assistance:* Sage A. Sharp, "So You Want to Apologize . . . Now What?," Software Freedom Conservancy, April 20, 2021, https://sfconservancy.org/blog/?author=sage.

42 *timeless disclaimer from Monty Python:* Internet Movie Database, *Monty Python's Flying Circus* (TV Series), "The War Against Pornography," 1972, https://www.imdb.com/title/tt0651002/characters/nm0001385.

Chapter 3: Sorry If, Sorry But, Sorry You: Things Not to Say

45 *Oakland's former mayor said she was "apologetic":* Internet Archive capture of KRON 4 News at 8, June 8, 2014, https://archive.org/details/KRON_20140609_030000_KRON_4_News_at_8.

46 *he put up Instagram posts:* Chris DeVille, "Questlove Apologizes for Racist Instagrams," Stereogum, December 30, 2013, https://www.stereogum.com/1615151/questlove-apologizes-for-racist-instagrams/news/.

47 *Sometimes, the failure of the other person to apologize:* Harriet Lerner, *Why Won't You Apologize?: Healing Big Betrayals and Everyday Hurts* (New York: Gallery Books, 2017), 4.

48 *the idea that apologizing is lily-livered and unmanly:* Edwin L. Battistella, *Sorry About That: The Language of Public Apology* (New York: Oxford University Press, 2014), 172–74.

49 A Fish Called Wanda: Movieclips, "A Fish Called Wanda (6/11) Movie Clip; Upside-Down Apology (1988)," May 13, 2015, YouTube video, https://www.youtube.com/watch?v=lwfuUyTMpVY.

51 *the example of sisters Iris and Marie:* Gary Chapman and Jennifer Thomas, *The Five Languages of Apology: How to Experience Healing in All Your Relationships* (Chicago: Northfield Publishing, 2006), 31.

54 *"had not understood the apology process":* Aaron Lazare, *On Apology* (Oxford: Oxford University Press, 2004), 169.

55 *Mark Wahlberg's 1993 press conference:* Michael Saunders, "Facing Protest, Wahlberg Apologizes for 'Racist' Action," *Boston Globe,* February

19, 1993, posted December 5, 2014, https://www.bostonglobe.com /metro/1993/02/19/facing-protest-wahlberg-apologizes-for-racist -action/C8QUpxtnexamtLjiSQIWxN/story.html.

55 *Wahlberg threw rocks and chanted:* Marlow Stern, "Mark Wahlberg's Pardon Plea: A Look Back at His Troubled, Violent, and Racist Rap Sheet," *Daily Beast,* December 7, 2014, updated April 14, 2017, https://www .thedailybeast.com/mark-wahlbergs-pardon-plea-a-look-back-at-his -troubling-violent-and-racist-rap-sheet.

56 *"but that's no excuse":* Saunders, "Facing Protest, Wahlberg Apologizes."

56 *"don't do it":* Saunders, "Facing Protest, Wahlberg Apologizes."

56 *"made it 10 times more difficult":* Megan Johnson, "Mark Wahlberg Reflects on His Criminal Past: 'I Made a Lot of Terrible Mistakes,'" Yahoo! News, March 23, 2020, https://ph.news.yahoo.com/mark-wahlberg-criminal -past-terrible-mistakes-115207988.html.

57 *"did not mean it in a racial sense":* "Presidential Hopeful Sen. Ernest Hollings, D-SC, Was in Trouble . . . ," UPI, October 12, 1983, https:// www.upi.com/Archives/1983/10/12/Presidential-hopeful-Sen-Ernest -Hollings-D-SC-was-in-trouble/6591434779200/.

60 *NASA launch integration manager Wayne Hale:* Marjorie Ingall, "Time for Another Unabashedly Fab Apology," SorryWatch.com, December 28, 2013, https://sorrywatch.com/time-for-another-unabashedly -fab-apology/.

62 *they only report on how the speaker feels:* Battistella, *Sorry About That,* 58.

Chapter 4: Blame It on the Brain:
The Science of Why We Say Such Dumb Stuff

66 Vanity Fair: Monica Lewinsky, "Monica Lewinsky: Emerging from 'the House of Gaslight' in the Age of #MeToo," *Vanity Fair,* March 2018, https://www.vanityfair.com/news/2018/02/monica-lewinsky-in-the -age-of-metoo.

67 The Chronology of Water: Lidia Yuknavitch, *The Chronology of Water: A Memoir* (Edinburgh: Canongate, 2010), 277–78.

69 *In one such study:* Emory University Health Sciences Center, "Emory Study Lights Up the Political Brain," ScienceDaily, January 31, 2006, www.sciencedaily.com/releases/2006/01/060131092225.htm.

69 *"Essentially, it appears as if partisans twirl the cognitive kaleidoscope":* Emory, "Emory Study Lights Up the Political Brain."

70 *Carol Tavris and Elliot Aronson write:* Carol Tavris and Elliot Aronson, *Mistakes Were Made (but Not by Me): Why We Justify Foolish Beliefs, Bad Decisions, and Hurtful Acts* (San Diego: Harcourt, 2007), 4.

70 *Without it, they note:* Tavris and Aronson, *Mistakes Were Made*, 9.

70 *"The brain is designed with blind spots":* Tavris and Aronson, *Mistakes Were Made*, 42.

70 *Tavris and Aronson again:* Tavris and Aronson, *Mistakes Were Made*, 44.

71 *In a seminal study:* Roy Baumeister, Arlene Stillwell, and Sara R. Wotman, "Victim and Perpetrator Accounts of Interpersonal Conflict: Autobiographical Narratives About Anger," *Journal of Personality and Social Psychology* 59, no. 5 (November 1990): 994–1005, https://doi.org/10.1037/0022-3514.59.5.994.

72 *"less prone to become angry":* Baumeister, Stillwell, and Wotman, "Victim and Perpetrator Accounts," 1000.

73 *"unnecessarily vindictive":* Baumeister, Stillwell, and Wotman, "Victim and Perpetrator Accounts," 1001.

79 *In a TED Talk:* Brené Brown, "The Power of Vulnerability," June 2010, TedXHouston, https://www.ted.com/talks/brene_brown_the_power_of_vulnerability.

80 *"a place of happiness":* Nicole Sperling, "Ellen DeGeneres Apologizes to Staff Members as WarnerMedia Investigates Show," *New York Times*, July 30, 2020, updated December 10, 2020, https://www.nytimes.com/2020/07/30/business/media/ellen-degeneres-apologizes.html.

81 *apologized on air:* John Koblin, "Ellen DeGeneres Returns to Show with

Apology for Toxic Workplace," *New York Times*, September 21, 2020, updated May 12, 2021, https://www.nytimes.com/2020/09/21/business/media/ellen-degeneres-show.html.

81   *"Being known as the 'Be Kind' Lady":* Emily Yahr, "Ellen DeGeneres Returns to TV, Addresses Controversy: 'Being Known as the "Be Kind" Lady Is a Tricky Position to Be In,' " *Washington Post*, September 21, 2020, https://www.washingtonpost.com/arts-entertainment/2020/09/21/ellen-degeneres-addresses-show-controversy/.

82   *The* New York Times *snarkily noted:* John Koblin, "Ellen DeGeneres Loses 1 Million Viewers After Apologies for Toxic Workplace," *New York Times*, March 22, 2021, https://www.nytimes.com/2021/03/22/business/media/ellen-degeneres-ratings-decline.html.

83   *Kennedy gave a speech:* Thomas W. Benson, *Writing JFK: Presidential Rhetoric and the Press in the Bay of Pigs Crisis* (College Station, TX: Texas A&M University Press, 2003), 83.

89   *Kevin Spacey's apology on Twitter:* Kevin Spacey (@KevinSpacey), October 29, 2017, Twitter, https://twitter.com/KevinSpacey/status/924848412842971136.

90   *2010 meta-study:* "Empathy: College Students Don't Have as Much as They Used To," Michigan News: University of Michigan, May 27, 2010, https://news.umich.edu/empathy-college-students-don-t-have-as-much-as-they-used-to/.

91   *"Japanese apologies":* Aaron Lazare, *On Apology* (Oxford: Oxford University Press, 2005), 33.

Chapter 5: "I'm Sorry I Chased You with a Booger": Teaching Children to Apologize

95   *Take Riley here:* Snarly, "This Booger-Related Apology Is Better Than the Daily Beast's Olympic Apology," SorryWatch.com, August 14, 2016, http://sorrywatch.com/tag/ciara/.

96 *Jack's regurgitation situation:* Julie Kliegman, "A Boy Vomited in a Bookstore and Then Sent the Staff the Best Apology Letter," BuzzFeed News, April 7, 2015, https://www.buzzfeednews.com/article/juliekliegman/attention-barf-cleaners#.llEPNNK6Bk.

99 *she never knew how reconciliation took place:* Kate Rossmanith, *Small Wrongs: How We Really Say Sorry in Love, Life and Law* (Melbourne: Hardie Grant Books, 2018), 133.

100 *making him stand up at the dinner table:* Deborah Anna Luepnitz, PhD, *Schopenhauer's Porcupines: Intimacy and Its Dilemmas; Five Stories of Psychotherapy* (New York: Basic Books, 2002), 133.

101 *"an apology that comes from your lips":* Irène Némirovsky, *The Wine of Solitude* (New York: Knopf Doubleday, 2014), 30–31.

101 *"If you were really sorry, you wouldn't have done it":* Harriet Lerner, *Why Won't You Apologize?: Healing Big Betrayals and Everyday Hurts* (New York: Gallery Books, 2017), 97–98.

101 *even the smallest error:* Rossmanith, *Small Wrongs*, 31.

101 *a life-size pastel of Leif Erikson:* Amber Ruffin and Lacey Lamar, *You'll Never Believe What Happened to Lacey: Crazy Stories About Racism* (New York: Grand Central Publishing, 2021), 81–84.

104 *They constructed a game:* Barbara Moran, "'It's Not Fair!': *Nature* Paper Studies Kids and Fairness in Seven Societies," *The Brink*: Boston University, November 18, 2015, https://www.bu.edu/articles/2015/child-development-fairness/.

104 *"Getting nothing seems better":* Katherine McAuliffe, Peter R. Blake, and Felix Warneken, "Do Kids Have a Fundamental Sense of Fairness?," *Scientific American*, August 23, 2017, https://blogs.scientificamerican.com/observations/do-kids-have-a-fundamental-sense-of-fairness/.

106 *1768 apology from twelve-year-old Charles FitzGerald:* Stella Tillyard, *Aristocrats: Caroline, Emily, Louisa, and Sarah Lennox, 1740–1832* (New York: Farrar, Straus and Giroux, 1994), 222.

107 *choose their own kind of morning greeting:* "Teacher Greeting Her Students

with Special Handshakes & Hugs Before Class," Twitter Clips, November 9, 2018, https://www.youtube.com/watch?v=TdukPkUo30c.

107   *a dap:* Eliza Murphy, "Teacher Has Personalized Handshakes with Every One of His Students," Yahoo! News, February 1, 2017, https://www.yahoo.com/gma/teacher-personalized-handshakes-every-one-students-200526323--abc-news-topstories.html.

110   *"Deez nuts!":* Jessica Roy, "Sixth Grader Pens Handwritten Apology for Calling 911 and Yelling 'Deez Nuts,'" *New York* magazine, May 29, 2015, https://nymag.com/intelligencer/2015/05/6th-grader-apologizes-for-yelling-deez-nuts.html.

111   *example of a British child:* East Midlands Ambulance Service NHS Trust (@EMASNHSTrust), August 9, 2016, Twitter, https://twitter.com/EMASNHSTrust/status/762965767935684608.

CHAPTER 6: "Sorry, Our Policy Is That We Are Never at Fault": The Odiousness That Is Corporate

121   *2006 Harvard hospital system report:* "When Things Go Wrong: Responding to Adverse Events; A Consensus Statement of the Harvard Hospitals," Massachusetts Coalition for the Prevention of Medical Errors, March 2006, 10, http://www.macoalition.org/documents/respondingToAdverseEvents.pdf.

122   *2019 study in the* Stanford Law Review: Benjamin J. McMichael, R. Lawrence Van Horn, and W. Kip Viscusi, "Sorry Is Never Enough: How State Apology Laws Fail to Reduce Medical Malpractice Liability Risk," *Stanford Law Review* 71 (February 2019): 344, https://review.law.stanford.edu/wp-content/uploads/sites/3/2019/02/McMichael-71-Stan.-L.-Rev.-341-2019.pdf.

122   *"illustrates the importance":* McMichael, Van Horn, and Viscusi, "Sorry Is Never Enough," 388.

123   *"Apologies and Medical Error":* Jennifer K. Robbennolt, "Apologies and

Medical Error," *Clinical Orthopaedics and Related Research* 467, no. 2 (February 2009): 376–82, https://doi.org/10.1007/s11999-008-0580-1.

124 After Harm: Medical Error and the Ethics of Forgiveness: Nancy Berlinger, *After Harm: Medical Error and the Ethics of Forgiveness* (Baltimore: Johns Hopkins University Press, 2005).

125 Health Affairs: Michelle M. Mello, Allen Kachalia, Stephanie Roche, Melinda Van Niel, Lisa Buchsbaum, Suzanne Dodson, Patricia Folcarelli, Evan M. Benjamin, and Kenneth E. Sands, "Outcomes in Two Massachusetts Hospital Systems Give Reason for Optimism About Communication-And-Resolution Programs," *Health Affairs* 36, no. 10 (2017): 1795.

125 *"How Do Patients Want Physicians to Handle Mistakes?":* Amy B. Witman, Deric M. Park, and Steven B. Hardin, "How Do Patients Want Physicians to Handle Mistakes?," *Archives of Internal Medicine* 156, no. 22 (December 1996): 2566, https://doi.org/10.1377/hlthaff.2017.0320.

125 *the Lancet:* Charles Vincent, Magi Young, and Angela Phillips, "Why Do People Sue Doctors? A Study of Patients and Relatives Taking Legal Action," *Lancet* 343, no. 8913 (June 25, 1994): 1609–13, https://doi.org/10.1016/s0140-6736(94)93062-7.

126 *thirty-two-year-old man who visited a rural Hawaiian ER:* "Huge Settlement for Family of Man with Sore Throat Who Died at Hawaii Clinic," Associated Press, September 14, 2016, https://www.cbsnews.com/news/huge-settlement-for-family-of-man-with-sore-throat-who-died-at-hawaii-clinic/.

127 *Wojcieszak writes:* Doug Wojcieszak, "Hawaii Medical Center Apologizes, Promises Changes Following Death of 32-Year-Old Man," Sorry Works!, n.d., https://sorryworks.net/hawaii-medical-center-apologizes.

127 *Remember that Stanford paper:* McMichael, Van Horn, and Viscusi, "Sorry Is Never Enough," 390.

128 *Physician Sara Manning Peskin:* Sara Manning Peskin, MD, "My Human Doctor," *New York Times,* October 4, 2018, https://www.nytimes.com/2018/10/04/well/live/doctors-errors-apologies.html.

129   To Err Is Human: Linda T. Kohn, Janet M. Corrigan, and Molla S. Donaldson, eds., *To Err Is Human: Building a Safer Health System*, U.S. Institute of Medicine, Committee on Quality of Health Care in America (Washington, DC: National Academies Press, 2000), https://doi.org/10.17226/9728.

129   *magnificent memoir:* Paul Kalanithi, *When Breath Becomes Air* (New York: Random House, 2016), 78–80.

130   *Reddit:* "Which Medical Specialty Has the Biggest Jerks?," posted by u/Laistrygonian, r/medicine, Reddit, February 16, 2017, https://www.reddit.com/r/medicine/comments/5ufnvf/which_medical_specialty_has_the_biggest_jerks/.

130   *90 percent of surgeons:* Robbennolt, "Apologies and Medical Error."

130   *training in apologies as part of the curriculum:* Ralph A. Gillies, Stacie H. Speers, Sara M. Young, and Christopher A. Fly, "Teaching Medical Error Apologies: Development of a Multi-Component Intervention," *Family Medicine* 43, no. 6 (June 2011): 400.

130   *a 2011 paper in the* Journal of Family Medicine: Gillies et al., "Teaching Medical Error Apologies," 400–406.

130   *apologies by female students:* Gillies et al., "Teaching Medical Error Apologies," 404.

131   *"We are making a moral argument":* "When Things Go Wrong," 3.

132   *beginning in 1999:* Amy Edmonson, "Psychological Safety and Learning Behavior in Work Teams," *Administrative Science Quarterly* 44, no. 2 (June 1, 1999): 350–83, https://doi.org/10.2307/2666999.

133   *Communicator of the Year:* "United Airlines CEO Oscar Munoz Named PRWeek U.S. Communicator of the Year," *PRWeek*, March 9, 2017, https://www.prweek.com/article/1426909/united-airlines-ceo-oscar-munoz-named-prweek-us-communicator-year.

134   *leaked to the press:* "Text of Letter from United CEO Defending Employees," Associated Press, April 10, 2017, https://apnews.com/article/4e461a8a2ea144a7a7c739366caa79f5?.

136 *yet another statement:* Erin McCann, "United's Apologies: A Timeline," *New York Times*, April 14, 2017, https://www.nytimes.com/2017/04/14 /business/united-airlines-passenger-doctor.html.

137 *commitment to real change:* McCann, "United's Apologies."

137 *United also stated that Munoz and the company called Dr. Dao:* McCann, "United's Apologies."

137 *full-page ads:* "JetBlue Goes on the Apology Offensive," CBS/AP, on CBS News, February 21, 2007, https://www.cbsnews.com/news/jetblue-goes -on-the-apology-offensive/.

139 *flight attendant yelling, "I'm done!":* Sean Gardiner, "Flight Attendant Grabs Two Beers, Slides Down the Emergency Chute," *Wall Street Journal*, August 10, 2010, https://www.wsj.com/articles/SB1000142405274870 4388504575419743157731062.

139 *first political donation after the January 6 attack:* Rich Thomaselli, "JetBlue Defends Political Donation That Prompted Boycott Calls," Travel Pulse, April 10, 2021, https://www.travelpulse.com/news/airlines /jetblue-defends-political-donation-that-prompted-boycott-calls.html.

139 *diversity initiative:* Ted Reed, "As United Airlines Acts on Diversity and Carbon Emissions, Tucker Carlson Squawks and Sara Nelson Applauds," *Forbes*, April 13, 2021, https://www.forbes.com/sites/ted reed/2021/04/13/as-united-airlines-acts-on-diversity-and-carbon -emissions-tucker-carlson-squawks-and-sara-nelson-applauds/?.

140 *"We at Engulf & Devour":* Engulf & Devour is the evil media conglomerate in Mel Brooks's *Silent Movie*.

141 *Mort Drucker's "The Empire Strikes Out":* Matthew Trzcinski, "How a Note from George Lucas Saved a 'Star Wars' Parody," Showbiz CheatSheet, June 14, 2020, https://www.cheatsheet.com/entertainment/how-a-note -from-george-lucas-saved-a-star-wars-parody.html/.

142 *"The lawyers hated the fact that I was doing it":* Kevin A. Stein, Wm. Bryan Paul, and Peter Erikson, "James Burke, Johnson & Johnson," Public Apol-

ogy Central, Southern Utah University, n.d., http://publicapologycentral
.com/apologia-archive/corporate-2/james-burke-johnson-johnson/.

143 *A cleverly constructed 2009 study:* "Saying Sorry Really Does Cost Nothing," ScienceDaily, September 23, 2009, https://www.sciencedaily.com
/releases/2009/09/090923105815.htm.

143 *link to a YouTube video:* "A Personal Apology (Just for You)," Mullen-
Lowe Group, July 28, 2012, YouTube video, https://www.youtube.com
/watch?v=cNsUZGvLnMY.

145 *"in normal people":* William Raspberry, "The Chief and the Choke Hold,"
Washington Post, May 17, 1982, https://www.washingtonpost.com
/archive/politics/1982/05/17/the-chief-and-the-choke-hold/e17fa90f
-c692-43c2-935f-463da9cab500/.

145 *Pew study:* Rich Morin, Kim Parker, Renee Stepler, and Andrew
Mercer, "Behind the Badge: 6, Police Views, Public Views," Pew Research Center, January 11, 2017, https://www.pewresearch.org/social
-trends/2017/01/11/police-views-public-views/.

146 *"Events over the past several years":* Tom Jackman, "U.S. Police Chiefs Group
Apologizes for 'Historical Mistreatment' of Minorities," *Washington Post,*
October 17, 2016, https://www.washingtonpost.com/news/true-crime
/wp/2016/10/17/head-of-u-s-police-chiefs-apologizes-for-historic
-mistreatment-of-minorities/.

147 *"The town of Windsor":* Neil Vigdor, "Officer Who Pepper-Sprayed a Black
Army Officer Is Fired," *New York Times,* April 12, 2021, updated April
13, 2001, https://www.nytimes.com/2021/04/12/us/virginia-police
-officer-gutierrez-pepper-spray.html.

148 *"further distances communities":* Thomas C. O'Brien, Tracey L. Meares,
and Tom R. Tyler, "Reconciling Police and Communities with Apologies,
Acknowledgements, or Both: A Controlled Experiment," *Annals of the
American Academy of Political and Social Science* 687, no. 1 (2020): 210,
https://journals.sagepub.com/doi/pdf/10.1177/0002716220904659.

149 *"I've been arrested and jailed about 40 times"*: Traci Lee, "Civil Rights Leader Rep. John Lewis Accepts Long-Awaited Police Apology," MSNBC, March 4, 2013, https://www.msnbc.com/rachel-maddow-show/civil -rights-leader-rep-msna19464.

150 *Ryan Stokes was killed*: Daniel Boothe and Mike McGraw, "Official Reports About the Shooting of Ryan Stokes Raise More Questions Than Answers. Here's Why," Flatland, July 30, 2015, https://www.flatlandkc .org/news-issues/official-police-story-shooting-ryan-stokes-raises -doubts-why/.

151 *"The result of the events"*: Caitlin Knute, " 'Ryan and John Wanted Us to Meet': Mothers Form Friendship, Seek Reform After Officers Killed Sons," KSHB, last updated November 2, 2021, https://www.kshb.com /news/local-news/investigations/ryan-and-john-wanted-us-to-meet -mothers-form-friendship-seek-reform-after-officers-killed-sons.

151 *Straub told local station*: Peggy Lowe, "Former Kansas City Police Officer Who Refuted Shooting Story Feels Forced Out, Apologizes to Victim's Mother," KCUR 89.3: NPR in Kansas City, May 29, 2020, https://www .kcur.org/news/2020-05-29/kansas-city-police-officer-who-refuted -shooting-story-feels-forced-out-apologizes-to-victims-mother.

152 *According to a 2016 study*: Rick Trinkner, Tom R. Tyler, and Phillip Atiba Goff, "Justice from Within: The Relations Between a Procedurally Just Organizational Climate and Police Organizational Efficiency, Endorsement of Democratic Policing, and Officer Well-Being," *Psychology, Public Policy, and Law* 22, no. 2 (2016): 158–72, https://doi.org/10.1037 /law0000085.

152 *Another study found that*: Rick Trinkner, Erin M. Kerrison, and Phillip Atiba Goff, "The Force of Fear: Police Stereotype Threat, Self-Legitimacy, and Support for Excessive Force," *Law and Human Behavior* 43, no. 5 (October 2019): 421–35, http://dx.doi.org/10.1037 /lhb0000339.

152 *"a really bad day"*: Margaret Sullivan, " 'Not Racially Motivated'?: The

Atlanta Spa Shootings Show Why the Media Should Be Wary of Initial Police Statements," *Washington Post*, March 18, 2021, https://www.washingtonpost.com/lifestyle/media/media-police-statements-atlanta-spa-shootings-jay-baker/2021/03/18/83f1b438-87ec-11eb-8a8b-5cf82c3dffe4_story.html?utm_source=reddit.com.

153 *"one of the hardest in his 28 years in law enforcement"*: "8 Dead in Atlanta Spa Shootings, with Fears of Anti-Asian Bias," *New York Times*, last updated March 26, 2021, https://www.nytimes.com/live/2021/03/17/us/shooting-atlanta-acworth.

153 *charges against cops are often dismissed:* Gabriel Sandoval and Greg B. Smith, "NYPD Commissioners Cleared Cops Found Guilty of Everything from Chokeholds to Pushing Man into Traffic," *The City*, March 14, 2021, https://www.thecity.nyc/2021/3/14/22330463/nypd-commissioners-cleared-guilty-cops-chokeholds-matrix.

153 *rarely convicted:* Mark Berman, "When Police Kill People, They Are Rarely Prosecuted and Hard to Convict," *Washington Post*, April 4, 2021, https://www.washingtonpost.com/nation/2021/04/04/when-police-kill-people-they-are-rarely-prosecuted-hard-convict/.

154 *The nonprofit Sentencing Project has found:* German Lopez, "Mass Incarceration in America, Explained in 22 Maps and Charts," *Vox*, updated October 11, 2016, https://www.vox.com/2015/7/13/8913297/mass-incarceration-maps-charts.

154 *nine out of ten calls to the police:* Rashawn Ray, "What Does 'Defund the Police' Mean and Does It Have Merit?," Brookings, June 19, 2020, https://www.brookings.edu/blog/fixgov/2020/06/19/what-does-defund-the-police-mean-and-does-it-have-merit/?fbclid=IwAR1XTmjGOLNZgLuEQRC-v-zEfUXpOLyQm4rr2t__b_KI4BuC_7meJ_NwxgE.

156 *"I know the intense pressures":* Sullivan, "'Not Racially Motivated'?"

157 *"By foregrounding the voices and perspectives":* William Critchley-Menor, S.J., "Interview: How the Jesuits Are Working to Confront Their History

of Slavery," *America: The Jesuit Review*, February 26, 2021, https://www
.americamagazine.org/politics-society/2021/02/26/black-history
-slavery-jesuits-catholic-reconciliation-240100.

157 *"We express our solemn contrition":* Daniel Burke, "In Emotional Service, Jesuits and Georgetown Repent for Slave Trading," CNN, updated
April 20, 2017, https://www.cnn.com/2017/04/18/living/georgetown
-slavery-service.

158 *"This is an opportunity":* Rachel L. Swarns, "Catholic Order Pledges
$100 Million to Atone for Slave Labor and Sales," *New York Times*,
March 15, 2021, last updated May 10, 2021, https://www.nytimes
.com/2021/03/15/us/jesuits-georgetown-reparations-slavery.html.

Chapter 7: The Government Feels Sad About How That
All Went Down: How Political Apologies Get Made

164 *"this turbulent priest":* Ben Johnson, "Thomas Becket," Historic UK,
accessed April 30, 2021, https://www.historic-uk.com/HistoryUK
/HistoryofEngland/Thomas-Becket/.

164 *"What miserable drones and traitors":* Katherine Har, "Murder in the
Cathedral," British Library, medieval manuscripts blog, April 16, 2015,
https://blogs.bl.uk/digitisedmanuscripts/2015/04/murder-in-the
-cathedral.html.

164 *Anyway, dead:* Lloyd de Beer and Naomi Speakman, "Who Killed Thomas
Becket?," April 22, 2021, https://blog.britishmuseum.org/who-killed
-thomas-becket/.

165 *Lao Tzu, in a translation by Stephen Mitchell:* Carol Tavris and Elliot
Aronson, *Mistakes Were Made (but Not by Me): Why We Justify Foolish
Beliefs, Bad Decisions, and Hurtful Acts* (Boston: Houghton Mifflin Har-
court, 2007), 323–24.

166 *no duty to make redress for slavery:* Brian A. Weiner, *Sins of the Parents: The*

Politics of National Apologies in the United States (Philadelphia: Temple University Press, 2005), 130–31.

166   *a referendum of Georgetown students:* Deepika Jonnalagadda, "Students Endorse Reconciliation Fee in GU272 Referendum," *The Hoya,* April 12, 2019, https://thehoya.com/students-endorse-reconciliation-fee-gu272 -referendum/.

167   *The famous promise:* Henry Louis Gates Jr., "The Truth Behind '40 Acres and a Mule,'" PBS, accessed December 17, 2021, https://www.pbs.org /wnet/african-americans-many-rivers-to-cross/history/the-truth -behind-40-acres-and-a-mule/.

167   *Never doubt that slavery's repercussions:* Sergio Peçanha, "These Numbers Show That Black and White People Live in Two Different Americas," *Washington Post,* June 23, 2020, https://www.washingtonpost.com /opinions/2020/06/22/what-numbers-say-whites-blacks-live-two -different-americas/.

168   *prevented from getting benefits under the G.I. Bill:* Joseph Thompson, "The GI Bill Should've Been Race Neutral, Politicos Made Sure It Wasn't," *Military Times,* November 9, 2019, https://www.militarytimes .com/military-honor/salute-veterans/2019/11/10/the-gi-bill-shouldve -been-race-neutral-politicos-made-sure-it-wasnt/.

168   *"millions of workers from Africa":* Yanan Wang, "'Workers' or Slaves? Textbook Maker Backtracks After Mother's Online Complaint," *Washington Post,* October 5, 2015, https://www.washingtonpost.com/news /morning-mix/wp/2015/10/05/immigrant-workers-or-slaves -textbook-maker-backtracks-after-mothers-online-complaint/.

168   *Texas's social studies curriculum was revamped:* Valerie Strauss, "Proposed Texas Textbooks Are Inaccurate, Biased and Politicized, New Report Finds," *Washington Post,* September 12, 2014, https://www.washington post.com/news/answer-sheet/wp/2014/09/12/proposed-texas-text books-are-inaccurate-biased-and-politicized-new-report-finds/.

168 *"unfortunate blemish"*: Joe Heim, "Teaching America's Truth," *Washington Post*, August 28, 2019, https://www.washingtonpost.com/education/2019/08/28/teaching-slavery-schools/.

169 *2011 Pew Research Center poll*: Russell Heimlich, "What Caused the Civil War?" Pew Research Center, May 18, 2011, https://www.pewresearch.org/fact-tank/2011/05/18/what-caused-the-civil-war/.

169 *controlled between 60 and 90 percent*: "Exhibition: Slavery and Justice; Slavery and the Slave Trade in Rhode Island," John Carter Brown Library, Brown University, n.d., https://www.brown.edu/Facilities/John_Carter_Brown_Library/exhibitions/jcbexhibit/Pages/exhibSlavery.html.

169 *Rhode Island slave trade*: Jay Coughtry, *The Notorious Triangle: Rhode Island and the African Slave Trade, 1700–1807* (Philadelphia: Temple University Press, 1981), 25.

169 *a white mob attacked a Black neighborhood in Tulsa*: A. G. Sulzberger, "As Survivors Dwindle, Tulsa Confronts Past," *New York Times*, June 19, 2011, https://www.nytimes.com/2011/06/20/us/20tulsa.html.

169 *survivor Buck Colbert Franklin*: Allison Keyes, "A Long-Lost Manuscript Contains a Searing Eyewitness Account of the Tulsa Race Massacre of 1921," *Smithsonian*, May 27, 2016, https://www.smithsonianmag.com/smithsonian-institution/long-lost-manuscript-contains-searing-eyewitness-account-tulsa-race-massacre-1921-180959251/.

170 *recommended reparations for survivors*: "Final Report of Findings and Recommendations of the 1921 Tulsa Race Riot Commission," *Tulsa World*, May 25, 2020, https://tulsaworld.com/final-report-of-findings-and-recommendations-of-the-1921-tulsa-race-riot-commission/html_1d8aaca1-5589-5666-90b4-47271f3c4523.html.

171 *resolution of apology for the 1887 burning down of their Chinatown*: Olga R. Rodriguez, Associated Press, "California City Apologizes for 1887 Chinatown Destruction," MSN.com, September 30, 2021, https://www.msn.com/en-ca/lifestyle/smart-living/california-city-apologizes-for-1887-chinatown-destruction/ar-AAOVEFo?.

171 *eventually paid out:* Michael Adler, "Water Fight: Archaeology, Litigation, and the Assessment of Pre-Contact Canal Irrigation Technologies in the Northern Rio Grande Region," in *Traditional Arid Lands Agriculture: Understanding the Past for the Future*, edited by Scott E. Ingram and Robert C. Hunt (Tucson: University of Arizona Press, 2015), 219.

172 *In 2000, Kevin Gover:* "Former Leader of BIA Reflects on Historic 'Never Again' Apology," Indianz.com, November 19, 2015, https://www .indianz.com/News/2015/11/19/former-leader-of-bia-reflects.asp.

172 *That's a revised version of the speech:* "Remarks of Kevin Gover at the Ceremony Acknowledging the 175th Anniversary of the BIA September 8, 2000," Tribal Court Clearinghouse, n.d., http://www.tribal-institute.org /lists/kevin_gover.htm.

173 *apology from Congress to Native Americans:* 111th Congress of the United States of America, First Session, January 26, 2009, Defense Appropriations Act, 2010 (H.R. 3326), Section 8113, pages 45–46, https:// www.govinfo.gov/content/pkg/BILLS-111hr3326enr/pdf/BILLS -111hr3326enr.pdf.

174 *Not publicly, not even out loud:* Rob Capriccioso, "A Sorry Saga: Obama Signs Native American Apology Resolution; Fails to Draw Attention to It," Indian Law Resource Center, January 13, 2010, https://indianlaw .org/node/529.

174 *the little-discussed enslavement of millions of Native Americans:* Joe Helm, "The Missing Pieces of America's Education," *Washington Post*, August 28, 2019, https://www.washingtonpost.com/education/2019/08/28 /historians-slavery-myths/.

175 *Clinton's apology in 1997:* "Remarks by the President in Apology for Study Done in Tuskegee," The White House, Office of the Press Secretary, May 16, 1997, https://clintonwhitehouse4.archives.gov/textonly/New /Remarks/Fri/19970516-898.html.

176 *harm from the Tuskegee Experiment:* Marcella Alsan and Marianne Wanamaker, "Tuskegee and the Health of Black Men," *Quarterly Journal of Eco-*

nomics 133, no. 1 (February 2018): 407–55, https://doi.org/10.1093/qje/qjx029.

177　*"I will never apologize"*: Edwin L. Battistella, *Sorry About That: The Language of Public Apology* (New York: Oxford University Press, 2014), 145.

177　*having gone on an "apology tour"*: Battistella, *Sorry About That*, 174.

177　*Those who examined the claim:* Glenn Kessler, "Obama's 'Apology Tour,'" *Washington Post*, February 22, 2011, http://voices.washingtonpost.com/fact-checker/2011/02/obamas_apology_tour.html.

178　*Martha Minow says when nations discuss how to respond to past evils:* Quoted in Weiner, *Sins of the Parents*, 9–10.

178　*"To apologize is to admit wrongdoing":* Weiner, *Sins of the Parents*, 11.

178　*a government declaring that it has changed:* Quoted in Battistella, *Sorry About That*, 118–19.

179　*argues that "detainment" or "incarceration" fit the facts better:* "Terminology," Densho, accessed December 18, 2021, https://densho.org/terminology/.

179　*Ronald Reagan resisted plans to apologize and make reparations:* Timothy P. Maga, "Ronald Reagan and Redress for Japanese-American Internment, 1983–88," *Presidential Studies Quarterly* 28, no. 3 (Summer 1998): 606–19, https://www.jstor.org/stable/i27551894.

179　*Ballet dancer Sono Osato:* Richard Goldstein, "Sono Osato, Japanese-American Ballet Star, Is Dead at 99," *New York Times*, December 26, 2018, https://www.nytimes.com/2018/12/26/obituaries/sono-osato-dead.html.

180　*In 1942, when George Takei was five:* "George Takei Recalls 'Degrading' Internment of Japanese Americans," *Los Angeles Times*, June 7, 2012 https://latimesblogs.latimes.com/lanow/2012/06/george-takei-recalls-japanese-internment.html.

180　*little George thought the barbed wire was to keep dinosaurs out:* George Takei, Justin Eisinger, Steven Scott, and Harmony Becker, *They Called Us Enemy* (Marietta, GA: Top Shelf Productions, 2019), 60–61.

180 *the fact that no sabotage:* J. Burton, M. Farrell, F. Lord, and R. Lord, "A Brief History of Japanese American Relocation During World War II," excerpts on "Confinement and Ethnicity: An Overview of World War II Japanese American Relocation Sites," Western Archeological and Conservation Center, National Park Service, U.S. Department of the Interior, *Publications in Anthropology* 74 (1999, revised July 2000), National Park Service, updated April 1, 2016, https://www.nps.gov /articles/historyinternment.htm. Complete text at https://www.nps .gov/parkhistory/online_books/anthropology74/index.htm.

181 *there were many Italian Americans in the fishing industry:* Stephen Fox, *The Unknown Internment: An Oral History of Italian Americans During World War II* (Boston: Twayne, 1990).

181 *Peruvian Nikkei:* Erika Lee, "The WWII Incarceration of Japanese Americans Stretched Beyond U.S. Borders," *Time*, December 4, 2019, https://time.com/5743555/wwii-incarceration-japanese-latin -americans/.

181 *Sarah Taber:* Dr Sarah Taber (@SarahTaber_bww), Twitter, thread from January 20, 2018, https://twitter.com/SarahTaber_bww/status /954774752970801152.

181 *"It's a question of whether the white man lives on the Pacific Coast or the brown men":* A. V. Krebs, "Bitter Harvest," *Washington Post*, February 2, 1992, https://www.washingtonpost.com/archive/opinions/1992/02/02 /bitter-harvest/c8389b23-884d-43bd-ad34-bf7b11077135/?.

181 *"Go for Broke" boys:* Go for Broke National Education Center, accessed December 18, 2021, https://www.goforbroke.org/learn/history/combat _history/world_war_2/european_theater/rescue_of_the_lost _battalion.php.

181 *the rescue of the "Lost Battalion":* "100th/442nd RCT and the Rescue of the 'Lost Battalion,' October 1944," Go for Broke National Research Center, n.d., https://www.goforbroke.org/learn/history/combat_history/world _war_2/european_theater/rescue_of_the_lost_battalion.php.

182   *ordered the 442nd mustered for an awards ceremony:* Duane Vachon, "442nd
      Regimental Combat Team," *Hawaii Reporter*, July 3, 2016, https://www
      .hawaiireporter.com/442nd-regimental-combat-team/.

182   *She got a threatening call:* Arthur A. Hansen, "Nikkei Agriculture in
      Orange County, California, the Masuda Farm Family, and the Ameri-
      can Way of Redressing Racism—Part 5 of 6," Discover Nikkei: Japanese
      Migrants and Their Descendants, December 21, 2012, http://www
      .discovernikkei.org/en/journal/2012/12/21/masuda-family-5/.

183   *President Gerald Ford figured the Bicentennial was a good time:* Battistella,
      Sorry About That, 113–16.

183   *"it was not the Japanese way":* Bilal Qureshi, "From Wrong to Right:
      A U.S. Apology for Japanese Internment," Codeswitch, National
      Public Radio, August 9, 2012, https://www.npr.org/sections/codeswitch
      /2013/08/09/210138278/japanese-internment-redress.

184   *"No funds shall be appropriated":* Weiner, *Sins of the Parents*, 63.

187   *"I cannot see that Japanese Canadians constitute the slightest menace":* James
      H. Marsh, "Japanese Canadian Internment: Prisoners in their own Coun-
      try," *The Canadian Encyclopedia*, February 23, 2012, updated by Eli
      Yarhi, September 17, 2020, https://www.thecanadianencyclopedia.ca
      /en/article/japanese-internment-banished-and-beyond-tears-feature.

188   *Mulroney—now Canada's prime minister—apologized:* Quoted in Mitch
      Miyagawa, "A Sorry State," *Walrus*, December 12, 2009, updated February
      18, 2021, https://thewalrus.ca/a-sorry-state/.

191   *the $20,000 he got was insulting:* Aaron Lazare, *On Apology* (Oxford:
      Oxford University Press, 2004), 131–32.

191   *She got $400 from the government of Switzerland:* Lazare, *On Apology*, 67.

192   *filed an amicus brief in an ACLU lawsuit:* David Inoue, "Oversight of
      the Trump Administration's Muslim Ban," Japanese American Citi-
      zens League, September 24, 2017, https://jacl.org/statements/over
      sight-of-the-trump-administrations-muslim-ban.

193   *The Aleuts were forced to work in the sealing industry:* Dorothy Knee Jones,

A Century of Servitude: Pribilof Aleuts Under U.S. Rule (Washington, DC: University Press of America, 1980), 44.

193 *abandoned cannery buildings:* Erin Blakemore, "The U.S. Forcibly Detained Native Alaskans During World War II," *Smithsonian*, February 22, 2017, https://www.smithsonianmag.com/smart-news/us-forcibly -detained-native-alaskans-during-world-war-ii-180962239/.

193 *"my and my agency's most sincere apology":* "We Are Aleuts. Let People Know," U.S. Fish & Wildlife Service, Alaska Region, n.d., www.fws.gov /Alaska/stories/we-are-aleuts-let-people-know.

194 *"I apologise to you for the failure to detect an abnormality":* Simon Carswell, "HSE head Apologizes to Limerick Woman for False Smear Test," *Irish Times*, April 27, 2018, https://www.irishtimes.com/news/ireland /irish-news/hse-head-apologises-to-limerick-woman-for-false-smear -test-1.3477001.

195 *The HSE had more tests than labs in Ireland could handle:* Bodger, "HSE Boss 'Dismissed My Concerns' About Cervical Screening Results," *Broadsheet*, April 30, 2018, https://www.broadsheet.ie/2018/04/30/hse-boss -dismissed-my-concerns-about-cervical-screening-results/.

195 *Vicky Phelan was told in 2011:* Rachael O'Connor, "Vicky Phelan Returns to United States for Cancer Treatment Following 'Bad News' That Tumors Have Grown," *Irish Post*, August 12, 2021, https://www.irishpost .com/news/vicky-phelan-returns-to-united-states-for-cancer-treatment -following-bad-news-that-tumours-have-grown-218040.

196 *She is also fighting for an Irish right-to-die law*: Blathin de Paor, "Vicky Phelan Backs Assisted Suicide Bill as She Doesn't Want Her Kids to Watch Her Die in Pain," RSVP Live, updated April 24, 2021, https://www .rsvplive.ie/news/celebs/vicky-phelan-backs-assisted-suicide-23974471.

196 *"Failures in communicating":* "CervicalCheck Update—Information for Women Concerned About Their Smear Test Results," CervicalCheck, updated May 5, 2018, https://web.archive.org/web/20180510094757 /http://www.cervicalcheck.ie/screening-information/cervicalcheck

-update.13550.html. This site was later updated with different wording and more information, as seen at https://www.cervicalcheck.ie/news /cervicalcheck-statement-1st-may-2018.13384.html.

196   *a day of fasting and atonement for the Salem witch trials:* Jess Blumberg, "A Brief History of the Salem Witch Trials: One Town's Strange Journey from Paranoia to Pardon," *Smithsonian*, October 23, 2007, https://www .smithsonianmag.com/history/a-brief-history-of-the-salem-witch-trials -175162489/.

196   *this personal statement read aloud in his church by his pastor:* Battistella, *Sorry About That,* 11–12.

198   *used the term "Armenian genocide" in 2021:* Katie Rogers and Carlotta Gall, "Breaking With Predecessors, Biden Declares Mass Killings of Armenians a Genocide," *New York Times,* April 24, 2021, https://www.nytimes .com/2021/04/24/us/politics/armenia-genocide-joe-biden.html.

198   *there can be no adequate response:* Martha Minow, *Between Vengeance and Forgiveness: Facing History After Genocide and Mass Violence* (Boston: Beacon Press, 1998), 5.

198   *Elizabeth II's proclamation:* "Proclamation Designating July 28 of Every Year as 'A Day of Commemoration of the Great Upheaval,' Commencing on July 28, 2005," Justice Laws Website, Government of Canada, modified December 23, 2021, https://laws-lois.justice.gc.ca/eng/regulations /si-2003-188/page-1.html.

200   *Have you apologized to Monica:* Jamie Ross, "Bill Clinton Meltdown on Monica Lewinsky Scandal: I Did the Right Thing," *Daily Beast,* June 4, 2018, https://www.thedailybeast.com/clinton-on-metoo-why-i-never-said -sorry-to-monica-lewinsky.

201   *Janet Reno:* "Reno Apologizes to Ex-Suspect in Bombing," Associated Press, in *New York Times,* August 1, 1997, https://www.nytimes .com/1997/08/01/us/reno-apologizes-to-ex-suspect-in-bombing .html.

201   *John Ashcroft:* Scott Charton, "Governor Apologizes for Wife's After-

-Hours Library," AP News, May 18, 1990, https://apnews.com/article/70ae4c5ce1c7ad9f81c59e2a2d472c3c.

201 *Andrew Cuomo:* "Read the Full Transcript of Gov. Andrew Cuomo's Resignation Speech," *New York Times,* August 10, 2021, https://www.nytimes.com/2021/08/10/nyregion/cuomo-resignation-speech-transcript.html.

202 *Hahns Copeland:* Steve Thompson, "Virginia House Candidate Condemned for Tweet Insulting Speaker's Appearance," *Washington Post,* September 17, 2021, https://www.washingtonpost.com/local/virginia-politics/virginia-house-candidate-condemned-for-tweet-insulting-speakers-appearance/2021/09/17/8bcfb34e-1829-11ec-9589-31ac3173c2e5_story.html.

Chapter 8: How to Accept an Apology and How to Forgive . . . and When to Do Neither

205 *Ramsey smartly suggests:* Chescaleigh (Franchesca Ramsey), "Getting Called Out: How to Apologize," September 6, 2013, YouTube video, https://www.youtube.com/watch?v=C8xJXKYL8pU.

206 *study author Marissa Drell:* Fariss Samarrai, "'Sorry' Doesn't Heal Children's Hurt, but It Mends Relations," UVA Today, University of Virginia, November 12, 2015, https://news.virginia.edu/content/sorry-doesnt-heal-childrens-hurt-it-mends-relations.

207 *John Kador suggests:* John Kador, *Effective Apology: Mending Fences, Building Bridges, and Restoring Trust* (Oakland: Berrett-Koehler, 2009), 165–66.

212 *"It is well established that":* "Forgiving a Wrong May Actually Make It Easier to Forget," ScienceDaily, Association for Psychological Science, May 13, 2014, https://www.sciencedaily.com/releases/2014/05/140513113609.htm.

213 *He knelt in front of her and said:* Claude Steiner with Paul Perry, *Achieving Emotional Literacy: A Personal Program to Increase Your Emotional Intelligence* (New York: Avon, 1997), 152–53.

214 *die by suicide:* Helene Schumacher, "Why More Men Than Women Die by Suicide," BBC, March 17, 2019, https://www.bbc.com/future/article /20190313-why-more-men-kill-themselves-than-women.

214 *95 percent of those who commit homicide: Global Study on Homicide* (Vienna: United Nations Office on Drugs and Crime, 2013), 11, https://www .unodc.org/documents/data-and-analysis/statistics/GSH2013/2014 _GLOBAL_HOMICIDE_BOOK_web.pdf.

216 *"What do victims' families want?":* Arzoo Osanloo, "Forgiveness Works: What We Can Learn from a Victim-Centered Justice System," Princeton University Press, July 27, 2020, https://press.princeton.edu/ideas /forgiveness-works-what-can-we-learn-from-a-victim-centered-justice -system.

226 *"forgiveness interventions":* Nathaniel G. Wade, William T. Hoyt, Julia E. M. Kidwell, and Everett L. Worthington, "Efficacy of Psychotherapeutic Interventions to Promote Forgiveness: A Meta-Analysis," *Journal of Consulting and Clinical Psychology* 82, no. 1 (February 2014): 154, http://dx .doi.org/10.1037/a0035268.

227 *nine steps toward forgiveness:* Jason Marsh, "Fred Luskin Explains How to Forgive," *Greater Good Magazine*, August 24, 2020, https://greatergood .berkeley.edu/article/item/fred_luskin_explains_how_to_forgive.

229 *forgiveness model he calls REACH:* Everett Worthington, "REACH Forgiveness of Others," Everett Worthington, n.d., http://www.evworthington -forgiveness.com/reach-forgiveness-of-others.

234 *"One of the problems right now is that social shame":* Ezra Klein, "A Different Way of Thinking About Cancel Culture," *New York Times*, April 18, 2021, https://www.nytimes.com/2021/04/18/opinion/cancel -culture-social-media.html.

235 *tweet by comedian Hari Kondabolu:* Hari Kondabolu (@harikond abolu), June 22, 2020, Twitter, https://twitter.com/harikondabolu /status/1275293854279712770?s=20.

235 *Kondabolu's 2021 response:* Hari Kondabolu (@harikondabolu), April 12,

2021, Twitter, https://twitter.com/harikondabolu/status/1381660996
390039552?s=20.

235 *"Whites Can No Longer Stand On The Side-lines"*: Cher (@cher),
April 2, 2021, Twitter, https://twitter.com/cher/status/13781455
90068928516?s=20.

236 *"today's call-out culture"*: Loretta Ross, "I'm a Black Feminist. I Think Call-
Out Culture Is Toxic," *New York Times*, August 17, 2019, https://www
.nytimes.com/2019/08/17/opinion/sunday/cancel-culture-call-out
.html.

Chapter 9: "What I Said on My Private Island Was Taken out of Context": An Evisceration of Celebrity Apologies

242 *She later apologized:* "Reese Witherspoon Apologizes, 'Deeply Embarrassed' After Arrest," CBS/AP, on CBS News, April 22, 2013, https:
//www.cbsnews.com/news/reese-witherspoon-apologizes-deeply
-embarrassed-after-arrest/.

242 *"aren't being nice to the Dalai Lama"*: Robert Booth and Justin McCurry,
"They Are Not Being Nice to the Dalai Lama, Who Is a Very Good
Friend of Mine," *Guardian*, May 29, 2008, https://www.theguardian.com
/world/2008/may/30/chinaearthquake.china.

243 *Stone responded:* "Sharon Stone Apologizes—Again—for China Remarks," *People*, updated June 4, 2008, https://people.com/celebrity
/sharon-stone-apologizes-again-for-china-remarks/.

243 *"I am deeply saddened"*: Cathy Horyn, "Actress Stone and Dior Differ
over Apology," *New York Times*, June 1, 2008, https://www.nytimes
.com/2008/06/01/fashion/01stone.html.

246 *"Every Single Public Male Apology"*: @MadameNovelette, Twitter, November 21, 2020, https://twitter.com/MadameNovelette/status/13448
10860288618497?s=20.

248 *"I'm sorry I bet on baseball"*: Kostya Kennedy, "Even After 25 Years, Pete

Rose's Ban from Baseball Is Money in the Bank," FiveThirtyEight, July 31, 2014, https://fivethirtyeight.com/features/even-after-25-years-pete-roses-ban-from-baseball-is-money-in-the-bank/.

249 *"A woman doing comedy"*: Gregg Kilday, "Jerry Lewis Drew Ire over His Comments About Female Comedians," *Hollywood Reporter*, August 23, 2017, https://www.hollywoodreporter.com/news/general-news/jerry-lewis-drew-ire-his-comments-female-comedians-1031730/.

249 *"Lewis ought to have realized"*: Tom Sime, "Joke's on Jerry Lewis in His Remarks on Female Comics," *Journal Times* (Racine, WI), updated February 29, 2000, updated October 4, 2017, https://journaltimes.com/jokes-on-jerry-lewis-in-his-remarks-about-female-comics/article_679ca5be-77b3-5609-b3dc-58c5a0a06df8.html.

249 *"You don't want to be pitied"*: Sheila Marikar, "Jerry Lewis Raises Millions, Causes Controversy," ABC News, January 7, 2009, https://abcnews.go.com/Entertainment/story?id=3556180&page=1.

250 *"The statement I made"*: "Jerry Lewis sorry for 'cripple' remark," *Morning Journal* (Lorain, OH), June 2, 2001, updated July 21, 2021, https://www.morningjournal.com/2001/06/02/jerry-lewis-sorry-for-cripple-remark/.

250 *response on Instagram*: Florence Pugh (@FlorencePugh), Instagram, June 26, 2020, https://www.instagram.com/p/CB6FNMcl5yf/.

253 *Brian Primack*: Brian A. Primack, Ariel Shensa, Jaime E. Sidani, Erin O. Whaite, Liu yi Lin, Daniel Rosen, Jason B. Colditz, Ana Radovic, and Elizabeth Miller, "Social Media Use and Perceived Social Isolation Among Young Adults in the U.S.," *American Journal of Preventative Medicine* 53, no. 1 (July 1, 2017), https://doi.org/10.1016/j.amepre.2017.01.010.

253 *Still another study*: Elizabeth M. Seabrook, Margaret L. Kern, and Nikki S. Rickard, "Social Networking Sites, Depression, and Anxiety: A Systematic Review," *JMIR Mental Health* 3, no. 4 (October–December 2016): e50, https://doi.org/.

254 *list of the most frequently banned and challenged books*: "Top 10 Most Chal-

lenged Books Lists: Top 10 Most Challenged Books of 2020," Banned & Challenged Books, American Library Association, https://www.ala.org /advocacy/bbooks/frequentlychallengedbooks/top10.

256 *"I don't feel that that is who I am as a person"*: "Woman Who Falsely Accused Black Teen of Stealing Her Phone Says She 'Could've Approached the Situation Differently,' " CBS News, January 8, 2021, https://www.cbsnews .com/news/miya-ponsetto-soho-karen-black-teen-theft-accusation/.

257 *"I came of age in the '60s and '70s"*: "Harvey Weinstein's Full Statement Following Sexual Harassment Allegations," CNN Business, October 5, 2017, https://money.cnn.com/2017/10/05/media/harvey-weinsteins-full -statement/index.html.

258 *"While our first instinct is to listen to every woman's story"*: Constance Grady, "Lena Dunham Accused a Woman of Lying About Her Rape. It Fits Her Controversial Past," *Vox*, November 21, 2017, https://www.vox.com /culture/2017/11/21/16679078/lena-dunham-accused-woman -lying-rape-murray-miller-aurora-perrineau.

258 *"I naively believed"*: Lena Dunham (@lenadunham), Twitter, November 18, 2017, https://twitter.com/lenadunham/status/932050109121 970176?s=20.

259 *initially seemed to blame:* Jill Disis, "Mario Batali Steps away from Business, TV Show amid Sexual Misconduct Allegations," CNN Business, December 11, 2017, https://money.cnn.com/2017/12/11/media /mario-batali-sexual-misconduct-allegations/index.html.

259 *"As many of you know"*: Tess Koman, "A Complete Timeline of Mario Batali's Downfall," Delish, May 23, 2019, https://www.delish.com/restaurants /g20884247/timeline-of-mario-batali-sexual-assault-allegations/.

259 *"Words cannot begin to express"*: Sean Michaels, "Chris Brown 'Sorry and Saddened' over Alleged Rihanna Assault," *Guardian*, February 16, 2009, https://www.theguardian.com/music/2009/feb/16/chris-brown -statement-alleged-rihanna-assault.

260 *apology video:* Simon Vozick-Levinson, "Chris Brown Apologizes for

Assaulting Rihanna," *Entertainment Weekly*, updated December 20, 2019, https://ew.com/article/2009/07/20/chris-brown-assault-apology/.

260   *"At the end of the day"*: Mariel Concepcion, "Chris Brown Done Apologizing for Rihanna Assault," *Billboard*, March 9, 2011, https://www.billboard.com/music/music-news/chris-brown-done-apologizing-for-rihanna-assault-472639/.

260   *smashed a window*: Mark Cina, "Chris Brown Smashes Window in Meltdown After 'GMA' Interview," *Hollywood Reporter*, March 22, 2011, https://www.hollywoodreporter.com/news/music-news/chris-brown-smashes-window-meltdown-169952/.

260   *"I want to apologize to anybody who was startled"*: Andrea Canning, Jessica Hopper, and Sheila Marikar, "Chris Brown Apologizes for 'GMA' Incident on BET," ABC News, March 23, 2011, https://abcnews.go.com/Entertainment/chris-brown-apologizes-robin-roberts-bet-106-park/story?id=13200434.

Chapter 10: Girl, Stop Apologizing, or Maybe Don't, Ugh, It's Complicated: Gender, Race, and Power

265   *"Why Women Apologize More Than Men"*: Karina Schumann and Michael Ross, "Why Women Apologize More Than Men: Gender Differences in Thresholds for Perceiving Offensive Behavior," *Psychological Science* 21, no. 11 (first published online September 20, 2010; issue published November 1, 2010): 1649–55, https://doi.org/10.1177/0956797610384150.

266   *"This is just how sexism works"*: Jude Ellison Sady Doyle, "Women Don't Need to Apologize Less—Men Need to Learn How to Apologize," *Elle*, April 13, 2017, https://www.elle.com/culture/career-politics/news/a44528/why-men-are-so-bad-at-apologizing/.

266   *she examined 183 apologies*: Janet Holmes, "Apologies in New Zealand

English," *Language in Society* 19, no. 2 (June 1990): 155–99, https://doi .org/10.1017/s0047404500014366.

269 *"double backlash":* York University, "Saying Sorry Not Enough When Trust, Gender Roles Broken—Just Ask Clinton and Trump," Science Daily, September 12, 2016, https://www.sciencedaily.com/releases /2016/09/160912132552.htm.

271 *"Dave, if I could":* Alexandra Petri, "Opinion: Famous Quotes, the Way a Woman Would Have to Say Them During a Meeting," *Washington Post,* October 13, 2015, https://www.washingtonpost.com/blogs/compost /wp/2015/10/13/jennifer-lawrence-has-a-point-famous-quotes-the -way-a-woman-would-have-to-say-them-during-a-meeting/.

272 *A 2017 study found:* Christine L. Nittrouer, Michelle R. Hebl, Leslie Ashburn-Nardo, Rachel C. E. Trump-Steele, David M. Lane, and Virginia Valian, "Gender Disparities in Colloquium Speakers at Top Universities," *Proceedings of the National Academy of Sciences of the United States of America* 115, no. 1 (January 2, 2018): 104–8, https://doi.org/10.1073 /pnas.1708414115.

272 *women are just as likely:* Bayes Business School, "New Study Suggests Women Do Ask for Pay Rises but Don't Get Them," September 6, 2016, https://www.bayes.city.ac.uk/news-and-events/news/2016/september /new-study-suggests-women-do-ask-for-pay-rises-but-dont-get-them.

273 *"When Saying Sorry May Not Help":* Gili Freedman, Erin M. Burgoon, Jason D. Ferrell, James W. Pennebaker, and Jennifer S. Beer, "When Saying Sorry May Not Help: The Impact of Apologies on Social Rejections," *Frontiers in Psychology* 8 (August 2017): 1375, https://doi.org/10.3389 /fpsyg.2017.01375.

277 *Lehrer wasn't nearly as bad as Enron:* Peter Sims, "Jonah Lehrer's Mistake— and Ours," *Harvard Business Review,* August 16, 2012, https://hbr .org/2012/08/jonah-lehrers-mistake-and-o.

279 *variety of scenarios in which someone committed wrongdoing:* P. H. Kim,

A. Mislin, E. Tuncel, R. Fehr, A. Cheshin, and G. A. van Kleef, "Power as an Emotional Liability: Implications for Perceived Authenticity and Trust After a Transgression," *Journal of Experimental Psychology: General* 146, no. 10 (2017): 1379–1401, https://doi.org/10.1037/xge0000292.

280 *"The assumption is that the CEO":* Rebecca Stadlen Amir, "The More Powerful You Are the Less Believable Your Apology," Israel21C, February 14, 2018, https://www.israel21c.org/the-more-powerful-you-are-the-less-believable-your-apology/.

280 *"The more senior the politician":* Amir, "The More Powerful You Are."

281 *"The mythology presumes all Black women":* Wendy Ashley, "The Angry Black Woman: The Impact of Pejorative Stereotypes on Psychotherapy with Black Women," *Social Work in Public Health* 29, no. 1 (2014): 28, https://doi.org/10.1080/19371918.2011.619449.

281 *Black girls are universally seen as more mature:* Rebecca Epstein, Jamilia J. Blake, and Thalia González, "Girlhood Interrupted: The Erasure of Black Girls' Childhood," Center on Poverty and Inequality, Georgetown Law, 2017, https://ssrn.com/abstract=3000695 or http://dx.doi.org/10.2139/ssrn.3000695.

282 *more than 80 percent of white women and men:* "The State of Black Women in Corporate America: 2020," Lean In, n.d., https://leanin.org/research/state-of-black-women-in-corporate-america/section-3-everyday-discrimination#!.

282 *"Being sorry is literally a lesson in our DNA":* Sonya Renee Taylor, *The Body Is Not an Apology: The Power of Radical Self-Love* (Oakland: Berrett-Koehler, 2018), 11.

282 *"contrary to popular belief":* J. Celeste Walley-Jean, "Debunking the Myth of the 'Angry Black Woman': An Exploration of Anger in Young African American Women," *Black Women, Gender + Families* 3, no. 2 (2009): 82, https://www.jstor.org/stable/10.5406/blacwomegendfami.3.2.0068.

283 *for every one hundred men:* "The State of Black Women in Corporate America: 2020."

283 *"Dear Trolls":* Ayanna Pressley (@AyannaPressley), Twitter, February 6, 2020, https://twitter.com/AyannaPressley/status/12254931840144 38400?s=20.

284 *"baby peanut":* Alexandria Ocasio-Cortez (@AOC), Twitter, February 6, 2020, https://twitter.com/AOC/status/1225527290978807810.

284 *a buffet of apologies:* Taylor, *The Body Is Not an Apology*, 12.

284 *"awaken daily to a planet":* Taylor, *The Body Is Not an Apology*, 13.

284 *"I'm done apologising":* Elizabeth Wright, "My Hips Are Wonky: Disability, Fashion and Body Apology," *Conscious Being*, February 23, 2021, https://medium.com/conscious-life/my-hips-are-wonky-disability -fashion-and-body-apology-7b5eeee6e1c1.

285 *"I've reckoned with this":* Lili Loofbourow, "Junot Díaz and the Problem of the Male Self-Pardon," *Slate*, June 24, 2018, https://slate.com/culture/2018/06/junot-diaz-allegations-and-the-male-self-pardon.html.

286 *"I thought of how many people go to their graves unforgiven":* Elizabeth Gilbert, *Eat, Pray, Love: One Woman's Search for Everything Across Italy, India and Indonesia* (New York: Penguin, 2007), 196.

287 *"Dear Evie":* Eve Ensler, *The Apology* (New York: Bloomsbury, 2019), 9–10.

288 *Queens-based cartoonist Yao Xiao:* Yao Xiao, "If You Want to Say Thank You, Don't Say Sorry," Yao Xiao, n.d., http://www.yao.nyc/shortcomics /2020/3/30/if-you-want-to-say-thank-you-dont-say-sorry.

289 Forbes *magazine offered a roundup of career coaches:* Forbes Coaches Council, "11 Alternatives to 'I'm Sorry' When Resolving a Professional Dispute," *Forbes*, May 6, 2019, https://www.forbes.com/sites/forbes coachescouncil/2019/05/06/11-alternatives-to-im-sorry-when -resolving-a-professional-dispute.

290 *"Swimming in that sea of Aloneness":* Monica Lewinsky, "Monica Lewinsky: Emerging from 'The House of Gaslight' in the Age of #MeToo," *Vanity Fair*, February 25, 2018, https://www.vanityfair.com/news/2018/02 /monica-lewinsky-in-the-age-of-metoo.

Chapter 11: Let the Moment Last; Let the Ripples Widen

296   *Lyubomirsky writes:* Sonja Lyubomirsky, *The How of Happiness: A Scientific Approach to Getting the Life You Want* (New York: Penguin Press, 2008), 94.

296   *"in the crib, wailing away":* Jennifer Weiner, *Little Earthquakes* (New York: Washington Square Press/Atria, 2005), 391.

297   *Kumar and Epley wrote:* Amit Kumar and Nicholas Epley, "Undervaluing Gratitude: Expressers Misunderstand the Consequences of Showing Appreciation," *Psychological Science* 29, no. 9 (2018): 2, https://doi.org/10.1177/0956797618772506.

298   *"So people's willingness":* Kumar, "Undervaluing Gratitude," 7.

299   *"participants underestimated the positive consequences":* Kumar, "Undervaluing Gratitude," 11.

299   *treated for depression or suicidal ideation:* Jerome A. Motto, MD, and Alan G. Bostrom, PhD, "A Randomized Controlled Trial of Postcrisis Suicide Prevention," *Psychiatric Services* 52, no. 6 (June 2001): 828–33, https://doi.org/10.1176/appi.ps.52.6.828.

300   *What is this "curse of knowledge"?:* Colin Camerer, George Loewenstein, and Martin Weber, "The Curse of Knowledge in Economic Settings: An Experimental Analysis," *Journal of Political Economy* 97, no. 5 (October 1989): 1232–54, https://doi.org/10.1086/261651.

303   *"Spending Money on Others Promotes Happiness":* Elizabeth W. Dunn, Lara B. Aknin, and Michael I. Norton, "Spending Money on Others Promotes Happiness," *Science* 319, no. 5870 (March 2008): 1687–88, https://doi.org/10.1126/science.1150952.

308   *changes of direction they are making:* Rachelle Hampton and Madison Malone Kircher, "The Creator of 'This Is White Privilege' Wouldn't Do It Again," *Slate*, April 10, 2021, https://slate.com/culture/2021/04/this-is-white-privilege-tumblr-creator-interview.html.

309   *she, too, has had some second thoughts:* Liat Kaplan, "My Year of Grief and

Cancellation," *New York Times*, February 25, 2021, https://www.nytimes
.com/2021/02/25/style/your-fave-is-problematic-tumblr.html.

311 *Which brings us to a related cultural shift in . . . macaques:* Frans B. M.
de Waal and Denise L. Johanowicz, "Modification of Reconciliation
Behavior Through Social Experience: An Experiment with Two Macaque
Species," *Child Development* 64, no. 3 (June 1993): 897–908, https://doi
.org/10.1111/j.1467-8624.1993.tb02950.x.

BIBLIOGRAPHY

Balistreri, Maggie. *The Evasion-English Dictionary*. New York: Em Dash Group, 2018.

Balkin, Richard S. *Practicing Forgiveness: A Path Toward Healing*. New York: Oxford University Press, 2020.

Battistella, Edwin L. *Sorry About That: The Language of Public Apology*. New York: Oxford University Press, 2014.

Browning, Guy. *Never Hit a Jellyfish with a Spade: How to Survive Life's Smaller Challenges*. New York: Gotham, 2005.

Chapman, Gary, and Jennifer Thomas. *The Five Languages of Apology: How to Experience Healing in All Your Relationships*. Chicago: Northfield Publishing, 2006.

Engel, Beverly. *The Power of Apology: Healing Steps to Transform All Your Relationships*. New York: John Wiley & Sons, 2001.

Enright, Robert. *The Forgiving Life: A Pathway to Overcoming Resentment and Creating a Legacy of Love*. Washington, DC: American Psychological Association, 2012.

Fox, Stephen. *The Unknown Internment: An Oral History of the Relocation of Italian Americans During World War II*. Boston: Twayne, 1990.

Howes, Molly, PhD. *A Good Apology: Four Steps to Make Things Right*. New York: Grand Central Publishing, 2020.

Hyde, Lewis. *A Primer for Forgetting: Getting Past the Past*. New York: Farrar, Straus and Giroux, 2019.

Jones, Dorothy Knee. *A Century of Servitude: Pribilof Aleuts Under U.S. Rule.* Washington, DC: University Press of America, 1980.

Kador, John. *Effective Apology: Mending Fences, Building Bridges, and Restoring Trust.* San Francisco: Berrett-Koehler Publishers, 2009.

Kalanithi, Paul. *When Breath Becomes Air.* New York: Random House, 2016.

Kor, Eva Mozes. *The Power of Forgiveness.* Las Vegas: Central Recovery Press, 2021.

Lazare, Aaron. *On Apology.* New York: Oxford University Press, 2004.

Lerner, Harriet. *Why Won't You Apologize?: Healing Big Betrayals and Everyday Hurts.* New York: Touchstone, 2017.

Luepnitz, Deborah Anna, PhD. *Schopenhauer's Porcupines: Intimacy and Its Dilemmas; Five Stories of Psychotherapy.* New York: Basic Books, 2002.

Luskin, Fred. *Forgive for Good: A Proven Prescription for Health and Happiness.* New York: HarperOne, 2001.

Lyubomirsky, Sonja. *The How of Happiness: A Scientific Approach to Getting the Life You Want.* New York: Penguin Press, 2008.

Minow, Martha. *Between Vengeance and Forgiveness: Facing History After Genocide and Mass Violence.* Boston: Beacon Press, 1998.

———. *When Should Law Forgive?* New York: W. W. Norton, 2019.

Murthy, Vivek H., MD. *Together: The Healing Power of Human Connection in a Sometimes Lonely World.* New York: Harper Ways/HarperCollins, 2020.

Némirovsky, Irène. *The Wine of Solitude.* New York: Knopf, 2014.

Potter, Shawna. *Making Spaces Safer: A Guide to Giving Harassment the Boot Wherever You Work, Play, and Gather.* Chico, CA: AK Press, 2019.

Ramsey, Franchesca. *Well, That Escalated Quickly: Memoirs and Mistakes of an Accidental Activist.* New York: Grand Central Publishing, 2018.

Rossmanith, Kate. *Small Wrongs: How We Really Say Sorry in Love, Life and Law.* Melbourne: Hardie Grant Books, 2018.

Ruffin, Amber, and Lacey Lamar. *You'll Never Believe What Happened to Lacey: Crazy Stories About Racism.* New York: Grand Central Publishing, 2021.

Stevens, William Oliver. *Pistols at Ten Paces: The Story of the Code of Honor in America.* Boston: Riverside Press/Houghton Mifflin, 1940.

Tavris, Carol, and Elliot Aronson. *Mistakes Were Made (but Not by Me): Why We Justify Foolish Beliefs, Bad Decisions, and Hurtful Acts.* Boston: Houghton Mifflin Harcourt, 2007.

Taylor, Sonya Renee. *The Body Is Not an Apology.* Oakland: Berrett-Koehler, 2018.

Tillyard, Stella. *Aristocrats: Caroline, Emily, Louisa, and Sarah Lennox, 1740–1832.* New York: Farrar, Straus and Giroux, 1994.

Weiner, Brian A. *Sins of the Parents: The Politics of National Apologies in the United States.* Philadelphia: Temple University Press, 2005.

Worthington, Everett. *Moving Forward: Six Steps to Forgiving Yourself and Breaking Free from the Past.* Colorado Springs, CO: Waterbrook, 2013.

ABOUT THE AUTHORS

Marjorie Ingall and Susan McCarthy have been analyzing apologies in the news, pop culture, literature, and politics at SorryWatch.com since 2012.

Marjorie, who goes by "Snarly" on SorryWatch.com, is the author of *Mamaleh Knows Best: What Jewish Mothers Do to Raise Creative, Empathetic, Independent Children* (Harmony) and *The Field Guide to North American Males* (Henry Holt), and is the coauthor of *Hungry* (Simon & Schuster), with plus-size model Crystal Renn. A former columnist for *Tablet* magazine and the *Forward*, she is a frequent contributor to *The New York Times Book Review* and has also written for *New York, Town & Country, Ms., Glamour, Self, Elle,* and *Sassy* (yes, that one). She lives in New York City.

Susan, who goes by "Sumac" on SorryWatch.com, is the coauthor (with Jeffrey Moussaieff Masson) of the international bestseller *When Elephants Weep: The Emotional Lives of Animals* (Delacorte), which has been translated into twenty-one languages. She's also the author of *Becoming a Tiger: How Baby Animals Learn to Live in the Wild* (HarperCollins). Publications she's written for include *Parade,* the *Guardian, Wired, Smithsonian* magazine, *Outside,* and *Salon.* Her work has been anthologized in *The Best American Science Writing* and in *Mirth of a Nation: The Best Contemporary Humor.* She lives in San Francisco.